ABOUT THIS PUBLICATION

FOR SERVICE ASSISTANCE

Customer Service
704.898.0770

North Carolina General Statues is published by The Muliti-Media Group of Greater Charlotte in Charlotte, North Carolina. Copyright 2015 by the Multi-Media Group of Greater Charlotte. This book or parts thereof may not be reproduced in any form, stored in a retrieval system, or transmitted in any form by any means—electronic, mechanical, photocopy, recording or otherwise—without prior written permission of the publisher, except as provided by United States of America copyright law.

The records required by U.S. Code 2257(a) through (c) and the pertinent regulations 28 C.F.R. Cli. 1, Part 75 with respect to this publication and all materials associated with such records are maintained by The Multi-Media Group of Greater Charlotte, Publisher and available for review by Attorney General.

www.visionbooks.org

Copyright © 2015 by MMGGC
All rights reserved!

TID: 5061681
ISBN (10) digit: 1502915030
ISBN (13) digit: 978-1502915030

123-4-56789-01239-Paperback
123-4-56789-01239-Hardback

First Edition

090520140547

Printed in the United States of America

2015 EDITION

North Carolina Criminal Law And Procedure-Pamphlet # 45

Printed In conjunction with the Administration of the Courts

North Carolina Criminal Law and Procedure
Pamphlet Reference Guide

Chapters	Pamphlet
Chapter 1 Civil Procedure	1
Chapter 1 Civil Procedure (Continue)	2
Chapter 1A Rules of Civil Procedure	2
Chapter 1B Contribution.	2
Chapter 1C Enforcement of Judgments.	2
Chapter 1D Punitive Damages.	2
Chapter 1E Eastern Band of Cherokee Indians.	2
Chapter 1F North Carolina Uniform Interstate Depositions and Discovery Act.	2
Chapter 2 - Clerk of Superior Court [Repealed and Transferred.]	3
Chapter 3 - Commissioners of Affidavits and Deeds [Repealed.]	3
Chapter 4 - Common Law	3
Chapter 5 - Contempt [Repealed.]	3
Chapter 5A - Contempt	3
Chapter 6 - Liability for Court Costs	3
Chapter 7 - Courts [Repealed and Transferred.]	3
Chapter 7A – Judicial Department	3
Chapter 7A – Continuation (Judicial Department)	4
Chapter 7A – Continuation (Judicial Department)	5
Chapter 7B - Juvenile Code	5
Chapter 8 - Evidence	6
Chapter 8A - Interpreters for Deaf Persons [Recodified.]	6
Chapter 8B - Interpreters for Deaf Persons	6
Chapter 8C - Evidence Code	6
Chapter 9 - Jurors	6
Chapter 10 - Notaries [Repealed.]	6
Chapter 10A - Notaries [Recodified.]	6
Chapter 10B - Notaries	6
Chapter 11 - Oaths	6
Chapter 12 - Statutory Construction	6
Chapter 13 - Citizenship Restored	6
Chapter 14 - Criminal Law	7
Chapter 14 –Criminal Law (Continuation)	8
Chapter 15 - Criminal Procedure	9
Chapter 15A - Criminal Procedure Act (Continuation)	10
Chapter 15A - Criminal Procedure Act (Continuation)	11
Chapter 15B - Victims Compensation	11
Chapter 15C - Address Confidentiality Program	11
Chapter 16 - Gaming Contracts and Futures	11
Chapter 17 - Habeas Corpus	11

Chapter 17A - Law-Enforcement Officers [Recodified.]	11
Chapter 17B - North Carolina Criminal Justice Education and Training System [Recodified.] Chapter 17C - North Carolina Criminal Justice Education and Training Standards Commission	11
	11
Chapter 17D - North Carolina Justice Academy	11
Chapter 17E - North Carolina Sheriffs' Education and Training Standards Commission	11
Chapter 18 - Regulation of Intoxicating Liquors [Repealed.]	12
Chapter 18A - Regulation of Intoxicating Liquors [Repealed.]	12
Chapter 18B - Regulation of Alcoholic Beverages	12
Chapter 18C - North Carolina State Lottery	12
Chapter 19 - Offenses against Public Morals	12
Chapter 19A - Protection of Animals	12
Chapter 20 - Motor Vehicles	13
Chapter 20 - Motor Vehicles (Continuation)	14
Chapter 20 - Motor Vehicles (Continuation)	15
Chapter 20 - Motor Vehicles (Continuation)	16
Chapter 21 - Bills of Lading	17
Chapter 22 - Contracts Requiring Writing	17
Chapter 22A - Signatures	17
Chapter 22B - Contracts Against Public Policy	17
Chapter 22C - Payments to Subcontractors	17
Chapter 23 - Debtor and Creditor	17
Chapter 24 – Interest	17
Chapter 25 – Uniform Commercial Code	18
Chapter 25 – Uniform Commercial Code (Continuation)	19
Chapter 25A – Retail Installment Sales Act	20
Chapter 25B - Credit	20
Chapter 25C - Sales of Artwork	20
Chapter 26 - Suretyship	20
Chapter 27 - Warehouse Receipts [Repealed.]	20
Chapter 28 - Administration [Repealed.]	20
Chapter 28A - Administration of Decedents' Estates	20
Chapter 28B - Estates of Absentees in Military Service	20
Chapter 28C - Estates of Missing Persons	20
Chapter 29 - Intestate Succession	21
Chapter 30 - Surviving Spouses	21
Chapter 31 - Wills	21
Chapter 31A - Acts Barring Property Rights	21
Chapter 31B - Renunciation of Property and Renunciation of Fiduciary Powers Act	21
Chapter 31C - Uniform Disposition of Community Property Rights at Death Act	21
Chapter 32 - Fiduciaries	21
Chapter 32A - Powers of Attorney	21
Chapter 33 - Guardian and Ward [Repealed and Recodified.]	21

Chapter 33A - North Carolina Uniform Transfers to Minors Act	21
Chapter 33B - North Carolina Uniform Custodial Trust Act	21
Chapter 34 - Veterans' Guardianship Act	22
Chapter 35 - Sterilization Procedures	22
Chapter 35A - Incompetency and Guardianship	22
Chapter 36 - Trusts and Trustees [Repealed.]	22
Chapter 36A - Trusts and Trustees	22
Chapter 36B - Uniform Management of Institutional Funds Act [Repealed.]	22
Chapter 36C - North Carolina Uniform Trust Code	22
Chapter 36D - North Carolina Community Third Party Trusts, Pooled Trusts	23
Chapter 36E - Uniform Prudent Management of Institutional Funds Act	23
Chapter 37 - Allocation of Principal and Income [Repealed.]	23
Chapter 37A - Uniform Principal and Income Act	23
Chapter 38 - Boundaries	23
Chapter 38A - Landowner Liability	23
Chapter 39 - Conveyances	23
Chapter 39A - Transfer Fee Covenants Prohibited	23
Chapter 40 - Eminent Domain [Repealed.]	23
Chapter 40A - Eminent Domain	23
Chapter 41 - Estates	23
Chapter 41A - State Fair Housing Act	23
Chapter 42 - Landlord and Tenant	23
Chapter 42A - Vacation Rental Act	23
Chapter 43 - Land Registration	23
Chapter 44 - Liens	24
Chapter 44A - Statutory Liens and Charges	24
Chapter 45 - Mortgages and Deeds of Trust	24
Chapter 45A - Good Funds Settlement Act	24
Chapter 46 - Partition	24
Chapter 47 - Probate and Registration	25
Chapter 47A - Unit Ownership	25
Chapter 47B - Real Property Marketable Title Act	25
Chapter 47C - North Carolina Condominium Act	25
Chapter 47D - Notice of Settlement Act [Expired.]	25
Chapter 47E - Residential Property Disclosure Act	25
Chapter 47F - North Carolina Planned Community Act	25
Chapter 47G - Option to Purchase Contracts	25
Chapter 47H - Contracts for Deed	25
Chapter 48 - Adoptions +	26
Chapter 48A - Minors	26
Chapter 49 - Bastardy	26
Chapter 49A - Rights of Children	26
Chapter 50 - Divorce and Alimony	26
Chapter 50A - Uniform Child-Custody Jurisdiction and	

Enforcement Act	26
Chapter 50B - Domestic Violence	26
Chapter 50C - Civil No-Contact Orders	26
Chapter 51 - Marriage	26
Chapter 52 - Powers and Liabilities of Married Persons	27
Chapter 52A - Uniform Reciprocal Enforcement of Support Act [Repealed.]	27
Chapter 52B - Uniform Premarital Agreement Act	27
Chapter 52C - Uniform Interstate Family Support Act	27
Chapter 53 - Banks	27
Chapter 53A - Business Development Corporations and North Carolina Capital Resource Corporations	28
Chapter 53B - Financial Privacy Act	28
Chapter 54 - Cooperative Organizations	28
Chapter 54A - Capital Stock Savings and Loan Associations [Repealed.]	28
Chapter 54B - Savings and Loan Associations	29
Chapter 54C - Savings Banks	29
Chapter 55 - North Carolina Business Corporation Act	30
Chapter 55A - North Carolina Nonprofit Corporation Act	31
Chapter 55B - Professional Corporation Act	31
Chapter 55C - Foreign Trade Zones	31
Chapter 55D - Filings, Names, and Registered Agents for Corporations, Nonprofit Corporations, and Partnerships	31
Chapter 56 - Electric, Telegraph and Power Companies [Repealed.]	31
Chapter 57 - Hospital, Medical and Dental Service Corporations [Recodified.]	31
Chapter 57A - Health Maintenance Organization Act [Recodified.]	31
Chapter 57B - Health Maintenance Organization Act [Recodified.]	31
Chapter 57C - North Carolina Limited Liability Company Act.	31
Chapter 58 - Insurance.	32
Chapter 58 - Insurance (Continuation)	33
Chapter 58 - Insurance (Continuation)	34
Chapter 58 - Insurance (Continuation)	35
Chapter 58 - Insurance (Continuation)	36
Chapter 58 - Insurance (Continuation)	37
Chapter 58 - Insurance (Continuation)	38
Chapter 58A - North Carolina Health Insurance Trust Commission [Recodified.]	38
Chapter 59 - Partnership	39
Chapter 59B - Uniform Unincorporated Nonprofit Association Act.	39
Chapter 60 - Railroads and Other Carriers [Repealed and Transferred.]	39
Chapter 61 - Religious Societies	39
Chapter 62 - Public Utilities	39

Chapter 62 - Public Utilities (Continuation)	40
Chapter 62A - Public Safety Telephone Service And Wireless Telephone Service	40
Chapter 63 - Aeronautics	40
Chapter 63A - North Carolina Global TransPark Authority	40
Chapter 64 - Aliens	40
Chapter 65 – Cemeteries	40
Chapter 66 - Commerce and Business	41
Chapter 67 - Dogs	41
Chapter 68 - Fences and Stock Law	41
Chapter 69 - Fire Protection	41
Chapter 70 - Indian Antiquities, Archaeological Resources and Unmarked Human Skeletal Remains Protection	42
Chapter 71 - Indians [Repealed.]	42
Chapter 71A - Indians	42
Chapter 72 - Inns, Hotels and Restaurants	42
Chapter 73 - Mills	42
Chapter 74 - Mines and Quarries	42
Chapter 74A - Company Police [Repealed.]	42
Chapter 74B - Private Protective Services Act [Repealed.]	42
Chapter 74C - Private Protective Services	42
Chapter 74D - Alarm Systems	42
Chapter 74E - Company Police Act	42
Chapter 74F - Locksmith Licensing Act	42
Chapter 74G - Campus Police Act	42
Chapter 75 - Monopolies, Trusts and Consumer Protection	42
Chapter 75A - Boating and Water Safety	43
Chapter 75B - Discrimination in Business	43
Chapter 75C - Motion Picture Fair Competition Act	43
Chapter 75D - Racketeer Influenced and Corrupt Organizations	43
Chapter 75E - Unlawful Activities in Connection With Certain Corporate Transactions	43
Chapter 76 - Navigation	43
Chapter 76A - Navigation and Pilotage Commissions	43
Chapter 77 - Rivers, Creeks, and Coastal Waters	43
Chapter 78 - Securities Law [Repealed.]	43
Chapter 78A - North Carolina Securities Act	43
Chapter 78B - Tender Offer Disclosure Act [Repealed.]	43
Chapter 78C - Investment Advisers	43
Chapter 78D - Commodities Act	43
Chapter 79 - Strays [Repealed.]	43
Chapter 80 - Trademarks, Brands, etc.	44
Chapter 81 - Weights and Measures [Recodified.]	44
Chapter 81A - Weights and Measures Act of 1975.	44
Chapter 82 - Wrecks [Repealed.]	44
Chapter 83 - Architects [Recodified.]	44

Chapter 83A - Architects	44
Chapter 84 - Attorneys-at-Law	44
Chapter 84A - Foreign Legal Consultants	44
Chapter 85 - Auctions and Auctioneers [Repealed.]	44
Chapter 85A - Bail Bondsmen and Runners [Recodified.]	44
Chapter 85B - Auctions and Auctioneers	44
Chapter 85C - Bail Bondsmen and Runners [Recodified.]	44
Chapter 86 - Barbers [Recodified.]	44
Chapter 86A - Barbers	44
Chapter 87 - Contractors	44
Chapter 88 - Cosmetic Art [Repealed.]	44
Chapter 88A - Electrolysis Practice Act	44
Chapter 88B - Cosmetic Art	45
Chapter 89 - Engineering and Land Surveying [Recodified.]	45
Chapter 89A - Landscape Architects	45
Chapter 89B - Foresters	45
Chapter 89C - Engineering and Land Surveying	45
Chapter 89D - Landscape Contractors	45
Chapter 89E - Geologists Licensing Act	45
Chapter 89F - North Carolina Soil Scientist Licensing Act	45
Chapter 89G - Irrigation Contractors	45
Chapter 90 - Medicine and Allied Occupations	45
Chapter 90 - Medicine and Allied Occupations (Continuation)	46
Chapter 90 - Medicine and Allied Occupations (Continuation)	47
Chapter 90 - Medicine and Allied Occupations (Continuation)	48
Chapter 90A - Sanitarians and Water and Wastewater Treatment Facility Operators	48
Chapter 90B - Social Worker Certification and Licensure Act	48
Chapter 90C - North Carolina Recreational Therapy Licensure Act	48
Chapter 90D - Interpreters and Transliterators	48
Chapter 91 - Pawnbrokers [Repealed.]	48
Chapter 91A - Pawnbrokers Modernization Act of 1989	48
Chapter 92 - Photographers [Deleted.]	48
Chapter 93 - Certified Public Accountants	48
Chapter 93A - Real Estate License Law	49
Chapter 93B - Occupational Licensing Boards	49
Chapter 93C - Watchmakers [Repealed.]	49
Chapter 93D - North Carolina State Hearing Aid Dealers and Fitters Board.	49
Chapter 93E - North Carolina Appraisers Act	49
Chapter 94 - Apprenticeship	49
Chapter 95 - Department of Labor and Labor Regulations	49
Chapter 95 - Department of Labor and Labor Regulations (Continuation)	50
Chapter 96 - Employment Security	50
Chapter 97 - Workers' Compensation Act	50
Chapter 97 - Workers' Compensation Act (Continuation)	51

Chapter 98 - Burnt and Lost Records	51
Chapter 99 - Libel and Slander	51
Chapter 99A - Civil Remedies for Criminal Actions	51
Chapter 99B - Products Liability	51
Chapter 99C - Actions Relating to Winter Sports Safety and Accidents	51
Chapter 99D - Civil Rights	51
Chapter 99E - Special Liability Provisions	51
Chapter 100 - Monuments, Memorials and Parks	51
Chapter 101 - Names of Persons	51
Chapter 102 - Official Survey Base	51
Chapter 103 - Sundays, Holidays and Special Days	51
Chapter 104 - United States Lands	51
Chapter 104A - Degrees of Kinship	51
Chapter 104B - Hurricanes or Other Acts of Nature	51
Chapter 104C - Atomic Energy, Radioactivity and Ionizing Radiation [Repealed and Recodified.]	51
Chapter 104D - Southern States Energy Compact	51
Chapter 104E - North Carolina Radiation Protection Act	51
Chapter 104F - Southeast Interstate Low-Level Radioactive Waste Management Compact [Repealed]	51
Chapter 104G - North Carolina Low-Level Radioactive Waste Management Authority Act of 1987 [Repealed]	51
Chapter 105 - Taxation	51
Chapter 105 - Taxation (Continuation)	52
Chapter 105 - Taxation (Continuation)	53
Chapter 105 - Taxation (Continuation)	54
Chapter 105A - Setoff Debt Collection Act	55
Chapter 105B - Defaulted Student Loan Recovery Act	55
Chapter 106 - Agriculture	55
Chapter 106 - Agriculture (Continue)	56
Chapter 106 - Agriculture (Continue)	57
Chapter 107 - Agricultural Development Districts [Repealed.]	57
Chapter 108 - Social Services [Repealed and Recodified.]	57
Chapter 108A - Social Services	57
Chapter 108B - Community Action Programs	58
Chapter 108C Medicaid and Health Choice Provider Requirements.	58
Chapter 108D Medicaid Managed Care for Behavioral Health Services.	58
Chapter 109 - Bonds [Recodified.]	58
Chapter 110 - Child Welfare	58
Chapter 111 - Aid to the Blind	58
Chapter 112 - Confederate Homes and Pensions [Repealed.]	58
Chapter 113 - Conservation and Development	58
Chapter 113 - Conservation and Development (Continuation)	59

Chapter 113A - Pollution Control and Environment	59
Chapter 113A - Pollution Control and Environment (Continuation)	60
Chapter 113B - North Carolina Energy Policy Act of 1975	60
Chapter 114 - Department of Justice	60
Chapter 115 - Elementary and Secondary Education [Repealed.]	60
Chapter 115A - Community Colleges, Technical Institutes, and Industrial Education Centers [Repealed.]	60
Chapter 115B - Tuition and Fee Waivers	60
Chapter 115C - Elementary and Secondary Education	60
Chapter 115C - Elementary and Secondary Education (Continuation)	61
Chapter 115C - Elementary and Secondary Education (Continuation)	62
Chapter 115C - Elementary and Secondary Education (Continuation)	63
Chapter 115D - Community Colleges	63
Chapter 115E - Private Educational Facilities Finance Act [Recodified]	63
Chapter 116 - Higher Education	63
Chapter 116 - Higher Education (Continuation)	63
Chapter 116A - Escheats and Abandoned Property [Repealed.]	64
Chapter 116B - Escheats and Abandoned Property	64
Chapter 116C - Continuum of Education Programs	64
Chapter 116D - Higher Education Bonds	64
Chapter 117 - Electrification	64
Chapter 118 - Firemen's and Rescue Squad Workers' Relief and Pension Funds [Recodified.]	64
Chapter 118A - Firemen's Death Benefit Act [Repealed.]	64
Chapter 118B - Members of a Rescue Squad Death Benefit Act [Repealed.]	64
Chapter 119 - Gasoline and Oil Inspection and Regulation	64
Chapter 120 - General Assembly	65
Chapter 120 - General Assembly (Continuation)	66
Chapter 120 - General Assembly (Continuation)	67
Chapter 120C - Lobbying	67
Chapter 121 - Archives and History	67
Chapter 122 - Hospitals for the Mentally Disordered [Repealed.]	67
Chapter 122A - North Carolina Housing Finance Agency	67
Chapter 122B - North Carolina Agricultural Facilities Finance Act [Repealed.]	67
Chapter 122C - Mental Health, Developmental Disabilities, and Substance Abuse Act of 1985	67
Chapter 122C - Mental Health, Developmental Disabilities, and Substance Abuse Act of 1985 (Continuation)	68
Chapter 122D - North Carolina Agricultural Finance Act	68

Chapter 122E - North Carolina Housing Trust and Oil Overcharge Act	68
Chapter 123 - Impeachment	69
Chapter 123A - Industrial Development [Repealed.]	69
Chapter 124 - Internal Improvements	69
Chapter 125 - Libraries	69
Chapter 126 - State Personnel System	69
Chapter 127 - Militia [Repealed.]	69
Chapter 127A - Militia	69
Chapter 127B - Military Affairs	69
Chapter 127C - Advisory Commission on Military Affairs	69
Chapter 128 - Offices and Public Officers	69
Chapter 128 - Offices and Public Officers (Continuation)	70
Chapter 129 - Public Buildings and Grounds	70
Chapter 130 - Public Health [Repealed.]	70
Chapter 130A - Public Health	70
Chapter 130A - Public Health (Continuation)	71
Chapter 130A - Public Health (Continuation)	72
Chapter 130B - Hazardous Waste Management Commission [Repealed.]	72
Chapter 131 - Public Hospitals [Repealed.]	72
Chapter 131A - Health Care Facilities Finance Act	72
Chapter 131B - Licensing of Ambulatory Surgical Facilities [Repealed.]	72
Chapter 131C - Charitable Solicitation Licensure Act [Repealed.]	72
Chapter 131D - Inspection and Licensing of Facilities	72
Chapter 131E - Health Care Facilities and Services	72
Chapter 131E - Health Care Facilities and Services (Continuation)	73
Chapter 131F - Solicitation of Contributions	73
Chapter 132 - Public Records	73
Chapter 133 - Public Works	74
Chapter 134 - Youth Development [Recodified.]	74
Chapter 134A - Youth Services [Repealed.]	74
Chapter 135 - Retirement System for Teachers and State Employees; Social Security; Health Insurance Program for Children	74
Chapter 135 - Retirement System for Teachers and State Employees; Social Security; Health Insurance Program for Children	75
Chapter 136 - Transportation	75
Chapter 136 - Transportation (Continuation)	76
Chapter 137 - Rural Rehabilitation [Repealed.]	76
Chapter 138 - Salaries, Fees and Allowances	76
Chapter 138A - State Government Ethics Act	76
Chapter 139 - Soil and Water Conservation Districts	76

Chapter 140 - State Art Museum; Symphony and Art Societies	76
Chapter 140A - State Awards System	76
Chapter 141 - State Boundaries	76
Chapter 142 - State Debt	76
Chapter 143 - State Departments, Institutions, and Commissions	77
Chapter 143 - State Departments, Institutions, and Commissions (Continuation)	78
Chapter 143 - State Departments, Institutions, and Commissions (Continuation)	79
Chapter 143 - State Departments, Institutions, and Commissions (Continuation)	80
Chapter 143A - State Government Reorganization	80
Chapter 143B - Executive Organization Act of 1973	80
Chapter 143B - Executive Organization Act of 1973 (Continuation)	81
Chapter 143B - Executive Organization Act of 1973 (Continuation)	82
Chapter 143C - State Budget Act	83
Chapter 143D - The State Governmental Accountability and Internal Control Act	83
Chapter 144 - State Flag, Official Governmental Flags, Motto, and Colors	83
Chapter 145 - State Symbols and Other Official Adoptions.	83
Chapter 146 - State Lands	83
Chapter 147 - State Officers	83
Chapter 148 - State Prison System	84
Chapter 149 - State Song and Toast	84
Chapter 150 - Uniform Revocation of Licenses [Repealed.]	84
Chapter 150A - Administrative Procedure Act [Recodified.]	84
Chapter 150B - Administrative Procedure Act	84
Chapter 151 - Constables [Repealed.]	84
Chapter 152 - Coroners	84
Chapter 152A - County Medical Examiner [Repealed.]	84
Chapter 152A - County Medical Examiner [Repealed.] (Continuation)	85
Chapter 153 - Counties and County Commissioners [Repealed.]	85
Chapter 153A - Counties	85
Chapter 153B - Mountain Resources Planning Act	85
Chapter 153C - Uwharrie Regional Resources Act	85
Chapter 154 - County Surveyor [Repealed.]	85
Chapter 155 - County Treasurer [Repealed.]	85
Chapter 156 - Drainage	85
Chapter 156 – Drainage (Continuation)	86

Chapter 157 - Housing Authorities and Projects	86
Chapter 157A - Historic Properties Commissions [Transferred.]	86
Chapter 158 - Local Development	86
Chapter 159 - Local Government Finance	86
Chapter 159 - Local Government Finance (Continuation)	87
Chapter 159A - Pollution Abatement and Industrial Facilities Financing Act [Unconstitutional.]	87
Chapter 159B - Joint Municipal Electric Power and Energy Act	87
Chapter 159C - Industrial and Pollution Control Facilities Financing Act	87
Chapter 159D - The North Carolina Capital Facilities Financing Act	87
Chapter 159E - Registered Public Obligations Act	87
Chapter 159F - North Carolina Energy Development Authority [Repealed.]	87
Chapter 159G - Water Infrastructure	87
Chapter 159H - [Reserved.]	87
Chapter 159I - Solid Waste Management Loan Program and Local Government Special Obligation Bonds	87
Chapter 160 - Municipal Corporations [Repealed And Transferred.]	87
Chapter 160A - Cities and Towns	88
Chapter 160A - Cities and Towns (Continuation)	89
Chapter 160B - Consolidated City-County Act	89
Chapter 160C - Baseball Park Districts [Repealed.]	90
Chapter 161 - Register of Deeds	90
Chapter 162 - Sheriff	90
Chapter 162A - Water and Sewer Systems	90
Chapter 162B Continuity of Local Government in Emergency.	90
Chapter 163 Elections and Election Laws.	90
Chapter 163 Elections and Election Laws. (Continuation)	91
Chapter 164 Concerning the General Statutes of North Carolina.	92
Chapter 165 Veterans.	92
Chapter 166 Civil Preparedness Agencies [Repealed.]	92
Chapter 166A North Carolina Emergency Management Act.	92
Chapter 167 State Civil Air Patrol [Repealed.]	92
Chapter 168 Persons with Disabilities.	92
Chapter 168A Persons With Disabilities Protection Act.	92

Chapter 88B.

Cosmetic Art.

§ 88B-1. Short title.

This chapter shall be known and may be cited as the North Carolina Cosmetic Art Act. (1998-230, s. 2.)

§ 88B-2. Definitions.

The following definitions apply in this Chapter:

(1) Apprentice. - A person who is not a manager or operator and who is engaged in learning the practice of cosmetic art under the direction and supervision of a cosmetologist.

(2) Board. - The North Carolina Board of Cosmetic Art Examiners.

(3) Booth. - A workstation located within a licensed cosmetic art shop that is operated primarily by one individual in performing cosmetic art services for consumers.

(4) Booth renter. - A person who rents a booth in a cosmetic art shop.

(5) Cosmetic art. - All or any part or combination of cosmetology, esthetics, natural hair care, or manicuring, including the systematic manipulation with the hands or mechanical apparatus of the scalp, face, neck, shoulders, hands, and feet. Practices included within this subdivision shall not include the practice of massage or bodywork therapy as set forth in Article 36 of Chapter 90 of the General Statutes.

(6) Cosmetic art school. - Any building or part thereof where cosmetic art is taught.

(7) Cosmetic art shop. - Any building or part thereof where cosmetic art is practiced for pay or reward, whether direct or indirect.

(8) Cosmetologist. - Any individual who is licensed to practice all parts of cosmetic art.

(8a) Cosmetology. - The act of arranging, dressing, curling, waving, cleansing, cutting, singeing, bleaching, coloring, or similar work upon the hair of a person by any means, including the use of hands, mechanical or electrical apparatus, or appliances or by use of cosmetic or chemical preparations or antiseptics.

(9) Cosmetology teacher. - An individual licensed by the Board to teach all parts of cosmetic art.

(10) Esthetician. - An individual licensed by the Board to practice only that part of cosmetic art that constitutes skin care.

(11) Esthetician teacher. - An individual licensed by the Board to teach only that part of cosmetic art that constitutes skin care.

(11a) Esthetics. - Refers to any of the following practices: giving facials; applying makeup; performing skin care; removing superfluous hair from the body of a person by use of creams, tweezers, or waxing; applying eyelashes to a person, including the application of eyelash extensions, brow or lash color; beautifying the face, neck, arms, or upper part of the human body by use of cosmetic preparations, antiseptics, tonics, lotions, or creams; surface manipulation in relation to skin care; or cleaning or stimulating the face, neck, ears, arms, hands, bust, torso, legs, or feet of a person by means of hands, devices, apparatus, or appliances along with the use of cosmetic preparations, antiseptics, tonics, lotions, or creams.

(12) Manicuring. - The care and treatment of the fingernails, toenails, cuticles on fingernails and toenails, and the hands and feet, including the decoration of the fingernails and the application of nail extensions and artificial nails. The term "manicuring" shall not include the treatment of pathologic conditions.

(13) Manicurist. - An individual licensed by the Board to practice only that part of cosmetic art that constitutes manicuring.

(14) Manicurist teacher. - An individual licensed by the Board to teach manicuring.

(14a) Natural hair care. - A service that results in tension on hair strands or roots by twisting, wrapping, extending, or locking hair by hand or mechanical device. For purposes of this definition, the phrase "natural hair care" shall include the use of artificial or natural hair.

(14b) Natural hair care specialist. - An individual licensed by the Board to practice only that part of cosmetic art that constitutes natural hair care.

(14c) Natural hair care teacher. - An individual licensed by the Board to teach natural hair care.

(15) Shampooing. - The application and removal of commonly used, room temperature, liquid hair cleaning and hair conditioning products. Shampooing does not include the arranging, dressing, waving, coloring, or other treatment of the hair. (1933, c. 179, ss. 2-4, 8, 9; 1963, c. 1257, s. 1; 1981, c. 615, ss. 3, 7; 1993, c. 22, s. 1; 1998-230, s. 2; 2006-212, s. 1; 2009-521, s. 1.1.)

§ 88B-3. Creation and membership of the Board; term of office; removal for cause; officers.

(a) The North Carolina Board of Cosmetic Art Examiners is established. The Board shall consist of six members who shall be appointed as follows:

(1) The General Assembly, upon the recommendation of the President Pro Tempore of the Senate, shall appoint a cosmetologist.

(2) The General Assembly, upon the recommendation of the Speaker of the House of Representatives, shall appoint a cosmetologist.

(3) The Governor shall appoint two cosmetologists, a cosmetology teacher, and a member of the public who is not licensed under this Chapter.

(b) Each cosmetologist member shall have practiced all parts of cosmetic art in this State for at least five years immediately preceding appointment to the Board and shall not have any connection with any cosmetic art school while serving on the Board. The cosmetology teacher member shall be currently employed as a teacher by a North Carolina public school, community college, or other public or private cosmetic art school and shall have practiced or taught cosmetic art for at least five years immediately preceding appointment to the Board.

(c)   Cosmetologist members of the Board shall serve staggered terms of three years. No Board member shall serve more than two consecutive terms, except that each member shall serve until a successor is appointed and qualified. All other board members shall serve three-year terms, but they shall not be staggered.

(d)   The Governor may remove any member of the Board for cause.

(e)   A vacancy shall be filled in the same manner as the original appointment, except that unexpired terms in seats appointed by the General Assembly shall be filled in accordance with G.S. 120-122. Appointees to fill vacancies shall serve the remainder of the unexpired term and until their successors have been duly appointed and qualified.

(f)   The Board shall elect a chair, a vice-chair, and other officers as deemed necessary by the Board to carry out the purposes of this Chapter. All officers shall be elected annually by the Board for one-year terms and shall serve until their successors are elected and qualified.

(g)   The Board shall not issue a teacher's license to any Board member during that member's term on the Board.

(h)   No Board member may be employed by the Board for at least one year after that member's term expires. (1933, c. 179, ss. 13, 14, 23; 1935, c. 54, ss. 2, 5; 1943, c. 354, s. 1; 1957, c. 1184, s. 1; 1969, c. 844, s. 4; 1971, c. 355, s. 1; c. 616, ss. 1, 2; 1973, c. 476, s. 128; c. 1360, s. 1; 1975, c. 857, ss. 2, 3, 9; 1981, c. 614, s. 1; c. 615, ss. 10, 14; c. 884, s. 7; 1987, c. 211, s. 1; 1989, c. 650, s. 1; 1995, c. 490, s. 13; (Reg. Sess., 1996), c. 605, s. 16; 1998-230, s. 2.)

§ 88B-4. Powers and duties of the Board.

(a)   The Board shall have the following powers and duties:

(1)   To administer and interpret this Chapter.

(2) To adopt, amend, and repeal rules to carry out the provisions of this Chapter.

(3) To examine and determine the qualifications and fitness of applicants for licensure under this Chapter.

(4) To issue, renew, deny, restrict, suspend, or revoke licenses.

(5) To conduct investigations of alleged violations of this Chapter or the Board's rules.

(6) To collect fees required by G.S. 88B-20 and any other monies permitted by law to be paid to the Board.

(7) To approve new cosmetic art schools.

(7a) To adopt rules for cosmetic art schools.

(8) To inspect cosmetic art schools and shops.

(9) To adopt rules for the sanitary management and physical requirements of cosmetic art shops and cosmetic art schools.

(10) To establish a curriculum for each course of study required for the issuance of a license issued under this Chapter.

(11) To employ an executive director and any additional professional, clerical, or special personnel necessary to carry out the provisions of this Chapter, and to purchase or rent necessary office space, equipment, and supplies.

(12) To adopt a seal.

(13) To carry out any other actions authorized by this Chapter.

(b) A member of the Board shall have the authority to inspect cosmetic art shops and cosmetic art schools at any reasonable hour to determine compliance with the provisions of this Chapter if the inspection is made: (i) at the request of the Board, or with the approval of the chair or the executive director as the result of a complaint made to the Board or a problem reported by an inspector, or (ii) at the request of an inspector who deems it necessary to request the assistance of a Board member and who has the prior approval of the chair or executive director to do so. A Board member who makes an inspection pursuant to this subsection shall file a report with the Board before requesting reimbursement for expenses.

(c)   The Board shall keep a record of its proceedings relating to the issuance, renewal, denial, restriction, suspension, and revocation of licenses. This record shall also contain each licensee's name, business and home addresses, license number, and the date the license was issued. (1933, c. 179, ss. 1, 14, 15, 17, 23, 29; 1935, c. 54, ss. 3-5; 1941, c. 234, s. 2; 1943, c. 354, ss. 1, 2; 1957, c. 1184, ss. 1, 2; 1969, c. 844, s. 5; 1971, c. 355, ss. 1-3; c. 616, ss. 1-3; 1973, c. 476, s. 128; c. 1360, ss. 2-4; c. 1481, ss. 1, 2; 1975, c. 7, s. 1; c. 857, ss. 1, 3-5, 9; 1977, cc. 155, 472; 1981, c. 614, s. 1; c. 615, ss. 1, 2, 11, 14; c. 884, s. 7; 1983, c. 913, s. 9; 1983 (Reg. Sess., 1984), c. 990; 1985, c. 125; 1985 (Reg. Sess., 1986), c. 833; 1987 (Reg. Sess., 1988), c. 965; 1989, c. 650, ss. 2, 3; 1989 (Reg. Sess., 1990), c. 1013, s. 1; 1991 (Reg. Sess., 1992), c. 1030, s. 20; 1993, c. 22, s. 2; c. 54, s. 1; 1995, c. 541, s. 2; 1995 (Reg. Sess., 1996), c. 605, ss. 15, 16; 1998-230, s. 2; 1999-348, s. 1.)

§ 88B-5. Meetings and compensation of the Board.

(a)   Each member of the Board shall receive compensation for services and expenses as provided in G.S. 93B-5, but shall be limited to payment for services deemed official business of the Board when such business exceeds three continuous hours per day. Official business of the Board includes meetings called by the chair and time spent inspecting cosmetic art shops and schools as permitted by this Chapter. No payment for per diem or travel expenses shall be authorized or paid for Board meetings other than those called by the chair. The Board may annually select one member to attend a national state board of cosmetic arts meeting on official business of the Board. No other Board members shall be authorized to attend trade shows or to travel out-of-state at the Board's expense.

(b)   The Board shall hold four regular meetings a year in the months of January, April, July, and October. The chair may call additional meetings whenever necessary. (1933, c. 179, ss. 15, 17; 1935, c. 54, ss. 3, 4; 1941, c. 234, s. 2; 1943, c. 354, s. 2; 1957, c. 1184, s. 2; 1971, c. 355, ss. 2, 3; c. 616, ss. 1, 3; 1973, c. 1360, ss. 2-4; 1975, c. 857, ss. 4, 5; 1981, c. 615, s. 11; 1983, c. 913, s. 9; 1989, c. 650, ss. 2, 3; 1995, c. 541, s. 2; 1998-230, s. 2.)

§ 88B-6. Board office, employees, funds, budget requirements.

(a)   The Board shall maintain its office in Raleigh, North Carolina.

(b)   The Board shall employ an executive director who shall not be a member of the Board. The executive director shall keep all records of the Board, issue all necessary notices, and perform any other duties required by the Board.

(c)   With the approval of the Director of the Budget and the Office of State Human Resources, the Board may employ as many inspectors, investigators, and other staff as necessary to perform inspections and other duties prescribed by the Board. Inspectors and investigators shall be experienced in all parts of cosmetic art and shall have authority to examine cosmetic art shops and cosmetic art schools during business hours to determine compliance with this Chapter.

(d)   The salaries of all employees of the Board, excluding the executive director, shall be subject to the North Carolina Human Resources Act. The executive director shall serve at the pleasure of the Board.

(e)   The executive director may collect in the Board's name and on its behalf the fees prescribed in this Chapter and shall turn these and any other monies paid to the Board over to the State Treasurer. These funds shall be credited to the Board and shall be held and expended under the supervision of the Director of the Budget only for the administration and enforcement of this Chapter. Nothing in this Chapter shall authorize any expenditure in excess of the amount credited to the Board and held by the State Treasurer as provided in this subsection.

(f)   The Executive Budget Act and the North Carolina Human Resources Act apply to the administration of this Chapter. (1933, c. 179, ss. 14, 15; 1935, c. 54, s. 3; 1941, c. 234, s. 2; 1943, c. 354, ss. 1, 2; 1957, c. 1184, ss. 1, 2; 1969, c. 844, s. 4; 1971, c. 355, ss. 1-3; c. 616, ss. 1-3; 1973, c. 1360, s. 2; 1975, c. 857, ss. 3, 4; 1981, c. 615, s. 11; c. 884, s. 7; 1983, c. 913, s. 9; 1989, c. 650, s. 2.; 1998-230, s. 2; 2009-471, ss. 2.1, 2.2; 2009-521, s. 1.2; 2013-382, s. 9.1(c).)

§ 88B-7. Qualifications for licensing cosmetologists.

The Board shall issue a license to practice as a cosmetologist to any individual who meets all of the following requirements:

(1) Successful completion of at least 1,500 hours of a cosmetology curriculum in an approved cosmetic art school, or at least 1,200 hours of a cosmetology curriculum in an approved cosmetic art school and completion of an apprenticeship for a period of at least six months under the direct supervision of a cosmetologist, as certified by sworn affidavit of three licensed cosmetologists or by other evidence satisfactory to the Board.

(2) Passage of an examination conducted by the Board.

(3) Payment of the fees required by G.S. 88B-20. (1933, c. 179, s. 12; 1953, c. 1304, s. 3; 1973, c. 450, s. 2; 1977, c. 899, s. 1; 1981, c. 615, s. 9; 1985, c. 559, s. 5; 1998-230, s. 2.)

§ 88B-8. Qualifications for licensing apprentices.

The Board shall issue a license to practice as an apprentice to any individual who meets all of the following requirements:

(1) Successful completion of at least 1,200 hours of a cosmetology curriculum in an approved cosmetic art school.

(2) Passage of an examination conducted by the Board.

(3) Payment of the fees required by G.S. 88B-20. (1933, c. 179, s. 10; 1941, c. 234, s. 1; 1953, c. 1304, ss. 1, 2; 1963, c. 1257, s. 2; 1973, c. 450, s. 1; 1981, c. 615, s. 8; 1998-230, s. 2.)

§ 88B-9. Qualifications for licensing as an esthetician.

The Board shall issue a license to practice as an esthetician to any individual who meets all of the following requirements:

(1) Successful completion of at least 600 hours of an esthetics curriculum in an approved cosmetic art school.

(2) Passage of an examination conducted by the Board.

(3) Payment of the fees required by G.S. 88B-20. (1998-230, s. 2; 2006-212, s. 3.)

§ 88B-10. Qualifications for licensing manicurists.

The Board shall issue a license to practice as a manicurist to any individual who meets all of the following requirements:

(1) Successful completion of at least 300 hours of a manicurist curriculum in an approved cosmetic art school.

(2) Passage of an examination conducted by the Board.

(3) Payment of the fees required by G.S. 88B-20. (1963, c. 1257, s. 4; 1973, c. 450, s. 4; 1981, c. 615, s. 19; 1985, c. 559, s. 4; 1998-230, ss. 2, 2.1.)

§ 88B-10.1. Qualifications for licensing natural hair care specialists.

The Board shall issue a license to practice as a natural hair care specialist to any individual who meets all of the following requirements:

(1) Successful completion of at least 300 hours of a natural hair care curriculum in an approved cosmetic art school.

(2) Passage of an examination conducted by the Board.

(3) Payment of the fees required by G.S. 88B-20. (2009-521, s. 2.)

§ 88B-11. Qualifications for licensing teachers.

(a) Applicants for any teacher's license issued by the Board shall meet all of the following requirements:

(1) Possession of a high school diploma or a high school graduation equivalency certificate.

(2) Payment of the fees required by G.S. 88B-20.

(b) The Board shall issue a license to practice as a cosmetology teacher to any individual who meets the requirements of subsection (a) of this section and who meets all of the following:

(1) Holds in good standing a cosmetologist license issued by the Board.

(2) Submits proof of either practice of cosmetic art in a cosmetic art shop, or any Board-approved employment capacity in the cosmetic arts industry, for a period equivalent to five years of full-time work immediately prior to application or successful completion of at least 800 hours of a cosmetology teacher curriculum in an approved cosmetic art school.

(3) Passes an examination for cosmetology teachers conducted by the Board.

(c) The Board shall issue a license to practice as an esthetician teacher to any individual who meets the requirements of subsection (a) of this section and who meets all of the following:

(1) Holds in good standing a cosmetologist or an esthetician license issued by the Board.

(2) Submits proof of either practice as an esthetician in a cosmetic art shop, or any Board-approved employment capacity in the cosmetic arts industry, for a period equivalent to three years of full-time work immediately prior to application or successful completion of at least 650 hours of an esthetician teacher curriculum in an approved cosmetic art school.

(3) Passes an examination for esthetician teachers conducted by the Board.

(d) The Board shall issue a license to practice as a manicurist teacher to any individual who meets the requirements of subsection (a) of this section and who meets all of the following:

(1) Holds in good standing a cosmetologist or manicurist license issued by the Board.

(2) Submits proof of either practice as a manicurist in a cosmetic art shop, or any Board-approved employment capacity in the cosmetic arts industry, for a period equivalent to two years of full-time work immediately prior to application or successful completion of at least 320 hours of a manicurist teacher curriculum in an approved cosmetic art school.

(3) Passes an examination for manicurist teachers conducted by the Board.

(e) The Board shall issue a license to practice as a natural hair care teacher to any individual who meets the requirements of subsection (a) of this section and who meets all of the following:

(1) Holds in good standing a natural hair care license issued by the Board.

(2) Submits proof of either practice as a natural hair care specialist in a cosmetic art shop or any Board-approved employment capacity in the cosmetic art industry for a period equivalent to two years of full-time work immediately prior to application or successful completion of at least 320 hours of a natural hair care teacher curriculum in an approved cosmetic art school. (1998-230, s. 2; 2006-212, s. 5; 2009-521, s. 3.)

§ 88B-12. Temporary employment permit; extensions; limits on practice.

(a) The Board shall issue a temporary employment permit to an applicant for licensure as an apprentice, cosmetologist, esthetician, natural hair care specialist, or manicurist who meets all of the following:

(1) Has completed the required hours of a cosmetic art school curriculum in the area in which the applicant wishes to be licensed.

(2) Has applied to take the examination within three months of completing the required hours.

(3) Is qualified to take the examination.

(b)　A temporary employment permit shall expire six months from the date of graduation from a cosmetic art school and shall not be renewed.

(c)　The holder of a temporary employment permit may practice cosmetic art only under the supervision of a licensed cosmetologist, manicurist, natural hair care specialist, or esthetician, as appropriate, and may not operate a cosmetic art shop. (1989 (Reg. Sess., 1990), c. 1013, s. 1; 1991 (Reg. Sess., 1992), c. 1030, s. 20; 1998-230, s. 2; 2009-521, s. 4.)

§ 88B-13.　Applicants licensed in other states.

(a)　The Board shall issue a license to an applicant licensed as an apprentice, cosmetologist, esthetician, natural hair care specialist, or manicurist in another state if the applicant shows:

(1)　The applicant is an active practitioner in good standing.

(2)　The applicant has practiced at least one of the three years immediately preceding the application for a license.

(3)　There is no disciplinary proceeding or unresolved complaint pending against the applicant at the time a license is to be issued by this State.

(4)　The licensure requirements in the state in which the applicant is licensed are substantially equivalent to those required by this State.

(b)　Instead of meeting the requirements in subsection (a) of this section, any applicant who is licensed as a cosmetologist, esthetician, natural hair care specialist, or manicurist in another state shall be admitted to practice in this State under the same reciprocity or comity provisions that the state in which the applicant is licensed grants to persons licensed in this State.

(c)　The Board may establish standards for issuing a license to an applicant who is licensed as a teacher in another state. These standards shall include a requirement that the licensure requirements in the state in which the teacher is licensed shall be substantially equivalent to those required in this State and that the applicant shall be licensed by the Board to practice in the area in which the applicant is licensed to teach. (1933, c. 179, s. 19; 1953, c. 1304, s. 4; 1957, c.

1184, s. 3; 1963, c. 1257, s. 3; 1973, c. 256, s. 1; 1981, c. 615, s. 12; c. 967; 1983, c. 438; 1998-230, s. 2; 2009-521, s. 5.)

§ 88B-14. Licensing of cosmetic art shops.

(a)   The Board shall issue a license to operate a cosmetic art shop to any applicant who submits a properly completed application, on a form approved by the Board, pays the required fee, and is determined, after inspection, to be in compliance with the provisions of this Chapter and the Board's rules.

(b)   The applicant shall list all licensees who practice cosmetic art in the shop and shall identify each as an employee or a booth renter.

(c)   A cosmetic art shop shall be allowed to operate for a period of 30 days while the Board inspects and determines the shop's compliance with this Chapter and the Board's rules. If the Board is unable to complete the inspection within 30 days, the shop will be authorized to operate until such an inspection can be completed.

(d)   A license to operate a cosmetic art shop shall not be transferable from one location to another or from one owner to another. (1933, c. 179, s. 1; 1973, c. 1481, ss. 1, 2; 1975, c. 7; c. 857, s. 1; 1977, cc. 155, 472; 1981, c. 615, ss. 1, 2; 1983 (Reg. Sess., 1984), c. 990; 1985, c. 125; 1985 (Reg. Sess., 1986), c. 833; 1987 (Reg. Sess., 1988), c. 965; 1993, c. 22, s. 2; c. 54, s. 1; 1995 (Reg. Sess., 1996), c. 605, s. 15; 1998-230, s. 2; 2009-521, s. 6.)

§ 88B-15. Practice outside cosmetic art shops.

(a)   Any individual licensed under this Chapter may visit the residences of individuals who are sick or disabled and confined to their places of residence in order to attend to their cosmetic needs. A licensed individual may also visit hospitals, nursing homes, rest homes, retirement homes, mental institutions, correctional facilities, funeral homes, and similar institutions to attend to the cosmetic needs of those in these institutions.

(b)   An individual licensed under this Chapter may practice in a licensed barbershop as permitted by G.S. 86A-14. (1933, c. 179, s. 1; 1973, c. 1481, ss.

1, 2; 1975, c. 7; c. 857, s. 1; 1977, cc. 155, 472; 1981, c. 615, ss. 1, 2, 6; 1983 (Reg. Sess., 1984), c. 990; 1985, c. 125; 1985 (Reg. Sess., 1986), c. 833; 1987 (Reg. Sess., 1988), c. 965; 1993, c. 22, s. 2; c. 54, s. 1; 1995 (Reg. Sess., 1996), c. 605, s. 15; 1998-230, s. 2.)

§ 88B-16. Licensing cosmetic art schools.

(a)   The Board shall issue a license to any cosmetic art school that submits a properly completed application, on a form approved by the Board, pays the required license fee, and is determined by the Board, after inspection, to be in compliance with the provisions of this Chapter and the Board's rules.

(b)   No one may open or operate a cosmetic art school before the Board has approved a license for the school. The Board shall not issue a license before a cosmetic art school has been inspected and determined to be in compliance with the provisions of this Chapter and the Board's rules.

(c)   Cosmetic art schools located in this State shall be licensed by the Board before any credit may be given for curriculum hours taken in the school. The Board may establish standards for approving hours from schools in other states that are licensed. (1933, c. 179, s. 23; 1935, c. 54, s. 5; 1973, c. 476, s. 128; 1975, c. 857, s. 9; 1981, c. 614, s. 1; c. 615, s. 14; 1995 (Reg. Sess., 1996), c. 605, s. 16.; 1998-230, s. 2.)

§ 88B-17. Bond required for private cosmetic art schools.

(a)   Each private cosmetic art school shall provide a guaranty bond unless the school has already provided a bond or an alternative to a bond under G.S. 115D-95. The Board may restrict, suspend, revoke, or refuse to renew or reinstate the license of a school that fails to maintain a bond or an alternative to a bond pursuant to this section or G.S. 115D-95.

(b)   (1)   The applicant shall file the guaranty bond with the clerk of superior court in the county in which the school is located. The bond shall be in favor of the students. The bond shall be executed by the applicant as principal and by a bonding company authorized to do business in this State. The bond shall be conditioned to provide indemnification to any student or the student's parent or guardian who has suffered loss of tuition or any fees by reason of the failure of the school to offer or complete student instruction, academic services, or other goods and services as related to course enrollment for any reason, including suspension, revocation, or nonrenewal of a school's approval, bankruptcy, foreclosure, or the school's ceasing to operate.

(2)   The bond amount shall be at least equal to the maximum amount of prepaid tuition held at any time by the school during the last fiscal year, but in no case shall be less than ten thousand dollars ($10,000). Each application for license or license renewal shall include a letter signed by an authorized representative of the school showing the calculations made and the method of computing the amount of the bond in accordance with rules prescribed by the Board. If the Board finds that the calculations made and the method of computing the amount of the bond are inaccurate or that the amount of the bond is otherwise inadequate to provide indemnification under the terms of the bond, the Board may require the applicant to provide an additional bond.

(3)   The bond shall remain in force and effect until canceled by the guarantor. The guarantor may cancel the bond upon 30 days' notice to the Board. Cancellation of the bond shall not affect any liability incurred or accrued prior to the termination of the notice period.

(c)   An applicant who is unable to secure a bond may seek from the Board a waiver of the guaranty bond requirement and approval of one of the guaranty bond alternatives set forth in this subsection. With the approval of the Board, an applicant may file one of the following instead of a bond with the clerk of court in the county in which the school is located:

(1)   An assignment of a savings account in an amount equal to the bond required that is in a form acceptable to the Board, and is executed by the applicant and a state or federal savings and loan association, state bank, or national bank that is doing business in this State and whose accounts are insured by a federal depositor's corporation, and access to the account is subject to the same conditions as those for a bond in subsection (b) of this section.

(2)   A certificate of deposit that is executed by a state or federal savings and loan association, state bank, or national bank that is doing business in this State and whose accounts are insured by a federal depositor's corporation and access to the certificate of deposit is subject to the same conditions as those for

a bond in subsection (b) of this section. (1989 (Reg. Sess., 1990), c. 824, s. 4; 1991, c. 636, s. 5; 1998-230, s. 2.)

§ 88B-18. Examinations.

(a)   Repealed by Session Laws 2006-212, s. 2, effective August 8, 2006.

(b)   Each examination shall have both a practical and a written portion.

(c)   Examinations for applicants for apprentice, cosmetologist, teacher, esthetician, natural hair care specialist, and manicurist licenses shall be given in at least three locations in the State that are geographically scattered. The examinations shall be administered in Board-approved facilities.

(d)   An applicant for a cosmetologist, esthetician, manicurist, natural hair care specialist, or teacher's license who fails to pass the examination three times may not reapply to take the examination again until after the applicant has successfully completed any additional requirements prescribed by the Board. (1933, c. 179, ss. 16, 17; 1935, c. 54, s. 4; 1973, c. 1360, ss. 3, 4; 1975, c. 857, s. 5; 1985, c. 559, s. 1; 1989, c. 650, s. 3; 1995, c. 541, s. 2; 1998-230, s. 2; 2006-212, s. 2; 2009-521, s. 7.)

§ 88B-19. Expired school credits.

No credit shall be approved by the Board if five years or more have elapsed from the date a person enrolled in a cosmetic art school unless the person completed the required number of hours and filed an application to take an examination administered by the Board. (1933, c. 179, s. 12; 1953, c. 1304, s. 3; 1973, c. 450, s. 2; 1977, c. 899, s. 1; 1981, c. 615, s. 9; 1985, c. 559, s. 5; 1998-230, s. 2.)

§ 88B-20. Fees required.

(a)   The Board may charge the applicant the actual cost of preparation, administration, and grading of examinations for cosmetologists, apprentices, manicurists, estheticians, natural hair care specialist, or teachers, in addition to its other fees.

(b) The Board may charge application fees as follows:

(1) Inspection of a newly established cosmetic art shop.......................... $ 25.00

(2) Reciprocity applicant under G.S. 88B-13.. $ 15.00.

(c) The Board may charge license fees as follows:

(1) Cosmetologist... $ 39.00 every 3 years

(2) Apprentice... $ 10.00 per year

(3) Esthetician.. $ 10.00 per year

(4) Manicurist... $ 10.00 per year

(4a) Natural hair care specialist... $ 10.00 per year

(5) Teacher... $ 10.00 every 2 years

(6) Cosmetic art shop per active booth.............................. $ 3.00 per year

(7) Cosmetic art school.. $ 50.00 per year

(8) Duplicate license.. $ 1.00.

(d) The Board may require payment of late fees and reinstatement fees as follows:

(1)....... Apprentice, cosmetologist, esthetician, manicurist,

    natural hair care specialist, and teacher late renewal.......................... $ 10.00

(2) Cosmetic art schools and shops late renewal....................................... $ 10.00

(3) Reinstatement - cosmetic art schools and shops................................ $ 25.00.

(e) The Board may prorate fees as appropriate. (1933, c. 179, ss. 1, 21; 1955, c. 1265; 1973, c. 256, s. 2; c. 1481, ss. 1, 2; 1975, c. 7; c. 857, ss. 1, 6; 1977, cc. 155, 472; 1981, c. 615, ss. 1, 2, 13; 1983, c. 523; (Reg. Sess., 1984), c. 990; 1985, c. 125; 1985, c. 559, s. 2; (Reg. Sess., 1986), c. 833; 1987 (Reg. Sess., 1988), c. 965; 1993, c. 22, s. 2; c. 54, s. 1; 1995, c. 541, s. 1; (Reg. Sess., 1996), c. 605, s. 15; 1998-230, s. 2; 1999-348, s. 2; 2009-521, s. 8.)

§ 88B-21. Renewals; expired licenses; inactive status.

(a) Each license to operate a cosmetic art shop shall be renewed on or before the first day of February of each year. As provided in G.S. 88B-20, a late fee shall be charged for licenses renewed after February 1. Any license not renewed by March 1 of each year shall expire. A cosmetic art shop whose license has been expired for one year or less shall have the license reinstated immediately upon payment of the reinstatement fee, the late fee, and all unpaid license fees. The licensee shall submit to the Board, as a part of the renewal process, a list of all licensed cosmetologists who practice cosmetic art in the shop and shall identify each as an employee or a booth renter.

(b) Cosmetologist licenses shall be renewed on or before October 1 every three years beginning October 1, 1998. A late fee shall be charged for renewals after that date. Any license not renewed shall expire on October 1 of the year that renewal is required. The Board may develop and implement a plan for staggered license renewal and may prorate license fees to implement such a plan.

(c) Apprentice, esthetician, natural hair care specialist, and manicurist licenses shall be renewed annually on or before October 1 of each year. A late fee shall be charged for the renewal of licenses after that date. Any license not renewed shall expire on October 1 of that year.

(d) Teacher licenses shall be renewed every two years on or before October 1. A late fee shall be charged for the renewal of licenses after that date. Any license not renewed shall expire on October 1 of that year.

(e) Prior to renewal of a license, a teacher, cosmetologist, esthetician, natural hair care specialist, or manicurist shall annually complete eight hours of Board-approved continuing education for each year of the licensing cycle. A cosmetologist may complete up to 24 hours of required continuing education at any time within the cosmetologist's three-year licensing cycle. Licensees shall submit written documentation to the Board showing that they have satisfied the requirements of this subsection. A licensee who is in active practice as a cosmetologist, esthetician, natural hair care specialist, or manicurist, has practiced for at least 10 consecutive years in that profession, and is 60 years of age or older does not have to meet the continuing education requirements of this subsection. A licensee who is in active practice as a cosmetologist and has at least 20 consecutive years of experience as a cosmetologist, does not have to meet the continuing education requirements of this subsection, but shall report any continuing education classes completed to the Board, whether the continuing education classes are Board-approved or not. Promotion of products and systems shall be allowed at continuing education given in-house or at trade shows. Continuing education classes may also be offered in secondary languages as needed. No member of the Board may offer continuing education courses as required by this section.

(f) If an apprentice, cosmetologist, esthetician, manicurist, natural hair care specialist, or teacher fails to renew his or her license within five years following the expiration date, the licensee shall be required to pass an examination as prescribed by the Board before the license will be reinstated.

(g) Cosmetic art school licenses shall be renewed on or before October 1 of each year. A late fee shall be charged for licenses renewed after that date. Any license not renewed by November 1 of that year shall expire. A cosmetic art school whose license has been expired for one year or less shall have its license reinstated upon payment of the reinstatement fee, the late fee, and all unpaid license fees.

(h) Upon request by a licensee for inactive status, the Board may place the licensee's name on the inactive list so long as the licensee is in good standing with the Board. An inactive licensee is not required to complete continuing education requirements. An inactive licensee shall not practice cosmetic art for consideration. However, the inactive licensee may continue to purchase supplies as accorded an active licensee. When the inactive licensee desires to be removed from the inactive list and return to active practice, the inactive licensee shall notify the Board of his or her desire to return to active status and pay the required fee as determined by the Board. As a condition of returning to active status, the Board may require the licensee to complete eight to 24 hours of continuing education pursuant to subsection (e) of this section. (1933, c. 179, ss. 1, 25; 1957, c. 1184, s. 4; 1973, c. 256, s. 3; c. 450, s. 3; c. 1481, ss. 1, 2; 1975, c. 7; c. 857, ss. 1, 7; 1977, cc. 155, 472; 1981, c. 615, ss. 1, 2; 1983 (Reg. Sess., 1984), c. 990; 1985, c. 125; 1985, c. 559, s. 3; (Reg. Sess., 1986), c. 833; 1987 (Reg. Sess., 1988), c. 965; 1993, c. 22, s. 2; c. 54, s. 1; 1995 (Reg. Sess., 1996), c. 605, s. 15; 1998-230, s. 2; 2004-142, s. 1; 2006-212, s. 6; 2007-198, s. 1; 2009-521, s. 9.)

§ 88B-22. Licenses required; criminal penalty.

(a) Except as provided in this Chapter, no person may practice or attempt to practice cosmetic art for pay or reward in any form, either directly or indirectly, without being licensed as an apprentice, cosmetologist, esthetician, natural hair care specialist, or manicurist by the Board.

(b) Except as provided in this Chapter, no person may practice cosmetic art or any part of cosmetic art, for pay or reward in any form, either directly or indirectly, outside of a licensed cosmetic art shop.

(c) No person may open or operate a cosmetic art shop in this State unless a license has been issued by the Board for that shop.

(d) An individual licensed as an esthetician, natural hair care specialist, or manicurist may practice only that part of cosmetic art for which the individual is licensed.

(d1) No person may teach cosmetic art in a Board-approved cosmetic art school unless the person is a teacher licensed under this Chapter. A guest lecturer may be exempt from the requirements of this subsection upon approval by the Board.

(e)   An apprentice licensed under the provisions of this Chapter shall apprentice under the direct supervision of a cosmetologist. An apprentice shall not operate a cosmetic art shop.

(f)   A violation of this Chapter is a Class 3 misdemeanor. (1933, c. 179, ss. 1, 11, 28; 1949, c. 505, s. 2; 1973, c. 476, s. 128; c. 1481, ss. 1, 2; 1975, c. 7; c. 857, ss. 1, 8; 1977, cc. 155, 472; 1981, c. 614, s. 2; c. 615, ss. 1, 2, 17; 1983 (Reg. Sess., 1984), c. 990; 1985, c. 125; 1985 (Reg. Sess., 1986), c. 833; 1987 (Reg. Sess., 1988), c. 965; 1989 (Reg. Sess., 1990), c. 1013, s. 3; 1993, c. 22, s. 2; c. 54, s. 1; c. 539, s. 608; 1994, Ex. Sess., c. 24, s. 14(c); 1995 (Reg. Sess., 1996), c. 605, s. 15; 1998-230, s. 2; 2006-212, s. 4; 2009-521, s. 10.)

§ 88B-23. Licenses to be posted.

(a)   Every apprentice, cosmetologist, esthetician, manicurist, natural hair care specialist, and teacher licensed under this Chapter shall display the certificate of license issued by the Board within the shop in which the person works.

(b)   Every certificate of license to operate a cosmetic art shop or school shall be conspicuously posted in the shop or school for which it is issued. (1933, c. 179, s. 24; 1998-230, s. 2; 2009-521, s. 11.)

§ 88B-24. Revocation of licenses and other disciplinary measures.

The Board may restrict, suspend, revoke, or refuse to issue, renew, or reinstate any license for any of the following:

(1)   Conviction of a felony shown by certified copy of the record of the court of conviction.

(2)   Gross malpractice or gross incompetency as determined by the Board.

(3)   Advertising by means of knowingly false or deceptive statements.

(4) Permitting any individual to practice cosmetic art without a license or temporary employment permit, with an expired license or temporary employment permit, or with an invalid license or temporary employment permit.

(5) Obtaining or attempting to obtain a license for money or other thing of value other than the required fee or by fraudulent misrepresentation.

(6) Practicing or attempting to practice by fraudulent misrepresentation.

(7) Willful failure to display a certificate of license as required by G.S. 88B-23.

(8) Willful violation of the rules adopted by the Board.

(9) Violation of G.S. 86A-15 by a cosmetologist, esthetician, natural hair care specialist, or manicurist licensed by the Board and practicing cosmetic art in a barber shop. (1933, c. 179, ss. 23, 26, 28; 1935, c. 54, s. 5; 1941, c. 234, s. 4; 1949, c. 505, s. 2; 1973, c. 476, s. 128; 1975, c. 857, ss. 8, 9; 1981, c. 614, ss. 1, 2; c. 615, ss. 14, 15, 17; 1989 (Reg. Sess., 1990), c. 1013, ss. 2, 3; 1993, c. 539, 608; 1994, Ex. Sess., c. 24, s. 14(c); 1995 (Reg. Sess., 1996), c. 605, s. 16.; 1998-230, s. 2; 2009-521, s. 12.)

§ 88B-25. Exemptions.

The following persons are exempt from the provisions of this Chapter while engaged in the proper discharge of their professional duties:

(1) Undertakers and funeral establishments licensed under G.S. 90-210.25.

(2) Persons authorized to practice medicine or surgery under Chapter 90 of the General Statutes.

(3) Nurses licensed under Chapter 90 of the General Statutes.

(4) Commissioned medical or surgical officers of the United States Army, Air Force, Navy, Marine, or Coast Guard.

(5) A person employed in a cosmetic art shop to shampoo hair. (1933, c. 179, ss. 1, 22; 1973, c. 1481, ss. 1, 2; 1975, c. 7; c. 857, s. 1; 1977, cc. 155, 472; 1981, c. 615, ss. 1, 2; 1983 (Reg. Sess., 1984), c. 990; 1985, c. 125; 1985 (Reg. Sess., 1986), c. 833; 1987 (Reg. Sess., 1988), c. 965; 1993, c. 22, s. 2; c. 54, s. 1; 1995 (Reg. Sess., 1996), c. 605, s. 15; 1998-230, s. 2.)

§ 88B-26. Rules to be posted.

(a) The Board shall furnish a copy of its rules relating to sanitary management of cosmetic art shops and cosmetic art schools to each shop and school licensed by the Board. Each shop and school shall post the rules in a conspicuous place.

(b) The Board shall furnish a copy of its rules relating to curriculum and schools to each licensed cosmetic art school. Each cosmetic art school shall make these rules available to all teachers and students. (1933, c. 179, s. 23; 1935, c. 54, s. 5; 1973, c. 476, s. 128; 1975, c. 857, s. 9; 1981, c. 614, s. 1; c. 615, s. 14; 1995 (Reg. Sess., 1996), c. 605, s. 16; 1998-230, s. 2.)

§ 88B-27. Inspections.

Any inspector or other authorized representative of the Board may enter any cosmetic art shop or school to inspect it for compliance with this Chapter and the Board's rules. All persons practicing cosmetic art in a shop or school shall, upon request, present satisfactory proof of identification. Satisfactory proof shall be in the form of a photographic driver's license or photographic identification card issued by any state, federal, or other government entity. The Board may require a cosmetic art shop or school to be inspected as a condition for license renewal. (1933, c. 179, ss. 15, 23; 1935, c. 54, ss. 3, 5; 1941, c. 234, s. 2; 1943, c. 354, s. 2; 1957, c. 1184, s. 2; 1971, c. 355, ss. 2, 3; c. 616, ss. 1, 3; 1973, c. 476, s. 128; c. 1360, s. 2; 1975, c. 857, ss. 4, 9; 1981, c. 614, s. 1; c. 615, ss. 11, 14; 1983, c. 913, s. 9; 1989, c. 650, s. 2; 1995 (reg. Sess., 1996), c. 605, s. 16; 1998-230, s. 2.)

§ 88B-28. Restraining orders.

The Board, the Department of Health and Human Services, or any county or district health director may apply to the superior court for an injunction to restrain any person from violating the provisions of this Chapter or the Board's rules. Actions under this section shall be brought in the county where the defendant resides or maintains his or her principal place of business or where the alleged acts occurred. (1949, c. 505, s. 1; 1973, c. 476, s. 128; 1975, c. 857, s. 10; 1981, c. 614, s. 3; c. 615, s. 18; 1997-443, s. 11A.118(a); 1997-502, s. 8; 1998-230, s. 2.)

§ 88B-29. Civil penalties.

(a) Authority to Assess Civil Penalties. - In addition to taking any of the actions permitted under G.S. 88B-24, the Board may assess a civil penalty not in excess of one thousand dollars ($1,000) for the violation of any section of this Chapter or the violation of any rules adopted by the Board. The clear proceeds of any civil penalty assessed under this section shall be remitted to the Civil Penalty and Forfeiture Fund in accordance with G.S. 115C-457.2.

(b) Consideration Factors. - Before imposing and assessing a civil penalty and fixing the amount thereof, the Board shall, as a part of its deliberations, take into consideration the following factors:

(1) The nature, gravity, and persistence of the particular violation.

(2) The appropriateness of the imposition of a civil penalty when considered alone or in combination with other punishment.

(3) Whether the violation was willful and malicious.

(4) Any other factors that would tend to mitigate or aggravate the violations found to exist.

(c) Schedule of Civil Penalties. - The Board shall establish a schedule of civil penalties for violations of this Chapter. The schedule shall indicate for each type of violation whether the violation can be corrected. Penalties shall be assessed for the first, second, and third violations of specified sections of this Chapter and for specified rules.

(d)   Costs. - The Board may in a disciplinary proceeding charge costs, including reasonable attorneys' fees, to the licensee against whom the proceedings were brought. (1998-230, s. 2; 2004-142, s. 2.)

Chapter 89.

Engineering and Land Surveying.

§§ 89-1 through 89-16. Recodified as §§ 89C-1 to 89C-28.

Chapter 89A.

Landscape Architects.

§ 89A-1. Definitions.

The following definitions apply in this Chapter:

(1)   Board. - The North Carolina Board of Landscape Architects.

(2)   Landscape architect. - A person who, on the basis of demonstrated knowledge acquired by professional education or practical experience, or both, has been granted, and holds a current certificate entitling him or her to practice "landscape architecture" and to use the title "landscape architect" in North Carolina under the authority of this Chapter.

(3)   Landscape architecture or the practice of landscape architecture. - The performance of services in connection with the development of land areas where, and to the extent that the dominant purpose of the services is the preservation, enhancement or determination of proper land uses, natural land features, ground cover and planting, naturalistic and aesthetic values, the settings, approaches or environment for structures or other improvements, natural drainage and the consideration and determination of inherent problems of the land relating to the erosion, wear and tear, blight or other hazards. This practice shall include the preparation of plans and specifications and supervising the execution of projects involving the arranging of land and the elements set forth in this subsection used in connection with the land for public and private use and enjoyment, embracing the following, all in accordance with the accepted professional standards of public health, safety and welfare:

a. The location and orientation of buildings and other similar site elements.

b. The location, routing and design of public and private streets, residential and commercial subdivision roads, or roads in and providing access to private or public developments. This does not include the preparation of construction plans for proposed roads classified as major thoroughfares or a higher classification.

c. The location, routing and design of private and public pathways and other travelways.

d. The preparation of planting plans.

e. The design of surface or incidental subsurface drainage systems, soil conservation and erosion control measures necessary to an overall landscape plan and site design. (1969, c. 672, s. 1; 1997-406, s. 1; 2001-496, s. 12.1(a).)

§ 89A-2. Practice of landscape architecture or use of title "landscape architect" without registration prohibited; use of seal.

(a) No person shall use the designation "landscape architect," "landscape architecture," or "landscape architectural," or advertise any title or description tending to convey the impression that he or she is a landscape architect or shall engage in the practice of landscape architecture unless the person is registered as a landscape architect in the manner hereinafter provided and thereafter complies with the provisions of this Chapter. Every holder of a certificate shall display it in a conspicuous place in his or her principal office, place of business or employment.

(a1) No firm, partnership, or corporation shall engage in the practice of landscape architecture unless the firm, partnership, or corporation registered with the Board and has paid the fee required by G.S. 89A-6. All landscape architecture performed by a firm, partnership, or corporation shall be under the direct supervision of an individual who is registered under this Chapter.

(b) Nothing in this Chapter shall be construed (i) to authorize a landscape architect to engage in the practice of architecture, engineering, or land surveying, (ii) to restrict from the practice of landscape architecture or otherwise affect the rights of any person licensed to practice architecture under Chapter 83A, or engineering or land surveying under Chapter 89C of the General Statutes if the person does not use the title landscape architect, landscape architecture, or landscape architectural, (iii) to restrict any person from engaging in the occupation of grading lands whether by hand tools or machinery, (iv) to restrict the planting, maintaining, or marketing of plants or plant materials or the drafting of plans or specifications related to the location of plants on a site, (v) to require a certificate for the preparation, sale, or furnishing of plans, specifications and related data, or for the supervision of construction pursuant thereto, where the project involved is a single family residential site, or a residential, institutional, or commercial site of one acre or less, or the project involved is a site of more than one acre where only planting and mulching is required, or (vi) to prevent any individual from making plans or data for their own building site or for the supervision of construction pursuant thereto.

(c) Each landscape architect shall, upon registration, obtain a seal of the design authorized by the Board, bearing the name of the registrant, number of certificate and the legend "N.C. Registered Landscape Architect". Such seal may be used only while the registrant's certificate is in full force and effect.

Nothing in this Chapter shall be construed as authorizing the use or acceptance of the seal of a landscape architect instead of or as a substitute for the seal of an architect, engineer, or land surveyor. (1969, c. 672, s. 2; 1989, c. 673, s. 3; 1997-406, s. 2.)

§ 89A-3. North Carolina Board of Landscape Architects; appointments.

(a) There is created the North Carolina Board of Landscape Architects, consisting of seven members appointed by the Governor for four-year staggered terms. Five members of the Board shall have been engaged in the practice of landscape architecture in North Carolina at least five years at the time of their respective appointments. Two members of the Board shall not be landscape architects and shall represent the interest of the public at large. Each member shall hold office until the appointment and qualification of his or her successor. Vacancies occurring prior to the expiration of the term shall be filled by appointment for the unexpired term. No member shall serve more than two complete consecutive terms.

The Board shall be subject to the provisions of Chapter 93B of the General Statutes.

(b)   The Board shall elect annually from its members a chair and a vice-chair and shall hold such meetings during the year as it may determine to be necessary, one of which shall consist of the annual meeting. A quorum of the Board shall consist of not less than three members.

(b1)   The members of the Board shall not be compensated. However, members shall be entitled to be reimbursed from Board funds for all proper traveling and incidental expenses incurred in carrying out the provisions of this Chapter.

(c), (d) Repealed by Session Laws 1997-406, s. 3. (1969, c. 672, s. 3; 1979, c. 872, s. 1; 1997-406, s. 3.)

§ 89A-3.1. Board's powers and duties.

The Board shall have the following powers and duties:

(1)   Administer and enforce the provisions of this Chapter.

(2)   Adopt rules to administer and enforce the provisions of this Chapter.

(3)   Examine and determine the qualifications and fitness of applicants for registration and renewal of registration.

(4)   Determine the qualifications of firms, partnerships, or corporations applying for a certificate of registration.

(5)   Issue, renew, deny, suspend, or revoke certificates of registration and conduct any disciplinary actions authorized by this Chapter.

(6)   Establish and approve continuing education requirements for persons registered under this Chapter.

(7)   Receive and investigate complaints from members of the public.

(8) Conduct investigations for the purpose of determining whether violations of this Chapter or grounds for disciplining registrants exist.

(9) Conduct administrative hearings in accordance with Article 3 of Chapter 150B of the General Statutes.

(10) Maintain a record of all proceedings conducted by the Board and make available to registrants and other concerned parties an annual report of all Board action.

(11) Employ and fix the compensation of personnel that the Board determines is necessary to carry out the provisions of this Chapter and incur other expenses necessary to perform the duties of the Board.

(12) Adopt and publish a code of professional conduct for all registrants.

(13) Adopt a seal containing the name of the Board for use on all certificates of registration and official reports issued by the Board.

(14) Retain private counsel subject to G.S. 114-2.3. (1997-406, s. 4; 1997-456, s. 27; 2002-168, s. 7.)

§ 89A-4. Application, examination, certificate.

(a) Any person hereafter desiring to be registered and licensed to use the title "landscape architect" and to practice landscape architecture in the State, shall make a written application for examination to the Board, on a form prescribed by the Board, together with such evidence of his or her qualifications as may be prescribed by rules of the Board. Minimum qualifications under such rules shall require that the applicant:

(1) Shall be at least 18 years of age.

(2) Shall be of good moral character.

(3) Shall be a graduate of a Landscape Architect's Accreditation Board (LAAB) accredited collegiate curriculum in landscape architecture as approved by the Board.

(4) Shall have at least four years' experience in landscape architecture.

(a1) Notwithstanding the requirements of subdivisions (a)(3) and (4) of this section, any person who has had a minimum of 10 years of education and experience in landscape architecture, in any combination deemed suitable by the Board, may make application to the Board for examination.

(b) If the application is satisfactory to the Board, and is accompanied by the fees required by this Chapter, then the applicant shall be entitled to an examination to determine his or her qualifications. If the result of the examination of any applicant shall be satisfactory to the Board, then the Board shall issue to the applicant a certificate to use the title "landscape architect" and to practice landscape architecture in North Carolina. Examinations shall be held at least once a year at a time and place to be fixed by the Board which shall determine the subjects and scope of the examination. The Board may adopt rules for administering the examination in one or more parts at the same time or at different times.

(c) The Board, within its discretion, may issue licenses without examination and licenses by reciprocity or comity to persons holding a license or certificate in landscape architecture from any legally constituted board of examiners in another state or country whose registration requirements are deemed to be equal or equivalent to those of this State.

(d) Repealed by Session Laws 1997-406, s. 5.

(e) The Board, within its discretion, may grant an honorific title license to persons who have held for a minimum of 20 years a license or certificate in landscape architecture issued by the Board or a legally constituted board of examiners in another state or country whose registration requirements are equal or equivalent to those of this State. The honorific title license shall allow the person to use the title "landscape architect emeritus", but the person shall not practice landscape architecture or provide expert testimony as a landscape architect in this State unless the person complies with the provisions of this Chapter. There shall be no fee charged for an honorific title license. (1969, c. 672, s. 4; 1971, c. 162; 1979, c. 872, ss. 2, 3; 1997-406, s. 5.)

§ 89A-5. Annual renewal of certificate.

Every registrant under this Chapter shall, on or before the first day of July in each year, obtain a renewal of a certificate for the ensuing year, by application, accompanied by the required fee. Upon failure to renew, the certificate shall be automatically revoked. The certificate may be renewed at any time within one year after its expiration if the applicant pays the required renewal fee and late renewal penalty, and the Board finds that the applicant has not used his or her certificate or title or engaged in the practice of landscape architecture after notice of revocation and is otherwise eligible for registration under the provisions of this Chapter. When necessary to protect the public health, safety, or welfare, the Board shall require such evidence as it deems necessary to establish the continuing competency of licensees as a condition of license renewal. (1969, c. 672, s. 5; 1979, c. 872, s. 4; 1997-406, s. 6.)

§ 89A-6. Fees.

Fees are to be determined by the Board, but shall not exceed the amounts specified herein, however; fees must reflect actual expenses of the Board.

Application... $100.00

License by reciprocity or comity... 250.00

Annual license renewal.. 100.00

Late renewal penalty... 50.00

Reissue of certificate... 25.00

Corporate certificate.. 250.00

In all instances where the Board uses the services of a testing service for preparation, administration, or grading of examinations, the Board may charge the applicant the actual cost of the examination services, in addition to its other fees. Fees shall be paid to the Board at the times specified by the Board. (1969, c. 672, s. 6; 1979, c. 872, s. 5; 1989, c. 673, s. 4; 1997-406, s. 7; 1999-315, s. 1.)

§ 89A-7. Disciplinary actions.

(a)   The Board may deny or refuse to renew a certificate of registration, suspend, or revoke a certificate of registration if the registrant or applicant:

(1)   Obtains a certificate of registration by fraudulent misrepresentation.

(2)   Uses or attempts to use another's certificate of registration to practice landscape architecture.

(3)   Uses or attempts to use another's name for purposes of obtaining a certificate of registration or practicing landscape architecture.

(4)   Has demonstrated gross malpractice or gross incompetency as determined by the Board.

(5)   Has been convicted of or pled guilty or no contest to a crime that indicates that the person is unfit or incompetent to practice landscape architecture or that indicates the person has deceived or defrauded the public.

(6)   Has been declared mentally incompetent by a court of competent jurisdiction.

(7)   Has willfully violated any of the provisions of this Chapter or the Board's rules.

(b)   The Board may require a registrant to take a written or oral examination if the Board finds evidence that the person is not competent to practice landscape architecture as defined in this Chapter.

(c) The Board may take any of the actions authorized in subsection (a) of this section against any firm, partnership, or corporation registered with the Board.

(d) In addition to taking any of the actions authorized in subsection (a) of this section, the Board may assess a civil penalty not in excess of two thousand dollars ($2,000) for the violation of any section of this Chapter or the violation of any rules adopted by the Board. All civil penalties collected by the Board shall be remitted to the school fund of the county in which the violation occurred. Before imposing and assessing a civil penalty and fixing the amount thereof, the Board shall, as a part of its deliberations, take into consideration the following factors:

(1) The nature, gravity, and persistence of the particular violation.

(2) The appropriateness of the imposition of a civil penalty when considered alone or in combination with other punishment.

(3) Whether the violation was willful.

(4) Any other factors that would tend to mitigate or aggravate the violations found to exist. (1969, c. 672, s. 7; 1973, c. 1331, s. 3; 1987, c. 827, ss. 1, 71; 1997-406, s. 8.)

§ 89A-8. Violation a misdemeanor; injunction to prevent violation.

(a) It shall be a Class 2 misdemeanor for any person to use, or to hold himself or herself out as entitled to practice under the title of landscape architect or landscape architecture or to practice landscape architecture unless he or she is duly registered under the provisions of this Chapter.

(b) The Board may appear in its own name in the courts of the State and apply for injunctions to prevent violations of this Chapter. (1969, c. 672, s. 8; 1973, c. 1331, s. 3; 1987, c. 827, s. 72; 1993, c. 539, s. 610; 1994, Ex. Sess., c. 24, s. 14(c); 1997-406, s. 9.)

Chapter 89B.

Foresters.

§ 89B-1. General provisions.

(a) No person shall use the designation "forester", "registered forester", or any other descriptive terms that include the words "forester" or "registered forester" and that directly convey that the person is a forester without first having been registered under this Chapter.

(b) This Chapter benefits and protects the public by improving the standards for the practice of professional forestry in North Carolina. (1975, c. 531, s. 1; 1998-157, s. 1.)

§ 89B-2. Definitions.

As used in this Chapter:

(1) "Board" means the State Board of Registration for Foresters, provided for by this Chapter.

(2) "Forester" means a person who by reason of special knowledge and training in natural sciences, mathematics, silviculture, forest protection, forest mensuration, forest management, forest economics, and forest utilization is qualified to engage in the practice of forestry.

(2a) "Forestry" means the professional practice embracing the science, business, and the art of creating, conserving, and managing forests and forestlands for the sustained use and enjoyment of their resources, material, or other forest produce.

(3) "Practice of forestry" means rendering professional forestry services, including but not limited to, consultation, investigation, evaluation, planning, or other forestry activities requiring knowledge, training, and experience in forestry principles and techniques.

(4) "Registered forester" means a person who has been registered pursuant to this Chapter.

(5) "Consulting forester" means a registered forester who:

a. through c. Repealed by Session Laws 1998-157, s.1.

d. Is competent to practice forest management, appraisal, development, marketing, protection, and utilization for the benefit of the general public on a fee, contractual, or contingency basis;

e. Has not engaged in any practice that constitutes a conflict of interest or in any way diminishes his ability to represent the best interests of his clients; and

f. Has filed annually an affidavit with the Board in accordance with G.S. 89B-14(b).

(6) "Urban forester" means a person who engages in the practice of forestry in an urban setting that involves municipal ownership, homesteads, parks and woodlots, and similar urban properties. (1975, c. 531, s. 2; 1989, c. 169; 1998-157, s. 1.)

§ 89B-3. State Board of Registration for Foresters; appointment of members; terms.

(a) A State Board of Registration for Foresters is created to administer the provisions of this Chapter. The Board shall have five members as follows:

(1) Four duly practicing registered foresters, at least three of whom hold a bachelors or higher degree from an accredited forestry school, and

(2) One public member.

Each member shall be appointed by the Governor for a three-year term. No member may serve more than two complete consecutive terms.

(b) Each member of the Board shall be a citizen of the United States and a resident of North Carolina.

(c) Vacancies in the membership of the Board shall be filled by appointment by the Governor for the unexpired term.

(d)   The Board shall elect annually the following officers: a chairman, and a vice-chairman, who shall be members of the Board, and a secretary who may be a member of the Board. A quorum of the Board shall consist of not less than three voting members of the Board. (1975, c. 531, s. 3; 1983, c. 103, s. 1; 1998-157, s. 1.)

§ 89B-4. Compensation and expenses of Board members.

Each member of the Board shall receive per diem and allowances as provided by G.S. 93B-5. (1975, c. 531, s. 4; 1998-157, s. 1.)

§ 89B-5. Organization and meetings of the Board.

The Board shall meet at least twice each year. In addition, special meetings may be held in accordance with the rules of the Board. (1975, c. 531, s. 5; 1998-157, s. 1.)

§ 89B-6. Powers of the Board.

The Board may adopt rules in accordance with Chapter 150B of the General Statutes for the proper performance of its duties and the regulation of the proceedings before it. The Board shall adopt an official seal. Any member of the Board may administer oaths or affirmations to witnesses appearing before the Board.

The Board may establish fees, subject to the maximum amounts prescribed by this Chapter. (1975, c. 531, s. 6; 1998-157, s. 1.)

§ 89B-7. Receipts and disbursements.

The secretary of the Board shall receive and account for all moneys derived under this Chapter, and shall keep these moneys in a separate fund known as the "Registered Foresters' Fund." Moneys in the Fund shall be expended to carry out the purposes of the Board. The secretary of the Board shall give surety bond to the Board in an amount determined by the Board. The premium for the surety bond is a proper expense of the Board and shall be paid from the Registered Foresters' Fund.

The Board may employ and fix the compensation of necessary clerical and other assistants. The compensation of these assistants shall be paid out of the Registered Foresters' Fund. (1975, c. 531, s. 7; 1998-157, s. 1.)

§ 89B-8. Records and reports.

The Board shall keep a record of its proceedings and a register of all applications for registration. The register shall show the name, age and residence of each applicant; the date of the application; the applicant's place of business; the applicant's educational and other qualifications; whether or not examination was required; whether the application was rejected or registration was granted; the date of action by the Board; and other information deemed necessary by the Board. Each July 1 the Board shall submit to the Governor a report of its transactions of the preceding year. (1975, c. 531, s. 8; 1998-157, s. 1.)

§ 89B-9. General requirements for registration.

(a)   An applicant for registration shall be registered upon satisfactory proof to the Board that the applicant is of good moral character and meets one of the following requirements:

(1)   Graduation with a bachelors or higher degree in a forestry curriculum from a school or college of forestry approved by the Board, passage of a comprehensive written examination, and the completion of two or more years' experience in forestry.

(2)   Passage of a comprehensive written examination designed to show knowledge approximating that obtained through graduation from a four-year curriculum in forestry in a university or college approved by the Board and the completion of six or more years of active practice in forestry work immediately

prior to the application. The work must be of a character acceptable to the Board. Graduation with an Associate Applied Science degree in a forestry curriculum in a school or college approved by the Board is the equivalent of one year of experience. The completion of the junior year of a curriculum in forestry in a college or school approved by the Board is the equivalent of two years of experience. The completion of the senior year of a curriculum in forestry in a school or college approved by the Board is equivalent to three years of experience.

(3)   Registration in good standing as a registered forester with the Board as of January 1, 1999.

(4)   Practice of urban forestry for six years immediately prior to January 1, 1999, if the applicant meets all of the following conditions:

a.   The applicant is a North Carolina resident at the time of filing the application.

b.   The applicant practiced under the title "urban forester" during the six-year period.

c.   The applicant, prior to June 30, 1999, applies to the Board for registration and submits an affidavit under oath to the Board showing experience and education equivalent to that of a forester, as determined by the Board.

(b)   Registration shall be determined upon the basis of individual personal qualification. No firm, company, partnership, corporation or public agency shall be registered as a registered forester.

(b1)   The Board may issue a forester-in-training certificate to an applicant who has completed the educational requirements under subdivision (a)(1) of this section.

(c)   A nonresident of North Carolina may become a registered forester under this Chapter by complying with its terms, and by filing a consent as to service of process and pleadings upon the Board secretary. In connection with the practice of forestry by such nonresident in North Carolina, the consent as to service of process and pleadings shall be held binding and valid in all courts, as if due service had been made personally upon said nonresident by the Board, when such process has been served upon the Board secretary.

(d)   A nonresident or person who has moved to North Carolina recently and who is registered as a registered forester in another jurisdiction may be registered under this Chapter, by written application to the Board, if that jurisdiction provides for the same or substantially the same registration for North Carolina foresters who are registered under this Chapter.

(e)   A nonresident of North Carolina may use the term "registered forester" or other titles otherwise prohibited by this Chapter in North Carolina without becoming registered under this Chapter if registered in another state which will reciprocate with the provision of this Chapter. (1975, c. 531, s. 9; 1998-157, s. 1.)

§ 89B-10. Application and registration fees.

(a)   Applications for registration shall be made on forms prescribed and furnished by the Board. The application fee for a certificate of registration as a registered forester shall be in an amount determined by the Board, not to exceed fifty dollars ($50.00), which shall accompany the application. An additional fee, not to exceed forty dollars ($40.00), shall be paid upon issuance of the certificate of registration. An applicant that does not remit the certificate fee within 30 days after being notified of qualification forfeits the right to have the certificate issued, and the applicant may be required again to submit an original application fee. If the Board denies a certificate of registration to any applicant, the initial application fee deposited by the applicant shall be retained by the Board.

(b)   It is unlawful for any person to provide false or forged information to the Board or a member of the Board in obtaining a certificate of registration. (1975, c. 531, s. 10; 1989, c. 245, s. 1; 1998-157, s. 1.)

§ 89B-11. Expiration and renewals; continuing education.

(a)   Registrations shall expire on the last day of June following issuance or renewal and shall become invalid after that date unless renewed. The secretary of the Board shall notify every person registered under this Chapter, at the person's last registered address, of the date of the expiration of registration and the amount of fee required for its renewal for one year. The notices shall be mailed at least 30 days prior to the expiration date of the registrations. The annual renewal fee for certificates shall be in an amount established by the Board, not to exceed fifty dollars ($50.00). The fee for issuance of replacement certificates of registration shall be five dollars ($5.00).

Any registration which has expired may be renewed by paying the registration fee plus one-twelfth of the annual renewal fee per calendar month from the date of expiration. Charges above the renewal fee shall not exceed an amount equal to the renewal fee.

(b) The Board shall require registered foresters to attend continuing education courses approved by the Board, not to exceed 12 hours per year, as a condition of renewal. (1975, c. 531, s. 11; 1989, c. 245, s. 2; 1998-157, s. 1.)

§ 89B-12. Examinations.

When written examinations are required, they shall be held at the time and places in the State of North Carolina as the Board shall determine. The methods of procedure will be described by the Board. A candidate failing an examination may apply for reexamination after six months and will be reexamined with payment of an additional fee established by the Board, not to exceed fifty dollars ($50.00). Subsequent examinations will be granted upon payment of this fee for each examination. The Board may limit an applicant to three examinations. (1975, c. 531, s. 12; 1998-157, s. 1.)

§ 89B-13. Revocations and reissuance of registration.

The Board may revoke or suspend the certificate of registration of any registrant who it finds has committed gross negligence, fraud, deceit or flagrant misconduct in the practice of forestry or has demonstrated incompetence as a practicing forester. The Board may designate a person or persons to investigate and report to it upon any charges of fraud, deceit, gross negligence, incompetency or other misconduct by a registrant in the practice of forestry.

Any person may prefer charges against a registrant. The charges shall be in writing, sworn to by the person making them, and filed with the secretary of the

Board. The time and place for a hearing before the Board shall be fixed by the Board. At any hearing the accused may appear in person or by counsel. The Board may reissue a certificate of registration to any person whose certificate of registration has been revoked or suspended. (1975, c. 531, s. 13; 1998-157, s. 1.)

§ 89B-14. Roster of registered foresters; consulting forester affidavit.

(a) A roster showing the names, registration numbers, and places of business residence of all registrants under this Chapter shall be prepared annually by the secretary of the Board. Copies of this roster shall be placed on file with the Secretary of State of North Carolina and each clerk of superior court in North Carolina. A copy shall be sent to each registrant, and copies may be furnished to the public upon request and upon payment of a fee set by the Board.

(b) Each consulting forester shall annually file with the Board an affidavit of its compliance with this Chapter. (1975, c. 531, s. 14; 1998-157, s. 1.)

§ 89B-15. Violation.

A violation of this Chapter is a Class 3 misdemeanor. (1975, c. 531, s. 15; 1993, c. 539, s. 611; 1994, Ex. Sess., c. 24, s. 14(c); 1998-157, s. 1.)

Chapter 89C.

Engineering and Land Surveying.

§ 89C-1. Short title.

This Chapter shall be known and may be cited as "The North Carolina Engineering and Land Surveying Act." (1951, c. 1084, s. 1; 1975, c. 681, s. 1.)

§ 89C-2. Declarations; prohibitions.

In order to safeguard life, health, and property, and to promote the public welfare, the practice of engineering and the practice of land surveying in this State are hereby declared to be subject to regulation in the public interest. It shall be unlawful for any person to practice or to offer to practice engineering or land surveying in this State, as defined in the provisions of this Chapter, or to use in connection with the person's name or otherwise assume or advertise any title or description tending to convey the impression that the person is either a professional engineer or a professional land surveyor, unless the person has been duly licensed. The right to engage in the practice of engineering or land surveying is a personal right, based on the qualifications of the person as evidenced by the person's certificate of licensure, which shall not be transferable. (1921, c. 1, s. 1; C.S., s. 6055(b); 1951, c. 1084, s. 1; 1975, c. 681, s. 1; 1998-118, s. 1.)

§ 89C-3. Definitions.

The following definitions apply in this Chapter:

(1) Board. - The North Carolina State Board of Examiners for Engineers and Surveyors provided for by this Chapter.

(1a) Business firm. - A partnership, firm, association, or another organization or group that is not a corporation and is acting as a unit.

(2) Engineer. - A person who, by reason of special knowledge and use of the mathematical, physical and engineering sciences and the principles and methods of engineering analysis and design, acquired by engineering education and engineering experience, is qualified to practice engineering.

(3) Engineer intern. - A person who complies with the requirements for education, experience and character, and has passed an examination on the fundamentals of engineering as provided in this Chapter.

(3a) Inactive licensee. - A licensee who is not engaged in the practice of engineering or land surveying in this State, but renews his or her license as "inactive" as provided in this Chapter.

(4) Land surveyor intern. - A person who complies with the requirements for education, experience, and character and has passed an examination on the fundamentals of land surveying as provided in this Chapter.

(5) Person. - Any natural person, firm, partnership, corporation or other legal entity.

(6) Practice of engineering. -

a. Any service or creative work, the adequate performance of which requires engineering education, training, and experience, in the application of special knowledge of the mathematical, physical, and engineering sciences to such services or creative work as consultation, investigation, evaluation, planning, and design of engineering works and systems, planning the use of land and water, engineering surveys, and the observation of construction for the purposes of assuring compliance with drawings and specifications, including the consultation, investigation, evaluation, planning, and design for either private or public use, in connection with any utilities, structures, buildings, machines, equipment, processes, work systems, projects, and industrial or consumer products or equipment of a mechanical, electrical, hydraulic, pneumatic or thermal nature, insofar as they involve safeguarding life, health or property, and including such other professional services as may be necessary to the planning, progress and completion of any engineering services.

A person shall be construed to practice or offer to practice engineering, within the meaning and intent of this Chapter, who practices any branch of the profession of engineering; or who, by verbal claim, sign, advertisement, letterhead, card, or in any other way represents the person to be a professional engineer, or through the use of some other title implies that the person is a professional engineer or that the person is licensed under this Chapter; or who holds the person out as able to perform, or who does perform any engineering service or work not exempted by this Chapter, or any other service designated by the practitioner which is recognized as engineering.

b. The term "practice of engineering" shall not be construed to permit the location, description, establishment or reestablishment of property lines or descriptions of land boundaries for conveyance. The term does not include the assessment of an underground storage tank required by applicable rules at closure or change in service unless there has been a discharge or release of the product from the tank.

(7) Practice of land surveying. -

a. Providing professional services such as consultation, investigation, testimony, evaluation, planning, mapping, assembling, and interpreting reliable scientific measurements and information relative to the location, size, shape, or physical features of the earth, improvements on the earth, the space above the earth, or any part of the earth, whether the gathering of information for the providing of these services is accomplished by conventional ground measurements, by aerial photography, by global positioning via satellites, or by a combination of any of these methods, and the utilization and development of these facts and interpretations into an orderly survey map, plan, report, description, or project. The practice of land surveying includes the following:

1. Locating, relocating, establishing, laying out, or retracing any property line, easement, or boundary of any tract of land;

2. Locating, relocating, establishing, or laying out the alignment or elevation of any of the fixed works embraced within the practice of professional engineering;

3. Making any survey for the subdivision of any tract of land, including the topography, alignment and grades of streets and incidental drainage within the subdivision, and the preparation and perpetuation of maps, record plats, field note records, and property descriptions that represent these surveys;

4. Determining, by the use of the principles of land surveying, the position for any survey monument or reference point, or setting, resetting, or replacing any survey monument or reference point;

5. Determining the configuration or contour of the earth's surface or the position of fixed objects on the earth's surface by measuring lines and angles and applying the principles of mathematics or photogrammetry;

6. Providing geodetic surveying which includes surveying for determination of the size and shape of the earth both horizontally and vertically and the precise positioning of points on the earth utilizing angular and linear measurements through spatially oriented spherical geometry; and

7. Creating, preparing, or modifying electronic or computerized data, including land information systems and geographic information systems relative to the performance of the practice of land surveying.

b. The term "practice of land surveying" shall not be construed to permit the design or preparation of specifications for (i) major highways; (ii) wastewater systems; (iii) wastewater or industrial waste treatment works; (iv) pumping or lift stations; (v) water supply, treatment, or distribution systems; (vi) streets or storm sewer systems except as incidental to a subdivision.

(8) Professional engineer. - A person who has been duly licensed as a professional engineer by the Board established by this Chapter.

(8a) Professional engineer, retired. - A person who has been duly licensed as a professional engineer by the Board and who chooses to relinquish or not to renew a license and who applies to and is approved by the Board after review of record, including any disciplinary action, to be granted the use of the honorific title "Professional Engineer, Retired".

(9) Professional land surveyor. - A person who, by reason of special knowledge of mathematics, surveying principles and methods, and legal requirements which are acquired by education and/or practical experience, is qualified to engage in the practice of land surveying, as attested by the person's licensure as a professional land surveyor by the Board.

(9a) Professional land surveyor, retired. - A person who has been duly licensed as a professional land surveyor by the Board and who chooses to relinquish or not to renew a license and who applies to and is approved by the Board after review of record, including any disciplinary action, to be granted the use of the honorific title "Professional Land Surveyor, Retired".

(10) Responsible charge. - Direct control and personal supervision, either of engineering work or of land surveying, as the case may be. (1951, c. 1084, s. 1; 1953, c. 999, s. 1; 1973, c. 449; 1975, c. 681, s. 1; 1993 (Reg. Sess., 1994), c. 671, s. 1; 1996, 2nd Ex. Sess., c. 18, s. 7.10(i); 1998-118, s. 2; 2011-304, s. 1; 2013-98, s. 1.)

§ 89C-4. State Board of Examiners for Engineers and Surveyors; appointment; terms.

A State Board of Examiners for Engineers and Surveyors, whose duty it is to administer the provisions of this Chapter, is created. The Board shall consist of four licensed professional engineers, three licensed professional land surveyors and two public members, who are neither professional engineers nor professional land surveyors. Of the land surveyor members, one and only one may hold dual licenses as a professional land surveyor and professional engineer. All of the members shall be appointed by the Governor. Appointments of the engineer and land surveyor members shall preferably, but not necessarily, be made from a list of nominees submitted by the professional societies for engineers and land surveyors in this State. Each member of the Board shall receive a certificate of appointment from the Governor and shall file with the Secretary of State a written oath or affirmation for the faithful discharge of the duties.

Members of the Board serve for staggered five-year terms, and no member may be appointed for more than two full terms. Members serve until the expiration of their respective terms and until their respective successors are appointed. If a vacancy occurs during a term, the Governor shall appoint a successor from the same classification as the person causing the vacancy to serve for the remainder of the unexpired term. If the vacancy is not filled within 90 days after it occurs, the Board may appoint a provisional member to serve until the appointment by the Governor becomes effective. The provisional member during his tenure has all the powers and duties of a regular member. (1921, c. 1, ss. 3-6; C.S., ss. 6055(d)-6055(g); 1951, c. 1084, s. 1; 1957, c. 1060, s. 1; 1963, c. 843; 1965, c. 940; 1975, c. 681, s. 1; 1979, c. 819, s. 1; 1998-118, s. 3.)

§ 89C-5. Board members; qualifications.

Each engineer member of the Board shall be a resident of North Carolina and shall be a licensed professional engineer engaged in the lawful practice of engineering in North Carolina for at least six years.

Each land surveyor member of the Board shall be a resident of North Carolina and shall be a licensed professional land surveyor engaged in the lawful practice of land surveying in North Carolina for at least six years.

Each public member of the Board shall be a resident of North Carolina. (1921, c. 1, ss. 3-6; C.S., ss. 6055(d)-6055(g); 1951, c. 1084, s. 1; 1957, c. 1060, s. 1; 1963, c. 843; 1965, c. 940; 1975, c. 681, s. 1; 1979, c. 819, s. 2; 1989, c. 108; 1998-118, s. 4.)

§ 89C-6. Compensation and expenses of Board members.

Each member of the Board, when attending to the work of the Board or any of its committees, shall receive as compensation for services the per diem and, in addition, shall be reimbursed for travel expenses and incidentals not exceeding the maximum set forth by law. In addition to per diem allowances, travel and incidentals, the secretary of the Board may, with the approval of the Board, receive such reasonable additional compensation as is compatible with the actual hours of work required by the duties of the office. (1921, c. 1, ss. 3-6; C.S., ss. 6055(d)-6055(g); 1951, c. 1084, s. 1; 1957, c. 1060, s. 1; 1963, c. 843; 1965, c. 940; 1975, c. 681, s. 1; 1998-118, s. 5.)

§ 89C-7. Vacancies; removal of member.

The Governor may remove any member of the Board for misconduct, incompetency, neglect of duty, or any sufficient cause, in the manner prescribed by law for removal of State officials. Vacancies in the membership of the Board shall be filled for the unexpired term by appointment by the Governor as provided in G.S. 89C-4. (1921, c. 1, ss. 3-6; C.S., ss. 6055(d)-6055(g); 1951, c. 1084, s. 1; 1957, c. 1060, s. 1; 1963, c. 843; 1965, c. 940; 1975, c. 681, s. 1.)

§ 89C-8. Organization of the Board; meetings; election of officers.

The Board shall hold at least two regular meetings each year. Special meetings may be held at such times and upon such notice as the rules and regulations of the Board may provide. The Board shall elect annually from its members a chair, a vice-chair, and a secretary. A quorum of the Board shall consist of not less than five members. The Board shall operate under its rules and regulations supplemented by Robert's Rules of Order. (1921, c. 1, ss. 3-6; C.S., ss. 6055(d)-6055(g); 1951, c. 1084, s. 1; 1957, c. 1060, s. 1; 1963, c. 843; 1965, c. 940; 1975, c. 681, s. 1; 1998-118, s. 6.)

§ 89C-9. Executive director; duties and liabilities.

The Board shall employ an executive director who is not a member of the Board. The executive director shall be a full-time employee of the Board and perform the duties assigned to the director by the secretary subject to the approval of the Board. The executive director shall receive a salary and compensation fixed by the Board. The executive director shall give a surety bond satisfactory to the Board conditioned upon the faithful performance of the director's duties assigned. The premium on the bond shall be a necessary and proper expense of the Board. (1921, c. 1, ss. 3-6; C.S., ss. 6055(d)-6055(g); 1951, c. 1084, s. 1; 1957, c. 1060, s. 1; 1963, c. 843; 1965, c. 940; 1975, c. 681, s. 1; 1998-118, s. 7.)

§ 89C-10. Board powers.

(a) The Board may adopt and amend all rules and rules of procedure as may be reasonably necessary for the proper performance of its duties, the regulation of its procedures, meetings, records, the administration of examinations, and the authority to enforce the rules of professional conduct as may be adopted by the Board pursuant to G.S. 89C-20.

The action by the Board in carrying out any of the powers specified in this section shall be binding upon all persons licensed under this Chapter, including corporations and business firms holding certificates of authorization.

(b) The Board shall adopt and have an official seal, which shall be affixed to each certificate issued.

(c) The Board may in the name of the State apply for relief, by injunction, in the established manner provided in cases of civil procedure, without bond, to enforce the provisions of this Chapter, or to restrain any violation of the provisions of this Chapter. In proceedings for injunctive relief, it shall not be necessary to allege or prove either that an adequate remedy at law does not exist, or that substantial or irreparable damage would result from the continued violation of the provisions of this Chapter. The members of the Board shall not be personally liable under this proceeding.

(d) The Board may subject an applicant for licensure to any examination necessary to determine the applicant's qualifications.

(e) The Board may issue an appropriate certificate of licensure to any applicant who, in the opinion of the Board, has met the requirements of this Chapter.

(f) It shall be the responsibility and duty of the Board to conduct a regular program of investigation concerning all matters within its jurisdiction under the provisions of this Chapter. The investigation of a licensee is confidential until the Board issues a citation to the licensee. The Board may expend its funds for salaries, fees, and per diem expenses, in connection with its investigations, provided that no funds other than per diem expenses shall be paid to any member of the Board in connection with its investigations, nor may any member of the Board give testimony and later sit in deciding on any matter which may directly involve punitive action for the testimony.

(g) The Board may use its funds to establish and conduct instructional programs for persons who are currently licensed to practice engineering or land surveying, as well as refresher courses for persons interested in obtaining adequate instruction or programs of study to qualify them for licensure to practice engineering or land surveying. The Board may expend its funds for these purposes and may not only conduct, sponsor, and arrange for instructional programs, but also may carry out instructional programs through extension courses or other media. The Board may enter into plans or agreements with community colleges, public or private institutions of higher learning, State and county boards of education, or with the governing authority of any industrial education center for the purpose of planning, scheduling or arranging courses, instruction, extension courses, or in assisting in obtaining courses of study or programs in the field of engineering and land surveying. The Board shall encourage the educational institutions in this State to offer courses necessary to complete the educational requirements of this Chapter. For the purpose of carrying out these objectives, the Board may adopt rules as may be necessary for the educational programs, instruction, extension services, or for entering into plans or contracts with persons or educational and industrial institutions.

(h) The Board may license sponsors of continuing professional competency activities who agree to conduct programs in accordance with standards adopted by the Board. Sponsors shall pay a license fee established by the Board, not to exceed two hundred fifty dollars ($250.00) for licensure under this subsection. The license fee shall accompany the application. Sponsors shall renew their licenses annually on a form provided by the Board.

(i) The Board shall have the power to acquire, hold, rent, encumber, alienate, and otherwise deal with real property in the same manner as a private person or corporation, subject only to approval of the Governor and the Council of State. Collateral pledged by the Board for an encumbrance is limited to the assets, income, and revenues of the Board. (1921, c. 1, ss. 3-6; C.S., ss. 6055(d)-6055(g); 1951, c. 1084, s. 1; 1957, c. 1060, s. 1; 1963, c. 843; 1965, c. 940; 1975, c. 681, s. 1; 1985 (Reg. Sess., 1986), c. 977, s. 16; 1993 (Reg. Sess., 1994), c. 671, s. 8; 1998-118, s. 8; 2003-347, s. 1.)

§ 89C-11. Secretary; duties and liabilities; expenditures.

The secretary of the Board shall receive and account for all moneys derived from the operation of the Board as provided in this Chapter, and shall deposit them in one or more special funds in banks or other financial institutions carrying deposit insurance and authorized to do business in North Carolina. The fund or funds shall be designated as "Fund of the Board of Examiners for Engineers and Surveyors" and shall be drawn against only for the purpose of implementing provisions of this Chapter as herein provided. All expenses certified by the Board as properly and necessarily incurred in the discharge of its duties, including authorized compensation, shall be paid out of this fund on the warrant signed by the secretary of the Board. At no time shall the total of warrants issued exceed the total amount of funds accumulated under this Chapter. The secretary of the Board shall give a surety bond satisfactory to the State Board of Examiners for Engineers and Surveyors, conditioned upon the faithful performance of the duties assigned. The premium on the bond is a proper and necessary expense of the Board. The secretary of the Board may delegate to the executive director certain routine duties, such as receipt and disbursement of funds in stated amounts by a written authorization, which has the majority approval of the Board. (1921, c. 1, s. 7; C.S., s. 6055(h); 1951, c. 1084, s. 1; 1959, c. 617; 1975, c. 681, s. 1; 1998-118, s. 9; 2011-304, s. 2.)

§ 89C-12. Records and reports of Board; evidence.

The Board shall keep a record of its proceedings and a register of all applicants for licensure, showing for each the date of application, name, age, education, and other qualifications, place of business and place of residence, whether the applicant was rejected or a certificate of licensure granted, and the date licensure was rejected or granted. The books and register of the Board shall be prima facie evidence of all matters recorded by the Board, and a copy duly certified by the secretary of the Board under seal shall be admissible in evidence as if the original were produced. A roster showing the names and places of business and of residence of all licensed professional engineers and all licensed professional land surveyors shall be prepared by the secretary of the Board current to the month of January of each year. On or before the first day of May of each year, the Board shall submit to the Governor a report on its transactions for the preceding year, and shall file with the Secretary of State a copy of the report, together with a complete statement of the receipts and expenditures of the Board attested by the chair and the secretary and a copy of the roster of licensed professional engineers and professional land surveyors. (1921, c. 1, s. 8; C.S., s. 6055(i); 1951, c. 1084, s. 1; 1975, c. 681, s. 1; 1998-118, s. 10; 2000-140, s. 18; 2011-304, s. 3.)

§ 89C-13. General requirements for licensure.

(a) Engineer Applicant. - The following shall be considered as minimum evidence satisfactory to the Board that the applicant is qualified for licensure as a professional engineer:

(1) To be certified as an engineer intern, an applicant shall (i) pass the fundamentals of engineering examination and make application to the Board, (ii) be of good character and reputation, (iii) submit three character references to the Board, one of whom is a professional engineer, (iv) comply with the requirements of this Chapter, and (v) meet one of the following requirements:

a. Education. - Be a graduate of an engineering curriculum or related science curriculum of four years or more, approved by the Board as being of satisfactory standing.

b. Education and experience. - Be a graduate of an engineering curriculum or related science curriculum of four years or more, other than curriculums approved by the Board as being of satisfactory standing, or possess equivalent education and engineering experience satisfactory to the Board with a specific record of four or more years of progressive experience on engineering projects of a grade and character satisfactory to the Board.

(1a) To be licensed as a professional engineer, an applicant shall (i) be of good character and reputation, (ii) submit five character references to the Board, three of whom are professional engineers or individuals acceptable to the Board with personal knowledge of the applicant's engineering experience, (iii) comply with the requirements of this Chapter, and (iv) meet one of the following requirements:

a. Licensure by Comity or Endorsement. - A person holding a certificate of licensure to engage in the practice of engineering, on the basis of comparable qualifications, issued to the person by a proper authority of a state, territory, or possession of the United States, the District of Columbia, or of any foreign country possessing credentials that, based on verifiable evidence, in the opinion of the Board, of a standard not lower than that in effect in this State at the time the certificate was issued, may upon application, be licensed without further examination, except as required to examine the applicant's knowledge of laws, rules, and requirements unique to North Carolina.

b. E.I. Certificate, Experience, and Examination. - A holder of a certificate of engineer intern and with a specific record of an additional four years or more of progressive experience on engineering projects of a grade and character which indicates to the Board that the applicant may be competent to practice engineering, shall be admitted to the principles and practice of engineering examination. Upon passing the examination, the applicant shall be granted a certificate of licensure to practice professional engineering in this State, provided the applicant is otherwise qualified.

c. Graduation, Experience, and Examination. - A graduate of an engineering curriculum of four years or more approved by the Board as being of satisfactory standing, shall be admitted to the fundamentals of engineering examination, and with a specific record of an additional four years or more of progressive experience on engineering projects of a grade and character that indicates to the Board that the applicant may be competent to practice engineering, the principles and practice of engineering examination. Upon passing the examinations, the applicant shall be granted a certificate of licensure to practice professional engineering in this State, provided the applicant is otherwise qualified.

d. Graduation, Experience, and Examination. - A graduate of an engineering or related science curriculum of four years or more, other than the ones approved by the Board as being of satisfactory standing or with an equivalent education and engineering experience satisfactory to the Board shall be admitted to the fundamentals of engineering examination and with a specific record of an additional eight years or more of progressive experience on engineering projects of a grade and character that indicates to the Board that the applicant may be competent to practice engineering, the principles and practice of engineering examination. Upon passing the examinations, the applicant shall be granted a certificate of licensure to practice professional engineering in this State, provided the applicant is otherwise qualified.

e. Long-Established Practice. - A person with a specific record of 20 years or more of progressive experience on engineering projects of a grade and character which indicates to the Board that the applicant may be competent to practice engineering shall be admitted to the principles and practice of engineering examination. Upon passing the examination, the applicant shall be granted a certificate of licensure to practice professional engineering in this State, provided the applicant is otherwise qualified.

f. Full-time faculty. - Full-time engineering faculty members who teach in an approved engineering program offering a four-year or more degree approved by the Board, may request and be granted waiver of the fundamentals of engineering examination. The faculty applicant shall document that the degree meets the Board's requirement. The faculty applicant shall then be admitted to the principles and practice of engineering examination.

g. Doctoral degree. - A person possessing an earned doctoral degree in engineering from an institution in which the same discipline undergraduate engineering program has been accredited by ABET (EAC) may request and be granted waiver of the fundamentals of engineering examination. The doctoral degree applicant shall document that the degree meets the Board's requirement. The doctoral degree applicant shall then be admitted to the principles and practice of engineering examination.

At its discretion the Board may require an applicant to submit exhibits, drawings, designs, or other tangible evidence of engineering work which the applicant personally accomplished or supervised.

(2) Repealed by Session Laws 2013-98, s. 2, effective June 12, 2013.

(b) Land Surveyor Applicant. - The evaluation of a land surveyor applicant's qualifications shall involve a consideration of the applicant's education, technical, and land surveying experience, exhibits of land surveying projects with which the applicant has been associated, and recommendations by references. The land surveyor applicant's qualifications may be reviewed at an interview if the Board determines it necessary. Educational credit for institute courses, correspondence courses, or other courses shall be determined by the Board.

The following shall be considered as minimum evidence satisfactory to the Board that the applicant is qualified for licensure as a professional land surveyor:

(1) To be certified as a land surveyor intern, an applicant shall (i) pass the fundamentals of land surveying examination and make application to the Board, (ii) be of good character and reputation, (iii) submit three character references to the Board, one of whom is a professional land surveyor, (iv) comply with the requirements of this Chapter, and (v) satisfy one of the following requirements related to education and experience:

a. Be a graduate of a surveying curriculum of four years or more or other equivalent curriculum in surveying approved by the Board.

b. Have rightful possession of an associate degree in surveying technology approved by the Board, a record satisfactory to the Board of four years of progressive practical experience, two years of which shall have been under a practicing professional land surveyor, and have satisfactorily passed a written and oral examination as required by the Board.

c. Have graduated from high school or completed a high school equivalency certificate with a record satisfactory to the Board of 10 years of progressive, practical experience, six years of which shall have been under a practicing licensed land surveyor, and have satisfactorily passed any oral and written examinations required by the Board.

(1a) To be licensed as a professional land surveyor, an applicant shall (i) be of good character and reputation, (ii) submit five character references to the Board, three of whom are professional land surveyors or individuals acceptable to the Board, with personal knowledge of the applicant's land surveying experience, (iii) comply with the requirements of this Chapter, and (iv) meet one of the following requirements:

a. Rightful possession of a bachelor of science degree in surveying or other equivalent curricula, all approved by the Board and a record satisfactory to the Board of two years or more of progressive practical experience, one year of which shall have been under a practicing professional land surveyor if the applicant has successfully passed the first examination (Fundamentals of Surveying) on or before January 1, 2013, or if the applicant has not successfully passed the first examination on or before January 1, 2013, two years of which shall have been under a practicing professional land surveyor, and satisfactorily passing any oral and written examination required by the Board, all of which shall determine and indicate that the applicant is competent to practice land surveying. Upon passing the first examination and successful completion of the experience required by this subdivision, the applicant may apply to take the second examination (Principles and Practice of Land Surveying). An applicant who passes both examinations and completes the educational and experience requirements of this subdivision shall be granted licensure as a professional land surveyor.

b. Rightful possession of an associate degree in surveying technology approved by the Board and a record satisfactory to the Board of four years of progressive practical experience, three years of which shall have been under a practicing licensed land surveyor if the applicant has successfully passed the first examination (Fundamentals of Surveying) on or before January 1, 2013, or if the applicant has not successfully passed the first examination on or before January 1, 2013, eight years of progressive practical experience, four years of which shall have been under a practicing professional land surveyor, and satisfactorily passing any written and oral examination required by the Board, all of which shall determine and indicate that the applicant is competent to practice land surveying. If the applicant has not successfully completed the first examination on or before January 1, 2013, the applicant may apply to the Board to take the first examination after obtaining the associate degree and completing four years of practical experience, two years of which shall have been under a practicing professional land surveyor at the first regularly scheduled examination thereafter. Upon passing the first examination and successfully completing the practical experience required under this subdivision, the applicant may apply to the Board to take the second examination (Principles and Practice of Land Surveying). An applicant who passes both examinations and successfully completes the educational and experience requirements of this subdivision shall be granted licensure as a professional land surveyor.

c. Repealed by Session Laws 1998-118, s. 11.

d. Graduation from a high school or the completion of a high school equivalency certificate and a record satisfactory to the Board of seven years of progressive practical experience, six years of which shall have been under a practicing licensed land surveyor if the applicant has successfully passed the first examination (Fundamentals of Surveying) on or before January 1, 2013, or if the applicant has not successfully passed the first examination on or before January 1, 2013, 16 years of progressive practical experience, nine years of which shall have been under a practicing professional land surveyor, and satisfactorily passing any oral and written examinations required by the Board, all of which shall determine and indicate that the candidate is competent to practice land surveying. If the applicant has not successfully passed the first examination on or before January 1, 2013, the applicant may be qualified by the Board to take the first examination upon graduation from high school or the completion of a high school equivalency certificate and successfully completing 10 years of progressive practice experience, six of which shall have been under a practicing licensed land surveyor.

  e. Repealed by Session Laws 1985 (Regular Session, 1986), c. 977, s. 7.

  f. Licensure by Comity or Endorsement. - A person holding a certificate of licensure to engage in the practice of land surveying issued on comparable qualifications from a state, territory, or possession of the United States or the District of Columbia, possessing credentials that, based on verifiable evidence, in the opinion of the Board, of a standard not lower than that in effect in this State at the time the certificate was issued, may upon application, be licensed without further examination, except to take any examinations as the Board requires to determine the applicant's qualifications, but in any event, the applicant shall be required to pass an examination which shall include questions on laws, procedures, and practices pertaining to the practice of land surveying in North Carolina.

  g. A licensed professional engineer who can satisfactorily demonstrate to the Board that the professional engineer's formal academic training in acquiring a degree and field experience in engineering includes land surveying, to the extent necessary to reasonably qualify the applicant in the practice of land surveying, may apply for and may be granted permission to take the principles and practice of land surveying examination and the fundamentals of land surveying examination. Upon satisfactorily passing the examinations, the applicant shall be granted a license to practice land surveying in the State of North Carolina.

  h. Professional Engineers in Land Surveying. - Any person presently licensed to practice professional engineering under this Chapter shall upon application be licensed to practice land surveying, providing a written application is filed with the Board within one year next after June 19, 1975.

i. Photogrammetrists. - Any person presently practicing photogrammetry with at least seven years of experience in the profession, two or more of which shall have been in responsible charge of photogrammetric mapping projects meeting National Map Accuracy Standards shall, upon application, be licensed to practice land surveying, provided:

1. The applicant submit certified proof of graduation from high school, high school equivalency, or higher degree;

2. The applicant submit proof of employment in responsible charge as a photogrammetrist practicing within the State of North Carolina to include itemized reports detailing methods, procedures, amount of applicant's personal involvement and the name, address, and telephone numbers of the client for five projects completed by the applicant with the State. A final map for one of the five projects shall also be submitted;

3. Five references to the applicant's character and quality of work, three of which shall be from professional land surveyors, are submitted to the Board; and

4. The application is submitted to the Board by July 1, 1999. After July 1, 1999, no photogrammetrist shall be licensed without meeting the same requirements as to education, length of experience, and testing required of all land surveying applicants.

j. Any person performing activities described in G.S. 89C-3(7)a.2. and 7. with at least seven years of experience in performing mapping science surveys, two or more of which have been in responsible charge of mapping science projects that meet the requirements of 21 NCAC 56.1608, shall, upon application, be licensed to practice surveying in their area of competence (mapping science) provided all of the following requirements are met:

1. The applicant submits certified proof of graduation from high school, high school equivalency, or higher degree.

2. The applicant submits proof of employment in responsible charge of mapping science projects within the State of North Carolina, including itemized reports detailing methods, procedures, amount of applicant's personal

involvement, and the name, address, and telephone numbers of the client for five projects completed by the applicant within the State. The applicant shall also submit a final map, report, or digital product for one of the five projects.

3. Five references as to the applicant's character and quality of work, three of which shall be from professional land surveyors, are submitted to the Board.

4. The application is submitted to the Board by July 1, 2014. After July 1, 2014, no individual performing surveys described in 21 NCAC 56.1608 shall be licensed without meeting the same requirements as to education, length of experience, and testing required of all land surveying applications.

(2) Repealed by Session Laws 2013-98, s. 2 effective June 12, 2013.

The Board shall require an applicant to submit exhibits, drawings, plats, or other tangible evidence of land surveying work executed by the applicant under proper supervision and which the applicant has personally accomplished or supervised.

Land surveying encompasses a number of disciplines including geodetic surveying, hydrographic surveying, cadastral surveying, engineering surveying, route surveying, photogrammetric (aerial) surveying, and topographic surveying. A professional land surveyor shall practice only within the surveyor's area of expertise.

The Board shall require an applicant to submit exhibits, drawings, plats, or other tangible evidence of land surveying work executed by the applicant under proper supervision and which the applicant has personally accomplished or supervised. (1921, c. 1, s. 9; C.S., s. 6055(j); 1951, c. 1084, s. 1; 1953, c. 999, s. 2; 1957, c. 1060, ss. 2, 3; 1975, c. 681, s. 1; 1985 (Reg. Sess., 1986), c. 977, ss. 1-15; 1993 (Reg. Sess., 1994), c. 671, s. 2; 1995, c. 509, s. 36.1; 1998-118, s. 11; 1998-217, s. 41; 2005-296, s. 1; 2011-304, s. 4; 2013-98, s. 2.)

§ 89C-14. Application for licensure; license fees.

(a) Application for licensure as a professional engineer or professional land surveyor shall be on a form prescribed and furnished by the Board. It shall contain statements made under oath, showing the applicant's education and a detailed summary of the applicant's technical and engineering or land surveying experience, and shall include the names and complete mailing addresses of the references, none of whom may be immediate members of the applicant's family or members of the Board.

The Board may accept the certified information on the copy of a current formal certificate of qualifications issued by the National Council of Examiners for Engineering and Surveying in lieu of the same information that is required for the form prescribed and furnished by the Board.

(b)   An applicant for licensure who is required to take the written examination shall pay to the Board an application fee not to exceed one hundred dollars ($100.00). The Board may charge any fee necessary to defray the cost of any required examinations. The fee shall accompany the application. The fee for comity licensure of engineers and land surveyors who hold unexpired certificates in another state or a territory of the United States or in Canada shall be the total current fee as fixed by the Board.

(c)   The certification fee for a corporation is the amount set by the Board but shall not exceed one hundred dollars ($100.00). The fee shall accompany the application. The certification fee for a business firm is the same as the fee for a corporation. The fee for renewal of a certificate of licensure of a corporation is the amount set by the Board but shall not exceed seventy-five dollars ($75.00). The fee for renewal of a certificate of licensure for a business firm is the same as the renewal fee for a corporation.

(d)   Should the Board deny the issuance of a certificate of licensure to any applicant, the unobligated portion of fees paid shall be returned by the Board to the applicant.

(e)   A candidate failing an examination may apply, and be considered by the Board, for reexamination at the end of six months. The Board shall make such reexamination charge as is necessary to defray the cost of the examination.

A candidate with a combination of three failures or unexcused absences on an examination shall only be eligible after submitting a new application with appropriate application fee and documented evidence of actions taken by the candidate to enhance the candidate's prospects for passing the exam. A candidate with a combination of three failures or unexcused absences may only be considered by the Board for reexamination at the end of 12 months following the third failure or unexcused absence. After the end of the 12-month period, the applicant may take the examination no more than once every calendar year.

(1921, c. 1, s. 9; C.S., s. 6055(j); 1951, c. 1084, s. 1; 1953, c. 999, s. 2; 1957, c. 1060, ss. 2, 3; 1975, c. 681, s. 1; 1981, c. 230; 1983, c. 183, ss. 1, 2; 1993 (Reg. Sess., 1994), c. 671, s. 5; 1996, 2nd Ex. Sess., c. 18, s. 7.10(k); 1998-118, s. 12; 2000-115, s. 1.)

§ 89C-15. Examinations.

(a) The examinations will be held at the times and places as the Board directs. The Board shall determine the passing grade on examinations. All examinations shall be approved by the entire Board.

(b) Examinations will be given as follows:

(1) Fundamentals of Engineering. - Consists of an examination on the fundamentals of engineering. Passing this examination qualifies the applicant for an engineer intern certificate, provided the applicant has met all other requirements for licensure required by this Chapter.

(2) Principles and Practice of Engineering. - Consists of an examination on applied engineering. Passing this examination qualifies the applicant for licensure as a professional engineer, provided the applicant has met the other requirements for licensure required by this Chapter.

(3) Fundamentals of Land Surveying. - Consists of an examination on the fundamentals of land surveying. Passing this examination qualifies the applicant for a land surveyor intern certificate provided the applicant has met all other requirements for certification required by this Chapter.

(4) Principles and Practice of Land Surveying. - Consists of an examination on the applied disciplines of land surveying and an examination on requirements specific to the practice of land surveying in North Carolina. Passing each of these examinations qualifies the applicant for a professional land surveyor certificate provided the applicant has met all other requirements for certification required by this Chapter. (1975, c. 681, s. 1; 1998-118, s. 13; 2013-98, s. 3.)

§ 89C-16. Certificates of licensure; effect; seals.

(a) The Board shall issue to any applicant, who, in the opinion of the Board, has met the requirements of this Chapter, a certificate of licensure giving the licensee proper authority to practice the profession in this State. The certificate of licensure for a professional engineer shall carry the designation "professional engineer," and for a land surveyor, "professional land surveyor," shall give the full name of the licensee with the Board designated licensure number and shall be signed by the chair and the secretary under the seal of the Board.

(b) This certificate shall be prima facie evidence that the person named on the certificate is entitled to all rights, privileges and responsibilities of a professional engineer or a professional land surveyor, while the certificate of licensure remains unrevoked or unexpired.

(c) Each licensee shall upon licensure obtain a seal of a design authorized by the Board bearing the licensee's name, license number, and the legend, "professional engineer," or "professional land surveyor." Final drawings, specifications, plans and reports prepared by a licensee shall, when issued, be certified and stamped with the seal or facsimile of the seal unless the licensee is exempt under the provisions of G.S. 89C-25(7). It shall be unlawful for a licensee to affix, or permit the licensee's seal and signature or facsimile of the seal and signature to be affixed to any drawings, specifications, plans or reports after the expiration of a certificate or for the purpose of aiding or abetting any other person to evade or attempt to evade any provision of this Chapter. A professional engineer practicing land surveying shall use the licensee's land surveyor seal. (1921, c. 1, s. 11; C.S., s. 6055(m); 1951, c. 1084, s. 1; 1957, c. 1060, s. 6; 1975, c. 681, s. 1; 1998-118, s. 14.)

§ 89C-17. Expirations and renewals of certificates.

Certificates for licensure of corporations and business firms that engage in the practice of engineering or land surveying shall expire on the last day of the month of June following their issuance or renewal and shall become invalid on that date unless renewed. All other certificates for licensure shall expire on the last day of the month of December next following their issuance or renewal, and shall become invalid on that date unless renewed. When necessary to protect the public health, safety, or welfare, the Board shall require any evidence necessary to establish the continuing competency of engineers and land surveyors as a condition of renewal of licenses. When the Board is satisfied as to the continuing competency of an applicant, it shall issue a renewal of the certificate upon payment by the applicant of a fee fixed by the Board but not to exceed seventy-five dollars ($75.00). The secretary of the Board shall notify by mail every person licensed under this Chapter of the date of expiration of the certificate, the amount of the fee required for its renewal for one year, and any requirement as to evidence of continued competency. The notice shall be mailed at least one month in advance of the expiration date of the certificate. Renewal shall be effected at any time during the month immediately following the month of expiration, by payment to the secretary of the Board of a renewal fee, as determined by the Board, which shall not exceed seventy-five dollars ($75.00). Failure on the part of any licensee to renew the certificate annually in the month immediately following the month of expiration, as required above, shall deprive the licensee of the right to practice until reinstatement of the license. The license may be reinstated at anytime during the first 12 months immediately following the date the license became invalid by payment of a reinstatement fee of one hundred dollars ($100.00) in addition to the established renewal fee. Failure of a licensee to reinstate the license during the first 12 months immediately following the date the license became invalid shall require the individual, prior to resuming practice in North Carolina, to submit an application on the prescribed form, and to meet all other requirements for licensure as set forth in Chapter 89C. The secretary of the Board is instructed to remove from the official roster of engineers and land surveyors the names of all licensees who have not effected their renewal by the first day of the month immediately following the renewal period. The Board may adopt rules to provide for renewals in distress or hardship cases due to military service, prolonged illness, or prolonged absence from the State, where the applicant for renewal demonstrates to the Board that the applicant has maintained active knowledge and professional status as an engineer or land surveyor, as the case may be. It shall be the responsibility of each licensee to inform the Board promptly concerning change in address. A licensee may request and be granted inactive status. No inactive licensee may practice in this State unless otherwise exempted in this Chapter. A licensee granted inactive status shall pay annual renewal fees but shall not be subject to annual continuing professional competency requirements. A licensee granted inactive status may return to active status by meeting all requirements of the Board, including demonstration of continuing professional competency as a condition of reinstatement. (1921, c. 1, s. 9; C.S., s. 6055(k); 1951, c. 1084, s. 1; 1953, c. 1041, s. 9; 1957, c. 1060, s. 4; 1973, c. 1321; c. 1331, s. 3; 1975, c. 681, s. 1; 1979, c. 819, ss. 3, 4; 1985, c. 373; 1998-118, s. 15; 2000-115, s. 2; 2003-347, s. 3.)

§ 89C-18. Duplicate certificates.

The Board may issue a duplicate certificate of licensure or certificate of authorization to replace any certificate that has been lost, destroyed, or mutilated and may charge a fee of up to twenty-five dollars ($25.00) for issuing the certificate. (1921, c. 1, s. 10; C.S., s. 6055(l); 1939, c. 218, s. 2; 1951, c. 1084, s. 1; 1953, c. 1041, s. 10; 1957, c. 1060, s. 5; 1973, c. 1331, s. 3; 1975, c. 681, s. 1; 1993 (Reg. Sess., 1994), c. 671, s. 3; 1998-118, s. 16.)

§ 89C-18.1. Licensing of nonresidents.

(a) Definitions. - The following definitions apply in this section:

(1) Delinquent income tax debt. - The amount of income tax due as stated in a final notice of assessment issued to a taxpayer by the Secretary of Revenue when the taxpayer no longer has the right to contest the amount.

(2) Foreign corporation. - Defined in G.S. 55-1-40.

(3) Foreign entity. - A foreign corporation, a foreign limited liability company, or a foreign partnership.

(4) Foreign limited liability company. - Has the same meaning as the term "foreign LLC" in G.S. 57D-1-03.

(5) Foreign partnership. - Either of the following that does not have a permanent place of business in this State:

a. A foreign limited partnership as defined in G.S. 59-102.

b. A general partnership formed under the laws of a jurisdiction other than this State.

(b) Licensing. - The Board shall not renew a certificate of licensure for a foreign corporation unless the corporation has obtained a certificate of authority from the Secretary of State pursuant to Article 15 of Chapter 55 of the General Statutes. The Board shall not renew a certificate of licensure for a foreign limited liability company unless the company has obtained a certificate of authority from the Secretary of State pursuant to Article 7 of Chapter 57D of the General Statutes.

(c)   Information. - Upon request, the Board shall provide the Secretary of Revenue on an annual basis the name, address, and tax identification number of every nonresident individual and foreign entity licensed by the Board. The information shall be provided in the format required by the Secretary of Revenue.

(d)   Delinquents. - If the Secretary of Revenue determines that any nonresident individual or foreign corporation licensed by the Board, a member of any foreign limited liability company licensed by the Board, or a partner in any foreign partnership licensed by the Board, owes a delinquent income tax debt, the Secretary of Revenue may notify the Board of these nonresident individuals and foreign entities and instruct the Board not to renew their certificates of licensure. The Board shall not renew the certificate of licensure of such a nonresident individual or foreign entity identified by the Secretary of Revenue unless the Board receives a written statement from the Secretary that the debt either has been paid or is being paid pursuant to an installment agreement. (1998-162, ss. 7, 13; 2013-157, s. 23.)

§ 89C-19. Public works; requirements where public safety involved.

This State and its political subdivisions such as counties, cities, towns, or other political entities or legally constituted boards, commissions, public utility companies, or authorities, or officials, or employees of these entities shall not engage in the practice of engineering or land surveying involving either public or private property where the safety of the public is directly involved without the project being under the supervision of a professional engineer for the preparations of plans and specifications for engineering projects, or a professional land surveyor for land surveying projects, as provided for the practice of the respective professions by this Chapter.

An official or employee of the State or any political subdivision specified in this section, holding the positions set out in this section as of June 19, 1975, shall be exempt from the provisions of this section so long as such official or employee is engaged in substantially the same type of work as is involved in the present position.

Nothing in this section shall be construed to prohibit inspection, maintenance and service work done by employees of the State of North Carolina, any political subdivision of the State, or any municipality including construction, installation, servicing, and maintenance by regular full-time employees of, secondary roads and drawings incidental to work on secondary roads, streets, street lighting, traffic-control signals, police and fire alarm systems, waterworks, steam, electric and sewage treatment and disposal plants, the services of superintendents, inspectors or foremen regularly employed by the State of North Carolina or any political subdivision of the State, or municipal corporation.

The provisions in this section shall not be construed to alter or modify the requirements of Article 1 of Chapter 133 of the General Statutes. (1975, c. 681, s. 1; 1998-118, s. 17.)

§ 89C-19.1. Engineer who volunteers during an emergency or disaster; qualified immunity.

(a)   A professional engineer who voluntarily, without compensation, provides structural, electrical, mechanical, or other engineering services at the scene of a declared disaster or emergency, declared under federal law or in accordance with the provisions of Article 1A of Chapter 166A of the General Statutes, at the request of a public official, law enforcement official, public safety official, or building inspection official, acting in an official capacity, shall not be liable for any personal injury, wrongful death, property damage, or other loss caused by the professional engineer's acts or omissions in the performance of the engineering services.

(b)   The immunity provided in subsection (a) of this section applies only to an engineering service:

(1)   For any structure, building, piping, or other engineered system, either publicly or privately owned.

(2)   That occurs within 45 days after the declaration of the emergency or disaster, unless the 45-day immunity period is extended by an executive order issued by the Governor under the Governor's emergency executive powers.

(c)   The immunity provided in subsection (a) of this section does not apply if it is determined that the personal injury, wrongful death, property damage, or other loss was caused by the gross negligence, wanton conduct, or intentional wrongdoing of the professional engineer, or arose out of the operation of a motor vehicle.

(d)   As used in this section:

(1)   "Building inspection official" means any appointed or elected federal, State, or local official with overall executive responsibility to coordinate building inspection in the jurisdiction in which the emergency or disaster is declared.

(2)   "Law enforcement official" means any appointed or elected federal, State, or local official with overall executive responsibility to coordinate law enforcement in the jurisdiction in which the emergency or disaster is declared.

(3)   "Public official" means any federal, State, or locally elected official with overall executive responsibility in the jurisdiction in which the emergency or disaster is declared.

(4)   "Public safety official" means any appointed or elected federal, State, or local official with overall executive responsibility to coordinate public safety in the jurisdiction in which the emergency or disaster is declared. (1995, c. 416, s. 1; 2012-12, s. 2(q).)

§ 89C-20. Rules of professional conduct.

In the interest of protecting the safety, health, and welfare of the public, the Board shall adopt rules of professional conduct applicable to the practice of engineering and land surveying. These rules, when adopted, shall be construed to be a reasonable exercise of the police power vested in the Board of Examiners for Engineers and Land Surveyors. Every person licensed by the Board shall subscribe to and observe the adopted rules as the standard of professional conduct for the practice of engineering and land surveying and shall cooperate fully with the Board in the course of any investigation. In the case of violation of the rules of professional conduct, the Board shall proceed in accordance with G.S. 89C-22. (1975, c. 681, s. 1; 1987, c. 827, s. 73; 1998-118, s. 18.)

§ 89C-21. Disciplinary action - Reexamination, revocation, suspension, reprimand, or civil penalty.

(a) The Board may reprimand the licensee, suspend, refuse to renew, refuse to reinstate, or revoke the certificate of licensure, require additional education or, as appropriate, require reexamination, for any engineer or land surveyor, who is found guilty of any of the following:

(1) Fraud or deceit in obtaining or renewing a certificate of licensure or certificate of authorization.

(2) Gross negligence, incompetence, or misconduct in the practice of the profession.

(3) Conviction of, or entry of a plea of guilty or nolo contendere to, any crime that is a felony, whether or not related to the practice of engineering or surveying; conviction of, or entry of a plea of guilty or nolo contendere to, any crime, whether a felony, misdemeanor, or otherwise, where an essential element of the crime is dishonesty or when the crime is directly related to the practice of engineering or surveying; or conviction of, or entry of a plea of guilty or nolo contendere, of any crime involving moral turpitude.

(4) Violation of any provisions of this Chapter, the Rules of Professional Conduct, or any rules as adopted by the Board.

(5) Being declared insane or incompetent by a court of competent jurisdiction and having not later been lawfully declared sane or competent.

(6) Professional incompetence. In the event the Board finds that a certificate holder is incompetent the Board may, in its discretion, require oral or written examinations, or other indication of the certificate holder's fitness to practice engineering or land surveying and suspend the license during any such period.

(b) The Board may (i) revoke a certificate of authorization, or (ii) to suspend a certificate of authorization for a period of time not exceeding two years, of any corporation or business firm where one or more of its officers or directors have committed any act or have been guilty of any conduct which would authorize a revocation or suspension of their certificates of licensure under the provision of this section.

(c) The Board may levy a civil penalty not in excess of five thousand dollars ($5,000) for any engineer or not in excess of two thousand dollars ($2,000) for any land surveyor who violates any of the provisions of subdivisions (1) through (4) of subsection (a) of this section. The clear proceeds of all civil penalties collected by the Board, including civil penalties collected pursuant to G.S. 89C-22(c), shall be remitted to the Civil Penalty and Forfeiture Fund in accordance with G.S. 115C-457.2.

(d) Before imposing and assessing a civil penalty and fixing the amount, the Board shall, as a part of its deliberation, take into consideration the following factors:

(1) The nature, gravity, and persistence of the particular violations;

(2) The appropriateness of the imposition of a civil penalty when considered alone or in combination with other punishment;

(3) Whether the violation(s) were done willfully and maliciously; and

(4) Any other factors which would tend to either mitigate or aggravate the violation(s) found to exist. (1921, c. 1, s. 10; C.S., s. 6055(l); 1939, c. 218, s. 2; 1951, c. 1084, s. 1; 1953, c. 1041, s. 10; 1957, c. 1060, s. 5; 1973, c. 1331, s. 3; 1975, c. 681, s. 1; 1989, c. 669, s. 1; 1993 (Reg. Sess., 1994), c. 671, s. 6; 1998-118, s. 19; 1998-215, s. 134; 2003-347, s. 2; 2011-304, s. 5.)

§ 89C-22. Disciplinary action - Charges; procedure.

(a) Any person may prefer charges of fraud, deceit, gross negligence, incompetence, misconduct, or violations of this Chapter, the rules of professional conduct, or any rules adopted by the Board against any Board licensee. The charges shall be in writing and shall be sworn to by the person or persons making them and shall be filed with the Board.

(b) All charges, unless dismissed by the Board as unfounded or trivial or unless settled informally, shall be heard by the Board as provided under the requirements of Chapter 150B of the General Statutes.

(c) If, after a hearing, a majority of the Board votes in favor of sustaining the charges, the Board shall reprimand, levy a civil penalty, suspend, refuse to renew, refuse to reinstate, or revoke the licensee's certificate, require additional education or, as appropriate, require reexamination.

(d)   A licensee who is aggrieved by a final decision of the Board may appeal for judicial review as provided by Article 4 of Chapter 150B.

(e)   The Board may, upon petition of an individual or an entity whose certificate has been revoked, for sufficient reasons as it may determine, reissue a certificate of licensure or authorization, provided that a majority of the members of the Board vote in favor of such issuance. (1921, c. 1, s. 10; C.S., s. 6055(l); 1939, c. 218, s. 2; 1951, c. 1084, s. 1; 1953, c. 1041, s. 10; 1957, c. 1060, s. 5; 1973, c. 1331, s. 3; 1975, c. 681, s. 1; 1981, c. 789; 1989, c. 669, s. 2; 1993 (Reg. Sess., 1994), c. 671, s. 7; 1998-118, s. 20; 2011-304, s. 6.)

§ 89C-23. Unlawful to practice engineering or land surveying without licensure; unlawful use of title or terms; penalties; Attorney General to be legal adviser.

Any person who shall practice, or offer to practice, engineering or land surveying in this State without first being licensed in accordance with the provisions of this Chapter, or any person, firm, partnership, organization, association, corporation, or other entity using or employing the words "engineer" or "engineering" or "professional engineer" or "professional engineering" or "land surveyor" or "land surveying," or any modification or derivative of those words in its name or form of business or activity except as licensed under this Chapter or in pursuit of activities exempted by this Chapter, or any person presenting or attempting to use the certificate of licensure or the seal of another, or any person who shall give any false or forged evidence of any kind to the Board or to any member of the Board in obtaining or attempting to obtain a certificate of licensure, or any person who shall falsely impersonate any other licensee of like or different name, or any person who shall attempt to use an expired or revoked or nonexistent certificate of licensure, or who shall practice or offer to practice when not qualified, or any person who falsely claims that the person is registered under this Chapter, or any person who shall violate any of the provisions of this Chapter, in addition to injunctive procedures set out hereinbefore, shall be guilty of a Class 2 misdemeanor. In no event shall there be representation of or holding out to the public of any engineering expertise by unlicensed persons. It shall be the duty of all duly constituted officers of the State and all political subdivisions of the State to enforce the provisions of this Chapter and to prosecute any persons violating them.

The Attorney General of the State or an assistant shall act as legal adviser to the Board and render any legal assistance necessary to carry out the provisions of this Chapter. The Board may employ counsel and necessary assistance to aid in the enforcement of this Chapter, and the compensation and expenses for the assistance shall be paid from funds of the Board. (1921, c. 1, s. 12; C.S., s. 6055(n); 1951, c. 1084, s. 1; 1975, c. 681, s. 1; 1993, c. 539, s. 612; 1994, Ex. Sess., c. 24, s. 14(c); 1998-118, s. 21.)

§ 89C-24. Licensure of corporations and business firms that engage in the practice of engineering or land surveying.

A corporation or business firm may not engage in the practice of engineering or land surveying in this State unless it is licensed by the Board and has paid an application fee established by the Board in an amount not to exceed one hundred dollars ($100.00). A corporation or business firm is subject to the same duties and responsibilities as an individual licensee. Licensure of a corporation or business firm does not affect the requirement that all engineering or land surveying work done by the corporation or business firm be performed by or under the responsible charge of individual registrants, nor does it relieve the individual registrants within a corporation or business firm of their design and supervision responsibilities. The Board may adopt rules regulating the operation of offices and places of business of corporations and business firms licensed under this section to ensure that professional engineering and land surveying services are performed under the supervision of licensed professional engineers and land surveyors.

This section applies to every corporation that is engaged in the practice of engineering or land surveying, regardless of when it was incorporated. A corporation that is not exempt from Chapter 55B of the General Statutes by application of G.S. 55B-15 must be incorporated under that Chapter. (1921, c. 1, s. 14; C.S., s. 6055(p); 1951, c. 1084, s. 1; 1969, c. 718, s. 18; 1975, c. 681, s. 1; 1993 (Reg. Sess., 1994), c. 671, s. 4; 1998-118, s. 22; 2000-115, s. 3.)

§ 89C-25. Limitations on application of Chapter.

This Chapter shall not be construed to prevent or affect:

(1)   The practice of architecture, landscape architecture, or contracting or any other legally recognized profession or trade.

(2)   Repealed by Session Laws 2011-304, s. 7, effective June 26, 2011.

(3)   Repealed by Session Laws 2011-304, s. 7, effective June 26, 2011.

(4)   Engaging in engineering or land surveying as an employee or assistant under the responsible charge of a professional engineer or professional land surveyor or as an employee or assistant of a nonresident professional engineer or a nonresident professional land surveyor provided for in subdivisions (2) and (3) of this section, provided that the work as an employee may not include responsible charge of design or supervision.

(5)   The practice of professional engineering or land surveying by any person not a resident of, and having no established place of business in this State, as a consulting associate of a professional engineer or professional land surveyor licensed under the provisions of this Chapter; provided, the nonresident is qualified for performing the professional service in the person's own state or country.

(6)   Practice by members of the Armed Forces of the United States; employees of the government of the United States while engaged in the practice of engineering or land surveying solely for the government on government-owned works and projects; or practice by those employees of the Natural Resources Conservation Service, county employees, or employees of the Soil and Water Conservation Districts who have federal engineering job approval authority that involves the planning, designing, or implementation of best management practices on agricultural lands.

(7)   The internal engineering or surveying activities of a person, firm or corporation engaged in manufacturing, processing, or producing a product, including the activities of public service corporations, public utility companies, authorities, State agencies, railroads, or membership cooperatives, or the installation and servicing of their product in the field; or research and development in connection with the manufacture of that product or their service; or of their research affiliates; or their employees in the course of their employment in connection with the manufacture, installation, or servicing of their product or service in the field, or on-the-premises maintenance of machinery, equipment, or apparatus incidental to the manufacture or installation of the product or service of a firm by the employees of the firm upon property owned,

leased or used by the firm; inspection, maintenance and service work done by employees of the State of North Carolina, any political subdivision of the State, or any municipality including construction, installation, servicing, maintenance by regular full-time employees of streets, street lighting, traffic-control signals, police and fire alarm systems, waterworks, steam, electric and sewage treatment and disposal plants; the services of superintendents, inspectors or foremen regularly employed by the State of North Carolina or any political subdivision of the State or a municipal corporation; provided, however, that the internal engineering or surveying activity is not a holding out to or an offer to the public of engineering or any service thereof as prohibited by this Chapter. Engineering work, not related to the foregoing exemptions, where the safety of the public is directly involved shall be under the responsible charge of a licensed professional engineer, or in accordance with standards prepared or approved by a licensed professional engineer.

(8) The (i) preparation of fire sprinkler planning and design drawings by a fire sprinkler contractor licensed under Article 2 of Chapter 87 of the General Statutes, or (ii) the performance of internal engineering or survey work by a manufacturing or communications common carrier company, or by a research and development company, or by employees of those corporations provided that the work is in connection with, or incidental to products of, or nonengineering services rendered by those corporations or their affiliates.

(9) The routine maintenance or servicing of machinery, equipment, facilities or structures, the work of mechanics in the performance of their established functions, or the inspection or supervision of construction by a foreman, superintendent, or agent of the architect or professional engineer, or services of an operational nature performed by an employee of a laboratory, a manufacturing plant, a public service corporation, or governmental operation.

(10) The design of land application irrigation systems for an animal waste management plan, required by G.S. 143-215.10C, by a designer who exhibits, by at least three years of relevant experience, proficiency in soil science and basic hydraulics, and who is thereby listed as an Irrigation Design Technical Specialist by the North Carolina Soil and Water Conservation Commission. (1921, c. 1, s. 13; C.S., s. 6055(o); 1951, c. 1084, s. 1; 1975, c. 681, s. 1; 1995, c. 146, s. 1; 1995 (Reg. Sess., 1996), c. 742, s. 35; 1997-454, s. 1; 1998-118, s. 23; 2007-536, s. 1; 2011-183, s. 53; 2011-304, s. 7.)

§ 89C-25.1. Supervision of unlicensed individuals by licensed person.

In all circumstances in which unlicensed individuals are permitted under this Chapter to perform engineering or land surveying work, or both, under the supervision of a licensed engineer, land surveyor, or both, the Board may by regulation establish a reasonable limit on the number of unlicensed individuals which a licensee of the Board may directly or personally supervise at one time. (1979, c. 819, s. 5; 1998-118, s. 24.)

§ 89C-25.2. Program of licensure by discipline.

The Board shall submit to the legislative committees of reference by July 1, 1981, a program of licensure by discipline and an analysis of the costs and merits thereof in order to permit the General Assembly to make a decision on the establishment of such a program. The "committees of reference" shall be the Senate and House Committees on State Government respectively or such other committees as the respective presiding officers may determine. (1979, c. 819, s. 5.)

§ 89C-26: Repealed by Session Laws 1997-309, s. 10.

§ 89C-27. Invalid sections; severability.

If any of the provisions of this Chapter, or if any rule, regulation or order thereunder, or if the application of such provision to any person or circumstance shall be held invalid, the remainder of this Chapter and the application of such provision of this Chapter or rule, regulation or order to persons or circumstances, other than those as to which it is held valid, shall not be affected thereby. (1975, c. 681, s. 1.)

§ 89C-28. Existing licensure not affected.

Nothing in this Chapter shall be construed as affecting the status of licensure of any professional engineer or land surveyor who is rightfully in possession of a certificate of licensure duly issued by the Board and valid as of July 1, 1975. (1951, c. 1084, s. 1; 1959, c. 1236, s. 2; 1975, c. 681, s. 1; 1998-118, s. 25.)

Chapter 89D.

Landscape Contractors.

§ 89D-1. Certificate required.

On and after December 1, 1975, it shall be unlawful for any person, partnership, association or corporation in this State to use the title "landscape contractor," or to advertise as such without first obtaining a certificate issued by the North Carolina Landscape contractors' Registration Board under provisions of this Chapter. (1975, c. 741, s. 1.)

§ 89D-2. Definition.

A "landscape contractor" within the meaning of this Chapter is any person, partnership, association or corporation who for compensation or valuable consideration or promise thereof engages in the business requiring the art, experience, ability, knowledge, science and skill to install, plant, repair and maintain gardens, lawns, shrubs, vines, bushes, trees and other decorative vegetation including the grading and preparation of plots and areas of land for decorative treatment and arrangement; who constructs or installs garden pools, fountains, pavilions, conservatories, hothouses and greenhouses, incidental retaining walls, fences, walks, drainage and sprinkler systems; or who engages in incidental construction in connection therewith, or does any part thereof in such a manner that, under an agreed specification, an acceptable landscaping project can be executed. (1975, c. 741, s. 2.)

§ 89D-3. Application of Chapter.

The provisions of this Chapter shall not apply to and shall not include any person, partnership, association or corporation who shall perform any of the acts aforesaid in G.S. 89D-2 with reference to any property, so long as that person, partnership, association or corporation shall not use the title "landscape contractor." (1975, c. 741, s. 3.)

§ 89D-4. Landscape Contractors' Registration Board created; membership; compensation; power, etc.

(a)   There is created the North Carolina Landscape Contractors' Registration Board (hereinafter called the Board) which shall issue registration certificates of title to landscape contractors. The Board shall be composed of nine members appointed as follows: Two by the Governor to represent the public at large; two by the Commissioner of Agriculture; two practicing nurserymen operating a nursery certified by the North Carolina Department of Agriculture and Consumer Services Plant Pest Inspection Program appointed by the Board of Directors of the North Carolina Association of Nurserymen, Inc.; two registered landscape contractors in the business of landscape contracting appointed by the Board of Directors of the North Carolina Landscape Contractors' Association, Inc.; and one registered landscape architect appointed by the Board of Directors of the North Carolina Chapter of the American Society of Landscape Architects. All appointments shall be for three-year terms and no member shall serve more than two complete consecutive terms.

Any vacancy on the Board created by death, resignation or otherwise shall be filled for the unexpired term by the initial appointing authority and all members shall serve until their successors are appointed and qualify.

(b)   From its funds, the Board shall pay its members at the rate set out in G.S. 93B-5: Provided, that at no time shall the expense exceed the cash balance on hand.

(c)   The Board shall have power to make such rules and regulations as are not inconsistent with the provisions of this Chapter and the laws of North Carolina. The Board shall not make rules or regulations regulating commissions, salaries, or fees to be charged by registrants under this Chapter. The Board shall adopt a seal for its use, which shall bear thereon the words "North Carolina Landscape Contractors' Registration Board."

(d)   The Board may employ a secretary-treasurer and such clerical assistance as may be necessary to carry out the provisions of this Chapter and to put into effect such rules and regulations as the Board may promulgate. The Board shall fix salaries for employees and shall require employees to make good and sufficient surety bond for the faithful performance of their duties.

(e)   The Board shall be entitled to the services of the Attorney General of North Carolina in connection with the affairs of the Board or may, on approval of the Attorney General, employ an attorney to assist or represent it in the enforcement of this Chapter, but the fee paid for such service shall be approved by the Attorney General. (1975, c. 741, s. 4; 1983, c. 108, s. 1; 1997-261, s. 109.)

§ 89D-5. Application for certificate; examination; renewal.

(a)   Any person, partnership, association or corporation hereinafter desiring to register and be titled as a landscape contractor shall make written application for a certificate of title to the Board on such forms as are prescribed by the Board. Each applicant for a certificate of title as a landscape contractor shall be at least 18 years of age. Prior to July 1, 1976, each applicant for a certificate shall have been actively engaged as an untitled landscape contractor for at least one year prior to date of application. After July 1, 1976, an applicant shall furnish evidence satisfactory to the Board of three years' experience in landscape contracting or the completion of a study or combination of study and experience in landscape contracting equivalent to three years' experience under a landscape contractor.

(b)   Any person who applies to the Board to be registered and titled as a landscape contractor shall be required to take an oral or written examination to determine his qualifications. Each application for registration by examination shall be accompanied by an application fee of seventy-five dollars ($75.00).

The Board shall compile a manual from which the examination will be prepared. The examination fee shall not exceed seventy-five dollars ($75.00). Any one failing to pass an examination may be reexamined upon payment of the same fee as that charged to persons taking the examination for the first time, in accordance with such rules as the Board may adopt pertaining to examinations and reexaminations.

If the results of the examination are satisfactory, the Board shall issue the applicant a certificate authorizing him to be titled as a landscape contractor in the State of North Carolina upon payment of the initial certification fee as outlined in subsection (c).

(c) All certificates granted and issued by the Board under the provisions of this Chapter shall expire annually on December 31. Renewal of such certificates may be effected at any time during the month preceding the expiration date of such certificates upon proper application to the Board accompanied by the payment to the secretary-treasurer of the Board of a renewal fee, as set by the Board, of not more than seventy-five dollars ($75.00). The fee for an initial certificate shall be the same as for a renewal certificate and is in addition to the application fee. All certificates reinstated after expiration date thereof shall be subject to a late filing fee of twenty-five dollars ($25.00). In the event a registrant fails to obtain a reinstatement of such certificate within 12 months from the date of expiration thereof, the Board may, in its discretion, consider such registrant subject to the provisions of this Chapter relating to the issuance of an original certificate. Duplicate certificates may be issued by the Board upon payment of a fee not to exceed five dollars ($5.00) by the registrant. The Board may charge a fee not to exceed thirty-five dollars ($35.00) for issuance of a duplicate parchment certificate. (1975, c. 741, s. 5; 1983, c. 108, ss. 2, 3; 1991, c. 180, s. 1; 2007-426, s. 1.)

§ 89D-6. Registers of applicants and certificate holders.

(a) The secretary-treasurer of the Board shall keep a register of all applicants for certificates of title. The register shall include the date of application, name, place of business, place of residence, and indicate whether the certificate of title was granted or refused.

(b) The secretary-treasurer of the Board shall also keep a current roster showing the names and places of business of all registered titled landscape contractors. The roster shall be kept on file in the office of the Board and be open to public inspection.

(c) On or before the first day of September of each year, the Board shall file with the Secretary of State a copy of the roster of landscape contractors holding certificates of title. At the same time the Board shall file with the Secretary of State a report containing a complete statement of receipts and disbursements of the Board for the preceding fiscal year ending June 30. Such statement shall be attested by the secretary-treasurer of the Board. (1975, c. 741, s. 6.)

§ 89D-7. Denial, revocation or suspension of certificate.

(a) The Board shall have power to revoke or suspend certificates of title herein provided. The Board may upon its own motion or upon a verified complaint in writing hold a hearing as hereinafter provided to investigate the actions of any titled landscape contractor. The Board shall have the power to suspend or revoke any certificate of title issued under the provisions of this Chapter if the registrant has by false or fraudulent representations obtained a certificate; if the registrant has been convicted or has entered a plea of nolo contendere to any crime involving moral turpitude in any court, State or federal; if the registrant is found to have committed any act which constitutes improper, fraudulent or dishonest dealing; or if the registrant violates any rule or regulation duly promulgated by the Board.

(b) Chapter 150B of the General Statutes applies to proceedings under this section to deny, revoke, or suspend a certificate. (1975, c. 741, s. 7; 1987, c. 827, s. 74.)

§ 89D-8. Out-of-state applicants.

An applicant from another state which offers registration privileges to residents of North Carolina may be registered by conforming to all the provisions of this Chapter and, in the discretion of the Board, such other terms and conditions as are required of North Carolina residents applying for a certificate in such other state. The Board may exempt from the examination prescribed in this Chapter a landscape contractor duly registered in another state if a similar exemption is extended to registered landscape contractors from North Carolina. (1975, c. 741, s. 8.)

§ 89D-9. Persons in practice prior to July 1, 1976.

Before July 1, 1976, any person, partnership, corporation or other legal entity submitting an application, application fee and evidence satisfactory to the Board that he has actively engaged in the practice of landscape contracting for one year prior to July 1, 1976, shall be issued a certificate of title without the requirement of examination. (1975, c. 741, s. 10.)

§ 89D-10. Injunctions for violation of Chapter.

The Board shall have authority to petition for, and the superior courts of the State shall have authority to issue, temporary restraining orders, and preliminary and permanent injunctions for violations of this Chapter. (1975, c. 741, s. 11.)

Chapter 89E.

Geologists Licensing Act.

§ 89E-1. Short title.

This Chapter shall be known as the North Carolina Geologists Licensing Act. (1983 (Reg. Sess., 1984), c. 1074, s. 1.)

§ 89E-2. Purpose.

The purposes of this Chapter are to protect life, property, health and public welfare through the regulation of the practice of geology in the State of North Carolina; to define the practice of geology as a profession, establishing minimum professional standards of ethical conduct, professional responsibility, educational and experience background; and to prevent abuses of the practice of geology by untrained or unprincipled individuals. (1983 (Reg. Sess., 1984), c. 1074, s. 1.)

§ 89E-3. Definitions.

When used in this Chapter, unless the context otherwise requires:

(1)   "Board" means the North Carolina Board for Licensing of Geologists.

(2)   "Geologist". The term "geologist", within the intent of this Chapter, shall mean a person who is trained and educated in the science of geology.

(3) The term "geologist-in-training" means a person who has taken and successfully passed the portion of professional examination covering fundamental or academic geologic subjects, prior to his completion of the requisite years of experience in geologic work as provided for in this Chapter.

(4) "Geology" means the science dealing with the earth and its history; investigation, prediction and location of the materials and structures which compose it; the natural processes that cause change in the earth; and the applied science of utilizing knowledge of the earth and its constituent rocks, minerals, liquids, gases and other materials for the benefit of mankind. This definition shall not include any of the following:

a. Service or creative works, the adequate performance of which requires engineering education, training, and experience.

b. The assessment of an underground storage tank required by applicable rules at closure or change in service unless there has been a discharge or release of the product from the tank.

(5) The term "good moral character" means such character as tends to ensure the faithful discharge of the fiduciary duties of the licensed geologist to his client.

(6) "License" means a certificate issued by the Board recognizing the individual named in this certificate as meeting the requirements for licensing under this Chapter.

(7) "Licensed geologist" means a person who is licensed as a geologist under the provisions of this Chapter.

(8) "Public practice of geology" means the performance for others of geological service or work in the nature of work or consultation, investigation, surveys, evaluations, planning, mapping and inspection of geological work, in which the performance is related to the public welfare of safeguarding of life, health, property and the environment, except as specifically exempted by this Chapter. The definition shall not include or allow the practice of engineering as defined in Chapter 89C of the North Carolina General Statutes.

(9) The term "qualified geologist" means a person who possesses all of the qualifications specified in this Chapter for licensing except that he or she is not licensed.

(10) The term "responsible charge of work" means the independent control and direction by the use of initiative, skill and independent judgment of geological work or the supervision of such work.

(11) The term "subordinate" means any person who assists a licensed geologist in the practice of geology without assuming the responsible charge of work. (1983 (Reg. Sess., 1984), c. 1074, s. 1; 1996, 2nd Ex. Sess., c. 18, s. 7.10(j).)

§ 89E-4. North Carolina Board for Licensing of Geologists; appointments; terms; composition.

(a) The North Carolina Board for Licensing of Geologists shall have the power and responsibility to administer the provisions of this Chapter in compliance with Chapter 150B of the General Statutes.

(b) The Board shall consist of five members appointed by the Governor in the manner hereinafter prescribed, and in addition the State geologist shall serve on the Board ex officio. The Governor may remove any member of the Board for neglect of duty or malfeasance or violation of this Chapter or conviction of a felony or other crime of moral turpitude, but for no other reason.

(c) Each member of the Board shall be a citizen of the United States and shall have been a resident of this State for at least six months immediately preceding his or her appointment.

(d) All members of the initial Board shall be appointed by the Governor and shall at the time of their appointment qualify for licensing under this Chapter except for the lay member appointee. At all times at least one member of the Board shall be an academic geologist; one member shall be a salaried company geologist; one member shall be an independent or consultant geologist; one member shall be a representative from the mining industry; one member shall be a consumer or lay member who is not a geologist; and in addition, the State geologist shall serve as a permanent ex officio member.

(e) After the establishment of the initial Board, all members, with the exception of the lay member, shall be so licensed under the provisions of this Chapter. The term of office of each member of the Board shall be three years; provided, however, that of the members first appointed, one shall be appointed for a term of one year; two for terms of two years; and two for terms of three years in the discretion of the Governor. No member shall serve more than two consecutive three-year terms without an interruption in service of at least one year.

(f)   Each term of service on the Board shall expire on the 30th day of June of the year in which the term expires. As the term of a member expires, the Governor shall make the appointment for a full term, or, if a vacancy occurs for any other reason, for the remainder of the unexpired term.

(g)   Members of the Board may receive compensation for their services and reimbursement for expenses incurred in the performance of duties required by this Chapter at the rates prescribed in G.S. 138-5, subject to availability of funds.

(h)   The Board may employ the necessary personnel for performance of its functions, and fix their compensation within the limits of funds available to the Board. (1983 (Reg. Sess., 1984), c. 1074, s. 1; 1987, c. 827, s. 75; 1989, c. 579, s. 1.)

§ 89E-5. Functions and duties of the Licensing Board.

(a)   The Board shall administer and enforce the provisions of this Chapter.

(b)   The Board shall elect from its membership a chairman, a vice-chairman and a secretary-treasurer, and adopt rules, consistent with the Administrative Procedures Act, to govern its proceedings. A majority of the membership of the Board shall constitute a quorum for all Board meetings.

(c)   The Board shall examine and pass on the qualifications of all applicants for licensing under this Chapter, and shall issue a license to each successful applicant therefor.

(d)   The Board may adopt a seal which may be affixed to all licenses issued by the Board.

(e)   The Board may authorize expenditures deemed necessary to carry out the provisions of this Chapter and all expenses shall be paid upon the warrant of the Board treasurer. The Board treasurer shall deposit funds received by the

Board in one or more funds in banks or other financial institutions carrying deposit insurance and authorized to do business in North Carolina. Interest earned on such funds may remain in the funds account and may be expended as authorized by the Board to carry out the provisions of this Chapter. In no event may expenditures exceed the revenues of the Board during any fiscal year. The Board is authorized and empowered to utilize the services of the Purchase and Contract Division of the Department of Administration for the procurement of personal property, in accordance with Article 3 of Chapter 143 of the General Statutes. The Board shall: (i) submit all proposed contracts for supplies, materials, printing, equipment, and contractual services that exceed one million dollars ($1,000,000) authorized by this subsection to the Attorney General or the Attorney General's designee for review as provided in G.S. 114-8.3; and (ii) include in all contracts to be awarded by the Board under this subsection a standard clause which provides that the State Auditor and internal auditors of the Board may audit the records of the contractor during and after the term of the contract to verify accounts and data affecting fees and performance. The Board shall not award a cost plus percentage of cost agreement or contract for any purpose.

(f) The Board shall hold a meeting within 30 days after a quorum of its members is first appointed and thereafter shall hold at least two regular meetings each year.

(g) The Board shall establish and receive fees as required by this Chapter. In establishing fees, the Board shall consider exemptions from fees or a reduction in licensing fees for those persons otherwise qualified for licensing under this Chapter but who perform geologic work or services less than 15 days per year.

(h) The Board shall have such other powers and duties as are necessary to carry out the provisions of this Chapter.

(i) The Board shall have the power to establish or approve reasonable standards for licensing and renewal of licenses of geologists, including, but not limited to the power to adopt or use examination materials and accreditation standards of any duly professionally recognized accrediting agency. The Board shall have the power to establish reasonable standards for continuing professional education for geologists, provided that for renewal of license no examination shall be required. (1983 (Reg. Sess., 1984), c. 1074, s. 1; 1989, c. 579, s. 2; 2010-194, s. 13; 2011-326, s. 15(m).)

§ 89E-6. Exemptions.

Any person except as specifically exempted below who shall publicly practice or offer to publicly practice geology in this State is subject to the provisions of this Chapter. The following persons are exempt:

(1) Persons engaged solely in teaching the science of geology or engaged solely in geologic research in this State may pursue their teaching and/or research without licensing. A teacher or researcher must, however, be a licensed geologist if he or she performs geologic work and services for which a licensed geologist is required by this Chapter.

(2) Officers and employees of the United States of America and the State of North Carolina practicing solely as such officers or employees.

(3) Officers and employees of petroleum companies practicing solely as such officers and employees and not offering their professional services to the public for hire.

(4) A subordinate to a geologist or a geologist-in-training licensed under this Chapter insofar as he or she acts solely in such capacity. This exemption does not permit any such subordinate to practice geology for others in his own right or use the term "licensed geologist". (1983 (Reg. Sess., 1984), c. 1074, s. 1.)

§ 89E-7. Limitations.

(a) This Chapter does not prohibit one or more geologists from practicing through the business organization of a sole proprietorship; partnership; corporation or professional association. In a partnership, the primary activity of which consists of geological services, at least one partner shall be a licensed geologist as defined in this Chapter. A corporation or professional association providing geological services shall comply with the provisions of Chapter 55B of the General Statutes.

(b) This Chapter shall not be construed to prevent or to affect:

(1) The practice of any profession or trade for which a license is required under any other law of this State, or the practice of registered professional engineers from lawfully practicing soils mechanics, foundation engineering and

other professional engineering as provided in the North Carolina General Statutes, or licensed architects or landscape architects from lawfully practicing architecture or landscape architecture, or the practice of soil science by professionals certified by the Soil Science Society of North Carolina, respectively as provided in the General Statutes;

(2) The public practice of geology by a person not a resident of and having no established place of business in this State, when such practice does not exceed in the aggregate more than 90 days in any calendar year, and provided such person is duly licensed to practice such profession in another state where the requirements for a license are not lower than those specified in this Chapter for obtaining the license required for such work; and provided further that such nonresident shall file with the Board within 10 days of entering this State for commencing of such work, a statement giving his name, residence, the number of his license, and by what authority issued, and upon the completion of the work, a statement of the time engaged in such work within the State; or

(3) The practice of a person not a resident and having no established place of business in this State, or who has recently become a resident hereof, practicing or offering to practice herein for more than 90 days in any calendar year the profession of geology, if he is licensed in another state or qualified as defined herein, if he shall have filed with the Board an application for a license and shall have paid the fee required by this Chapter. Such practice shall be deemed a provisional practice and shall continue only for such time as the Board requires reasonably for the consideration of the applicant for licensing under this Chapter as a geologist. (1983 (Reg. Sess., 1984), c. 1074, s. 1; 1991, c. 205, s. 5.)

§ 89E-8. Applications.

An application for licensing as a geologist shall be made under oath, shall show the applicant's education and a summary of his geological work, plus other relevant criteria to be determined by the Board. The Board shall have the power to determine a reasonable application fee which shall accompany each application. (1983 (Reg. Sess., 1984), c. 1074, s. 1.)

§ 89E-9. Minimum qualifications.

An applicant shall be eligible for a license as a geologist in North Carolina provided that each applicant meets the following minimum qualifications:

(1) Be of good moral and ethical character.

(2) Have graduated from an accredited college or university, and have a degree with a major in geology, engineering geology or geological engineering or related geologic science; or have completed 30 semester hours or the equivalent in geological science courses leading to a major in geology, of which at least 24 hours of the equivalent were upper level undergraduate courses or graduate courses. The Board shall waive the academic requirements for a person already practicing geology at the time this Chapter is enacted, provided application for license is made not later than one year after appointment of the initial Board and provided further that the applicant can provide evidence to satisfy the Board that he or she is competent to engage in the public practice of geology.

(3) Successfully pass such examination established by the Board which shall be designed to demonstrate that the applicant has the necessary knowledge and requisite skill to exercise the responsibilities of the public practice of geology. The Board shall waive the examination for licensing as a geologist of an applicant who makes written application to the Board not later than one year after appointment of the initial Board, and who otherwise meets the qualification of this Chapter.

(4) Have at least five years of professional geological work which shall include a minimum of three years of professional geological work under the supervision of a licensed geologist; or a minimum of three cumulative years work in responsible charge of geological work satisfactory to the Board. The following criteria of education and experience qualify as specified toward accumulation of the required five years of professional geological work:

a. Each full year of undergraduate study in the geological sciences shall count as one-half year of training up to a maximum of two years, and each year of graduate study shall count as one year of work.

b. Credit for undergraduate study, graduate study, graduate courses, individually or in any combination thereof, shall in no case exceed a total of four years toward meeting the requirements for at least five years of professional geological work as set forth above.

c. The Board may consider in lieu of the above professional geological work the cumulative total of professional geological work or geological research of persons teaching upper level geology courses at the college or university level, provided such work or research can be demonstrated to be of a sufficiently responsible nature to be equivalent to the professional requirements set forth in this section.

d. The ability of the applicant shall have been demonstrated by his having performed the work in a responsible position as determined by the Board. The adequacy of the required supervision and the experience shall be determined by the Board in accordance with the standards set forth in regulations adopted by it. (1983 (Reg. Sess., 1984), c. 1074, s. 1; 1989, c. 579, s. 3.)

§ 89E-10. Examinations.

(a) Examinations shall be formulated and conducted by the Board at such time and place as the Board shall determine, but shall be held at least annually.

(b) The Board shall determine the fee required for examination. (1983 (Reg. Sess., 1984), c. 1074, s. 1.)

§ 89E-11. Comity.

A person holding a license to engage in the practice of geology, on the basis of comparable licensing requirements issued to him by a proper authority by the State, territory, or possession of the United States or the District of Columbia, and who, in the opinion of the Board otherwise meets the requirements of this Chapter based upon verified evidence may, upon application, be licensed without further examination. (1983 (Reg. Sess., 1984), c. 1074, s. 1.)

§ 89E-12. Issuance, renewal and replacement of licenses.

(a) The Board shall issue a license upon payment of the license fee as fixed by the Board to any applicant who has satisfactorily met all the requirements of the Chapter as administered by the Board. Licenses shall show the full name of the registrant, shall give a serial number, and shall be signed by the chairman and secretary of the Board under the seal of the Board. The issuance of a license by the Board shall be prima facie evidence that the person named therein is entitled to all the rights and privileges of a licensed geologist while the license remains in full force and effect.

(b) All licenses shall expire at such interval as may be determined by the Board, unless licenses are renewed. All applications for renewal shall be filed with the Board under rules and regulations it shall adopt and which renewal shall be accompanied by the renewal fee prescribed by the Board. A license which has expired for failure to renew may only be restored after application and payment of the prescribed restoration fee, provided the renewal applicant meets all other provisions of this Chapter.

(c) A new license to replace any license lost, destroyed or mutilated may be issued, subject to the rules of the Board and payment of a fee set by the Board. (1983 (Reg. Sess., 1984), c. 1074, s. 1.)

§ 89E-13. Seals; requirements.

Each geologist licensed hereunder, upon the issuance of a license, shall obtain from the secretary at a cost prescribed by the Board, a seal of the design authorized by the Board bearing the licensee's name and the legend "Licensed Geologist - State of North Carolina". All drawings, reports or other geologic papers or documents involving geologic work as defined in this Chapter which shall have been prepared or approved by a licensed geologist or a subordinate employee under his direction for the use of or for delivery to any person or for public record within this State shall be signed by him or her and impressed with the said seal or the seal of a nonresident practicing under the provisions of this Chapter, either of which shall indicate his or her responsibility therefor. (1983 (Reg. Sess., 1984), c. 1074, s. 1.)

§ 89E-14. Records.

(a) The Board shall keep a public record of its proceedings and a register of all applications for licensing.

(b) The register shall show:

(1) The name, the age and the residency of each applicant;

(2) The date of application;

(3) The place of business of such applicant;

(4) His or her education and other qualifications;

(5) Whether or not an examination was required;

(6) Whether the applicant was licensed;

(7) Whether a license was granted;

(8) The dates of the action by the Board; and

(9) Such other information as may be deemed necessary by the Board. All official records of the Board or affidavits by the secretary as to the content of such records shall be prima facie evidence of all matters required to be kept therein.

(c) The Board shall treat as confidential and not subject to disclosure except to the extent required by law or by rule or regulation of the Board individual test scores and applications and material relating thereto, including letters of reference relating to an application. (1983 (Reg. Sess., 1984), c. 1074, s. 1.)

§ 89E-15. Roster of licensed geologists.

The secretary shall keep a record and shall publish annually a roster showing the names and places of business and residence addresses of all licensed geologists. Copies of this roster shall be made available to the public upon request and payment of reasonable fee for copying established by the Board. (1983 (Reg. Sess., 1984), c. 1074, s. 1.)

§ 89E-16. Code of professional conduct.

This Board shall cause to have prepared and shall adopt a code of professional conduct which shall be made known in writing to every licensee and applicant for licensing under this Chapter and which shall be published by the Board. Such publication shall constitute due notice to all licensees. The Board may revise and amend this code of ethics from time to time after due notice and opportunity for hearing to all licensed members and the public for comment before adoption of the revision or amendments. (1983 (Reg. Sess., 1984), c. 1074, s. 1.)

§ 89E-17. Complaints and investigations.

(a)   Any person may file written charges with the Board against any licensee pursuant to rules and regulations adopted by the Board; provided however, such charges or allegations shall be in writing and shall be sworn to by the person or persons making them and shall be filed with the secretary. The Board shall have the authority and shall be under a duty to investigate reasonably all valid complaints.

(b)   The Board may appoint, employ, or retain investigators for the purpose of examining or inquiring into any acts committed in this State that may violate the provisions of this Chapter, the Board's code of professional conduct, or the Board's rules. The Board may expend funds for salaries and fees in connection with an investigation conducted pursuant to this Chapter.

(c)   Investigations by the Board shall be confidential until the Board takes disciplinary action against a licensee or corporate registrant. Records, papers, and other documents containing information collected or compiled by the Board, its members, or employees as a result of an investigation, inquiry, or interview conducted pursuant to this Chapter shall not be a public record within the meaning of Chapter 132 of the General Statutes, except any notice or statement of charges or notice of hearing in any proceeding conducted by the Board and any records, papers, or other documents containing information collected and compiled by the Board and admitted into evidence in a hearing before the Board shall be a public record. (1983 (Reg. Sess., 1984), c. 1074, s. 1; 1999-355, s. 1.)

§ 89E-18. Prohibitions; unlawful acts.

After the effective date of this Chapter:

(1) It shall be unlawful for any person other than a licensed geologist or a subordinate under his direction to prepare any geologic plans, reports or documents in which the performance is related to the public welfare or safeguarding of life, health, property or the environment.

(2) It shall be unlawful for any person to publicly practice, or offer to publicly practice, geology in this State as defined in the provisions of this Chapter, or to use in connection with his or her name or otherwise assume, or advertise any title or description tending to convey the impression that he or she is a licensed geologist, unless such person has been duly licensed or exempted under the provisions of this Chapter.

(3) After one year following the effective date of this act, it shall be unlawful for anyone other than a geologist licensed under this Chapter to stamp or seal any plans, plats, reports or other documents with the seal or stamp of a licensed geologist, or to use in any manner the title "Licensed Geologist" unless that person is licensed hereunder.

(4) It shall be unlawful for any person to affix his or her signature to or to stamp or seal any plans, plats, reports, or other documents after the licensing of the person named thereon has expired or has been suspended or revoked unless the license has been renewed or reissued. (1983 (Reg. Sess., 1984), c. 1074, s. 1.)

§ 89E-19. Disciplinary procedures.

(a) The Board, consistent with the provisions of Article 3A of Chapter 150B of the General Statutes, may refuse to grant a license to any applicant who does not meet the qualifications required by this Chapter, the Board's code of professional conduct, or the Board's rules, or to any corporate registrant that does not meet such qualifications and the requirements of Chapter 55B of the General Statutes. The Board, consistent with the provisions of Article 3A of Chapter 150B of the General Statutes, may refuse to renew, suspend, or revoke a license or certificate of registration if a licensee or corporate registrant:

(1) Violates the provisions of this Chapter, the Board's code of professional conduct, the Board's rules, or an order issued by the Board.

(2) Has been convicted of a misdemeanor under G.S. 89E-22.

(3) Has been convicted of a felony.

(4) Engages in gross unprofessional conduct, dishonest practice, or professional incompetence.

(5) Commits fraud or deceit in obtaining a license or certificate of registration or in assisting another person in obtaining a license or certificate of registration.

(b) If the Board finds that a licensee is professionally incompetent, the Board may require the licensee to take an oral or written examination or to meet other requirements to demonstrate the licensee's fitness to practice geology, and the Board may suspend the licensee's license until he or she establishes professional competence to the satisfaction of the Board.

(c) In addition to the authority granted in subsections (a) and (b) of this section, the Board may levy a civil penalty not in excess of five thousand dollars ($5,000) for any licensee or corporate registrant who violates the provisions of this Chapter, the Board's code of professional conduct, the Board's rules, or any order issued by the Board. All civil penalties collected by the Board shall be remitted to the school fund of the county in which the violation occurred. Before assessing a civil penalty, the Board shall consider the following:

(1) The nature, gravity, and persistence of the violation.

(2) The appropriateness of the imposition of a civil penalty when considered alone or in combination with other action taken by the Board.

(3) Whether the violation was willful.

(4) Any other factors that tend to mitigate or aggravate the violation.

(d) The Board may bring a civil action in the superior court of the county in which the violation occurred to recover a civil penalty if a licensee or corporate registrant does one of the following:

(1) Fails to request a hearing on the imposition of a civil penalty and fails to pay the civil penalty within 30 days after being notified that a civil penalty has been imposed.

(2) Requests and receives a hearing on the imposition of a civil penalty but fails to pay the civil penalty within 30 days after service of a written copy of the Board's decision. (1983 (Reg. Sess., 1984), c. 1074, s. 1; 1987, c. 827, s. 1; 1999-355, s. 2.)

§ 89E-20. Hearing procedures.

(a) The Board shall develop procedures for investigation, prehearing and hearing of disciplinary actions; such disciplinary actions shall be conducted pursuant to the provisions of Chapter 150B of the General Statutes.

(b) Any person aggrieved by a decision of the Board other than a decision in a disciplinary action may petition the Board for a hearing pursuant to the provisions of Chapter 150B of the General Statutes.

(c) Judicial review of a final agency decision is available in the manner prescribed by Article 4, Chapter 150B of the General Statutes. (1983 (Reg. Sess., 1984), c. 1074, s. 1; 1987, c. 827, ss. 1, 76.)

§ 89E-21. Reissuance of license.

The Board, by a majority vote of the quorum, may reissue a license to any person whose license has been revoked when the Board finds upon written application by the applicant that there is good cause to justify such reissuance. (1983 (Reg. Sess., 1984), c. 1074, s. 1.)

§ 89E-22. Misdemeanor.

Any person who shall willfully practice publicly, or offer to practice publicly, geology for other natural or corporate persons in this State without being licensed in accordance with the provisions of this Chapter, or any person presenting or attempting to use as his own the license or the seal of another, or any person who shall give any false or forged evidence of any kind in obtaining a license, or any person who shall falsely impersonate any other licensee of like or different name, or any person who shall attempt to use an expired or revoked license or practice at any time during a period the Board has suspended or revoked the license, or any person who shall violate the provisions of this Chapter shall be guilty of a Class 2 misdemeanor. (1983 (Reg. Sess., 1984), c. 1074, s. 1; 1993, c. 539, s. 613; 1994, Ex. Sess., c. 24, s. 14(c).)

§ 89E-23. Injunction.

As an additional remedy, the Board shall have the authority to proceed in a superior court appropriate jurisdiction to enjoin and restrain any natural or corporate person from violating the prohibitions of this Chapter. The Board shall not be required to post bond in connection with obtaining either provisional, preliminary or permanent injunctive relief pursuant to the North Carolina Rules of Civil Procedure or G.S. 1-485 et seq. (1983 (Reg. Sess., 1984), c. 1074, s. 1.)

§ 89E-24. Attorney General as legal advisor.

The Attorney General or any assistant or associate in the Department of Justice selected by him shall act as legal advisor to the Board. (1983 (Reg. Sess., 1984), c. 1074, s. 1.)

Chapter 89F.

North Carolina Soil Scientist Licensing Act.

§ 89F-1. Short title.

This Chapter may be cited as the North Carolina Soil Scientist Licensing Act. (1995, c. 414, s. 1.)

§ 89F-2. Purposes.

The purposes of this Chapter are to protect life, property, health, and public welfare through regulation of the practice of soil science in the State; to define the practice of soil science as a profession by establishing minimum standards of ethical conduct and professional responsibility and by establishing professional education and experience requirements; and to prevent abuses in the practice of soil science by untrained or unprincipled individuals. (1995, c. 414, s. 1.)

§ 89F-3. Definitions.

As used in this Chapter, unless the context otherwise requires:

(1)   "Board" means the North Carolina Board for Licensing of Soil Scientists.

(2)   "License" means a certificate issued by the Board to an individual who meets the requirements established for a licensed soil scientist by this Chapter and rules adopted pursuant to this Chapter.

(3)   "Licensed soil scientist" means a person who is licensed as a soil scientist under this Chapter.

(4)   "Practice of soil science" means any service or work, the adequate performance of which requires education in the physical, chemical, and biological sciences, as well as soil science; training and experience in the application of special knowledge of these sciences to the use and management of soils by accepted principles and methods; and investigation, evaluation, and consultation; and in which the performance is related to the public welfare by safeguarding life, health, property, and the environment. "Practice of soil science" includes, but is not limited to, investigating and evaluating the interaction between water, soil, nutrients, plants, and other living organisms that are used to prepare soil scientists' reports for: subsurface ground absorption systems, including infiltration galleries; land application of residuals such as sludge, septage, and other wastes; spray irrigation of wastewater; soil remediation at conventional rates; land application of agricultural products; processing residues, bioremediation, and volatilization; soil erodibility and sedimentation; and identification of hydric soil and redoximorphic features.

(5)   "Responsible charge of work" means the independent control and direction by the use of initiative, skill, and independent judgment in the practice

of soil science or supervision of the practice of soil science by soil scientists-in-training and subordinates.

(6) "Soil" means the site or environmental setting consisting of soil material, saprolite, weathered materials, and soil rock interface. "Soil" includes the solid materials, waters, gases, and other biological, chemical, and contaminant materials in the soil environment.

(7) "Soil science" means the science dealing with soils as an environmental resource. "Soil science" includes the following tasks: soil characterization, classification, and mapping, and the physical, chemical, hydrologic, mineralogical, biological, and microbiological analysis of soil per se, and to its assessment, analysis, modeling, testing, evaluation, and use for the benefit of mankind when specifically required to complete the investigation and evaluation of interactions between water, soil, nutrients, plants, and other living organisms described in subdivision (5) of this section. "Soil science" does not include design or creative works, the adequate performance of which requires extensive geological, engineering, or land surveying education, training, and experience or requires licensing as a geologist under Chapter 89E of the General Statutes or as a professional engineer or land surveyor under Chapter 89C of the General Statutes.

(8) "Soil scientist" means a person who practices soil science.

(9) "Soil scientist-in-training" means a person who has passed the examination and satisfied all other requirements for licensure under this Chapter except for the professional work experience requirement.

(10) "Subordinate" means any person who assists a licensed soil scientist in the practice of soil science without assuming the responsible charge of work. (1995, c. 414, s. 1.)

§ 89F-4. North Carolina Board for Licensing of Soil Scientists.

(a) Creation; Membership. - The North Carolina Board for Licensing of Soil Scientists is created. The Board shall consist of seven members appointed as follows:

(1) One member appointed by the Governor, who shall be a soil scientist employed by a federal or State agency.

(2) One member appointed by the Governor, who shall be a soil scientist employed by a local government agency.

(3) One member appointed by the Governor, who shall be a soil scientist employed by an institution of higher education.

(4) One member appointed by the General Assembly upon recommendation of the Speaker of the House of Representatives, who shall be a soil scientist who is privately employed.

(5) One member appointed by the General Assembly upon recommendation of the Speaker of the House of Representatives, who shall be a member of the public who is not a soil scientist.

(6) One member appointed by the General Assembly upon recommendation of the President Pro Tempore of the Senate, who shall be a soil scientist who is privately employed.

(7) One member appointed by the General Assembly upon recommendation of the President Pro Tempore of the Senate, who shall be a member of the public who is not a soil scientist.

(b) Ex Officio Member. - In addition to the members of the Board appointed pursuant to subsection (a) of this section, the President of the Soil Science Society of North Carolina, or a member of the Society appointed by its President, shall serve as a nonvoting ex officio member of the Board.

(c) Terms. - Members shall serve staggered terms of office of three years. No member shall serve more than six consecutive years without an interruption in service of at least one year. The terms of office of members filling positions four and six shall expire on 30 June of years evenly divisible by three. The terms of office of members filling positions five and seven shall expire on 30 June of years that follow by one year those years that are evenly divisible by three. The terms of office of members filling positions one, two, and three shall expire on 30 June of years that precede by one year those years that are evenly divisible by three. Terms shall expire as provided by this subsection except that members of the Board shall serve until their successors are appointed and duly qualified as provided by G.S 128-7.

(d) Vacancies; Removal. - Vacancies in appointments shall be filled for the unexpired term. Vacancies in appointments made by the General Assembly shall be filled in accordance with G.S. 120-122. The Governor shall have the power to remove, in accordance with G.S 143B-13, any member appointed by the Governor. The General Assembly shall have the power to remove, in accordance with G.S 143B-13, any member appointed by the General Assembly.

(e) Quorum. - A majority of the members of the Board appointed pursuant to subsection (a) of this section shall constitute a quorum for the transaction of business.

(f) Compensation; Expenses. - Subject to the availability of funds, members of the Board may receive compensation for their services and be reimbursed for expenses incurred in the performance of duties required by this Chapter at the rates prescribed in G.S. 138-5. (1995, c. 414, s. 1.)

§ 89F-5. Powers and duties of the Board.

(a) The Board shall:

(1) Administer and enforce the provisions of this Chapter.

(2) Elect from its membership a Chair, a Vice-Chair, and a Secretary-Treasurer.

(3) Examine and pass on the qualifications of all applicants for licensing under this Chapter and issue a license to each successful applicant.

(4) Hold at least two regular meetings each year.

(5) Establish and receive fees as required by this Chapter. In establishing fees, the Board may provide for reduced fees or an exemption from fees for persons licensed under this Chapter who practice soil science for less than 15 days per calendar year.

(6) Adopt rules that establish standards or approve reasonable standards for licensing and renewal of licenses of soil scientists, including adopting

examination materials and accreditation standards of any recognized accrediting agency.

(7)   Establish reasonable standards for continuing professional education for soil scientists. No examination shall be required for a renewal of a license.

(8)   Submit two nominees to the appropriate appointing authority for each position to be filled on the Board.

(9)   Have any other powers and duties as are necessary to implement the provisions of this Chapter and adopt any rules needed to implement this Chapter.

(b)   The Board may adopt a seal that may be affixed to all licenses issued by the Board.

(c)   The Secretary-Treasurer shall deposit funds received by the Board, except for the clear proceeds of civil penalties assessed pursuant to G.S. 89F-20(b), in one or more funds in banks or other financial institutions carrying deposit insurance and authorized to do business in the State. Interest earned on funds may remain in the account and may be expended as authorized by the Board to carry out the provisions of this Chapter. The Board may authorize expenditures deemed necessary to carry out the provisions of this Chapter, and all expenses shall be paid upon the warrant of the Secretary-Treasurer. During any fiscal year, expenditures shall not exceed the revenues of the Board.

The clear proceeds of civil penalties shall be remitted to the Civil Penalty and Forfeiture Fund in accordance with G.S. 115C-457.2.

(d)   The Board may employ the necessary personnel for the performance of its functions and shall fix their compensation within the limits of funds available to the Board. The Board may procure personal property in accordance with the provisions of Article 3 of Chapter 143 of the General Statutes. The Board shall: (i) submit all proposed contracts for supplies, materials, printing, equipment, and contractual services that exceed one million dollars ($1,000,000) authorized by this subsection to the Attorney General or the Attorney General's designee for review as provided in G.S. 114-8.3; and (ii) include in all contracts to be awarded by the Board under this subsection a standard clause which provides that the State Auditor and internal auditors of the Board may audit the records of the contractor during and after the term of the contract to verify accounts and data affecting fees and performance. The Board shall not award a cost plus percentage of cost agreement or contract for any purpose.

(e) The Board may adopt rules in accordance with Chapter 150B of the General Statutes and shall administer this Chapter in accordance with Chapter 150B of the General Statutes. (1995, c. 414, s. 1; 1998-215, s. 135; 2010-194, s. 14; 2011-326, s. 15(n).)

§ 89F-6. Corporate, limited liability company, partnership, or sole proprietorship practice of soil science.

A corporation organized under Chapter 55B of the General Statutes, a limited liability company organized under Chapter 57D of the General Statutes, a partnership, or a sole proprietorship may engage in the practice of soil science in this State. A licensed soil scientist shall be in responsible charge of all practice of soil science by the corporation, limited liability company, partnership, or sole proprietorship. (1995, c. 414, s. 1; 2000-115, s. 7; 2013-157, s. 24.)

§ 89F-7. Exemptions.

(a) Except as provided in subsection (b) of this section, any person who practices or offers to practice soil science in this State is subject to the provisions of this Chapter.

(b) The following are exempt from the provisions of this Chapter:

(1) Persons engaged solely in teaching soil science or engaged solely in soil science research.

(2) Officers and employees of the United States, the State, and units of local government who practice soil science solely in the capacity of their office or employment.

(3) Officers and employees of companies engaged in the practice of soil science, when the officers and employees practice soil science solely in the capacity of their employment and who do not offer their services to the public for hire. (1995, c. 414, s. 1.)

§ 89F-8. Limitations.

This Chapter shall not prevent:

(1) The practice of any profession or trade for which a license is required under any other law of this State.

(2) Registered professional engineers from lawfully practicing soil mechanics, foundation engineering, or other professional engineering practices for which a license is required pursuant to Chapter 89C of the General Statutes.

(3) Registered land surveyors licensed pursuant to Chapter 89C of the General Statutes from practicing surveying.

(4) Architects licensed pursuant to Chapter 83A of the General Statutes or landscape architects licensed pursuant to Chapter 89A of the General Statutes from lawfully practicing architecture or landscape architecture.

(5) Geologists licensed pursuant to Chapter 89E of the General Statutes from practicing geology.

(6) The practice of soil science for 30 days or less in any calendar year by a person who is not a resident of this State and who has no established place of business in this State if the person:

a. Is licensed to practice soil science in another state where the requirements for a license equal or exceed the requirements for licensure under this Chapter;

b. Files a statement giving the person's name, address, the license number, and issuing authority with the Board within 10 days of commencing the practice of soil science in this State; and

c. Files a statement with the Board detailing the total time that the person engaged in the practice of soil science in the State within 10 days of the day on which the practice of soil science is completed.

(7) The practice of soil science by a person who is not a resident of this State and who has no established place of business in this State, the practice of soil science by a person who has become a resident of this State within the preceding 30 days, or the practice or an offer to practice soil science for more

than 30 days in any calendar year by a person who is licensed as a soil scientist in another state, who meets the licensing requirements of this Chapter, and who has filed an application for a license with the Board and paid the application fee. The practice of soil science under this subdivision shall continue only until the Board acts on the application for licensure under this Chapter.

(8) Soil sampling solely for the purpose of determining plant nutrient and lime application rates for gardening and agricultural purposes by persons who are not licensed soil scientists. (1995, c. 414, s. 1.)

§ 89F-9. Applications.

An application for a license as a soil scientist shall be made under oath, shall show the applicant's education and a summary of the applicant's professional work experience as a soil scientist, and shall show any other relevant criteria as determined by the Board. (1995, c. 414, s. 1.)

§ 89F-10. Minimum qualifications.

(a) To be eligible for a license as a soil scientist in this State, an applicant shall satisfy the following minimum qualifications:

(1) Be of good moral and ethical character as attested to by (i) four letters of reference, two of which shall be written by licensed soil scientists or persons who are eligible for licensure under this Chapter, and (ii) an agreement signed by the applicant to adhere to the Code of Professional Conduct adopted pursuant to G.S. 89F-17. For purposes of this requirement, "good moral and ethical character" means character that tends to ensure faithful discharge of the duties of a licensed soil scientist.

(2) Hold at least a bachelor of science degree from an accredited college or university with a minimum of 30 semester hours or 45 quarter hours in agricultural, biological, physical, or earth sciences and at least 15 semester hours or an equivalent number of quarter hours in soil science. The Board may adopt rules specifying combinations of education and experience that an applicant may substitute for a bachelor of science degree.

(3) Successfully pass an examination established by the Board. The examination shall be designed to demonstrate whether the applicant has the necessary knowledge and requisite skill to exercise the responsibilities of the practice of soil science.

(4) Subject to subsection (b) of this section, have at least three years of professional work experience as a soil scientist under the supervision of a licensed soil scientist, or a soil scientist who is eligible for licensure, under this Chapter, or a minimum of three cumulative years of professional work experience as a soil scientist in responsible charge of work satisfactory to the Board and in accordance with standards established by the Board by rule.

(b) An applicant may substitute an advanced degree in soil science for a portion of the professional work experience requirement. The Board, in its discretion, may allow an applicant to substitute a masters degree in soil science for one year of professional work experience and to substitute a doctoral degree in soil science for two years of professional work experience. The Board, in its discretion, may allow an applicant to substitute experience gained through teaching upper level soil science courses at the college or university level or research in soil science for all or any portion of the professional work experience requirement if the Board finds the teaching or research to be equivalent to the responsible charge of work by a soil scientist.

(c) The Board shall designate an applicant who meets all the requirements for a license under this Chapter except the professional work experience requirement as a soil scientist-in-training. A soil scientist-in-training may apply for a license upon completion of the professional work experience requirement. (1995, c. 414, s. 1.)

§ 89F-11. Examinations.

Examinations shall be formulated and conducted by the Board at the time and place as determined by the Board, and shall be held at least annually. (1995, c. 414, s. 1.)

§ 89F-12. Comity.

A person who holds a license to engage in the practice of soil science on the basis of comparable licensing requirements issued to that person by a proper authority by another state, by a territory, or by a possession of the United States or the District of Columbia, and who, as determined by the Board, meets the requirements of this Chapter based upon verified evidence, may, upon application, be licensed without taking an examination pursuant to G.S. 89F-10(a)(3). (1995, c. 414, s. 1.)

§ 89F-13. Issuance, renewal, and replacement of licenses.

(a) The Board shall issue a license to any applicant who has satisfactorily met the requirements of this Chapter including the payment of the license fee. A license shall be valid for the period of time established by the Board by rule. Each license shall state the full name of the registrant, shall have a serial number, shall state the date on which the license expires, shall be signed by the Chair and Secretary-Treasurer of the Board, and shall bear the seal of the Board. The issuance of a license by the Board shall be prima facie evidence that the person named on the license is entitled to all the rights and privileges of a licensed soil scientist for the period the license remains in effect.

(b) The Board shall renew the license of any licensee who continues to meet the requirements of this Chapter and who pays the renewal fee prior to the expiration of the license. The Board shall reinstate the license of any licensee whose license has expired, who continues to meet the requirements of this Chapter, and who pays the restoration fee.

(c) If a license is lost, destroyed, or mutilated, the Board may issue a replacement license subject to rules adopted by the Board. (1995, c. 414, s. 1.)

§ 89F-14. Seals; requirements.

Upon the issuance of a license, each soil scientist shall obtain from the Secretary-Treasurer a seal bearing the licensee's name and the legend "Licensed Soil Scientist - State of North Carolina". The Board shall ensure that the design of the seal is easily distinguished from other professional seals. All drawings, reports, or other soil science papers or documents involving the practice of soil science that are prepared or approved by a licensed soil scientist or a subordinate under his or her direction shall be signed by the soil scientist and impressed with the seal. The impression of the seal indicates his or her responsibility for the practice of soil science. (1995, c. 414, s. 1.)

§ 89F-15. Records.

(a) The Board shall maintain a record of its proceedings and a register of all applications for licensure under this Chapter. For each applicant the register shall show:

(1) The name, age, and home address of the applicant.

(2) The date of application.

(3) The applicant's place of business.

(4) The applicant's education, professional work experience, and other qualifications.

(5) Whether the applicant was required to take an examination.

(6) Whether a license was issued to the applicant.

(7) Whether the applicant is currently licensed.

(8) The date and nature of any action by the Board with respect to the applicant or licensee.

(9) Any other information that the Board determines to be necessary to meet the requirements of this Chapter or rules adopted pursuant to this Chapter.

(b) The Board shall treat as confidential and not subject to disclosure, except to the extent required by law or by rule of the Board, individual applications, related information, and examination scores. (1995, c. 414, s. 1.)

§ 89F-16. Roster of licensed soil scientists.

The Secretary-Treasurer of the Board shall keep a record and shall publish annually a roster showing the names, places of business, and residence addresses of all soil scientists licensed under this Chapter. Copies of this roster shall be made available to the public upon request and payment of a reasonable fee, established by the Board, for copying. (1995, c. 414, s. 1.)

§ 89F-17. Code of Professional Conduct.

The Board shall prepare and adopt by rule a Code of Professional Conduct that shall be made known in writing to every licensee and applicant for licensing under this Chapter and that shall be published by the Board. Publication of the Code of Professional Conduct is due notice to all licensees of its contents. The Board may revise and amend this Code of Professional Conduct. Prior to adoption of any revision or amendments, all licensed members and the public shall receive due notice and an opportunity to be heard. (1995, c. 414, s. 1.)

§ 89F-18. Complaints.

Any person may file written charges of violations of this Chapter or any rules adopted pursuant to this Chapter with the Board against any licensee. Any charges or allegations shall be in writing, shall be sworn to by the person making them, and shall be filed with the Secretary-Treasurer of the Board. The Board shall investigate reasonably all valid complaints. (1995, c. 414, s. 1.)

§ 89F-19. Prohibitions; unlawful acts.

(a)   It is unlawful for any person other than a licensed soil scientist or a subordinate under the soil scientist's direction to conduct or participate in any practice of soil science or prepare any soil science reports, maps, or documents related to the public welfare or the safeguarding of life, health, property, or the environment.

(b)   It is unlawful for any person, including a soil scientist-in-training or a subordinate, to practice, or offer to practice, soil science in this State, or to use in connection with his or her name, otherwise assume, or advertise any title or description tending to convey the impression that he or she is a licensed soil scientist, unless that person has been duly licensed or is exempted under the provisions of this Chapter.

(c)   It is unlawful for anyone other than a licensed soil scientist to stamp or seal any soils-related plans, maps, reports, or other soils-related documents with the seal or stamp of a licensed soil scientist, or use in any manner the title "soil scientist", unless that person is licensed under this Chapter.

(d)   It is unlawful for any person to affix his or her signature to, stamp, or seal any soils-related plans, maps, reports, or other soils-related documents after the license of the person has expired, been suspended, or revoked.

(e)   It is unlawful for a licensed soil scientist to prepare plats and maps so as to engage in the practice of land surveying by a registered land surveyor, as defined in G.S. 89C-3, unless the licensed soil scientist is also a registered land surveyor, as defined in G.S 89C-3.

(f)   It is unlawful for a licensed soil scientist to engage in the design of engineering works and systems, as that phrase is used in G.S. 89C-3(6), unless the licensed soil scientist is also a registered professional engineer, as defined in G.S. 89C-3. (1995, c. 414, s. 1.)

§ 89F-20. Disciplinary procedures.

(a)   The Board may, consistent with the provisions of Chapter 150B of the General Statues, refuse to grant or to renew, suspend, or revoke the license of any person licensed under this Chapter who:

(1)   Violates the provisions of this Chapter or a rule adopted by the Board.

(2)   Has been convicted of a misdemeanor under this Chapter.

(3)   Has been convicted of a felony.

(4)   Has been found by the Board to have engaged in unprofessional conduct, dishonest practice, incompetence, fraud or deceit in obtaining a license, or who aids another person who obtains or attempts to obtain a license by fraud or deceit.

(b) In lieu of revoking a license, the Board may enter a probationary order and assess a civil penalty not to exceed one thousand dollars ($1,000). In determining the amount of a penalty under this section, the Board shall consider the following factors:

(1) The degree and extent of harm to the natural resources of the State, to the public health, or to private property resulting from the violation.

(2) The duration and gravity of the violation.

(3) The effect on water quality.

(4) The cost of rectifying the damage.

(5) The cost to the State of enforcement procedures.

(6) The prior record of the violator in complying or failing to comply with this Chapter or a rule adopted pursuant to this Chapter. (1995, c. 414, s. 1.)

§ 89F-21. Reissuance of license.

The Board may, by a vote of the quorum, reissue a license to any person whose license has been revoked if the Board finds, after written application by the applicant, that there is good cause to justify the reissuance of the license. (1995, c. 414, s. 1.)

§ 89F-22. Misdemeanors.

A person who does any of the following shall be guilty of a Class 2 misdemeanor:

(1) Willfully practices soil science or offers to practice soil science for any other person in this State without being licensed in accordance with the provisions of this Chapter.

(2) Presents, or attempts to use as his or her own, the license or the seal of any other soil scientist.

(3)   Gives any false or forged evidence in the course of applying for a license under this Chapter.

(4)   Impersonates a licensed soil scientist.

(5)   Attempts to use an expired or revoked license, or practice at any time while the license is suspended or revoked.

(6)   Violates the provisions of this Chapter or rules adopted pursuant to this Chapter. (1995, c. 414, s. 1.)

§ 89F-23. Injunctive relief.

The Board may seek injunctive relief to enjoin and restrain any natural or corporate person from violating this Chapter. The Board shall not be required to post bond in connection with obtaining either provisional, preliminary, or permanent injunctive relief. (1995, c. 414, s. 1.)

§ 89F-24. Legal advisor.

The Attorney General or his designee shall act as legal advisor to the Board. (1995, c. 414, s. 1.)

§ 89F-25. Fees.

(a)   The Board shall determine fees for the following services that shall not exceed the amounts specified in this section:

Application $ 50.00

License
85.00

Renewal
85.00

Restoration
110.00

Replacement license
50.00

Seal
30.00.

(b) The Board may charge the applicant the actual cost of preparation, administration, and grading of examinations for soil scientists, in addition to its other fees. (1995, c. 414, s. 1; 2013-360, s. 13.8.)

Chapter 89G.

Irrigation Contractors.

§ 89G-1. Definitions.

The following definitions apply in this Chapter:

(1) Board. - The North Carolina Irrigation Contractors' Licensing Board.

(1a) Business entity. - A corporation, association, partnership, limited liability company, limited liability partnership, or other legal entity that is not an individual or a foreign entity.

(1b) Foreign corporation. - Defined in G.S. 55-1-40.

(1c) Foreign entity. - A foreign corporation, a foreign limited liability company, or a foreign partnership.

(1d) Foreign limited liability company. - Defined in G.S. 57C-1-03.

(1e) Foreign partnership. - One of the following that does not have a permanent place of business in this State:

a. A foreign limited partnership as defined in G.S. 59-102.

b. A general partnership formed under the laws of a jurisdiction other than this State.

(2) Irrigation construction or irrigation contracting. - The act of providing services as an irrigation contractor for compensation or other consideration.

(3) Irrigation contractor. - Any person who, for compensation or other consideration, constructs, installs, expands, services, or repairs irrigation systems.

(4) Irrigation system. - All piping, fittings, sprinklers, drip tubing, valves, control wiring of 30 volts or less, and associated components installed for the delivery and application of water for the purpose of irrigation that are downstream of a well, pond or other surface water, potable water or groundwater source, or grey water source and downstream of a backflow prevention assembly. Surface water, potable water or groundwater sources, water taps, utility piping, water service lines, water meters, backflow prevention assemblies, stormwater systems that service only the interior of a structure, and sanitary drainage systems are not part of an irrigation system.

(4a) Nonresident individual. - An individual who is not a resident of this State.

(5) Person. - An individual, firm, partnership, association, corporation, or other legal entity. (2008-177, s. 1; 2013-383, s. 1.)

§ 89G-2. License required.

Except as otherwise provided in this Chapter, no person shall engage in the practice of irrigation construction or irrigation contracting, use the designation "irrigation contractor," or advertise using any title or description that implies licensure as an irrigation contractor unless the person is licensed as an irrigation contractor as provided by this Chapter. All irrigation construction or irrigation contracting performed by an individual, partnership, association, corporation, firm, or other group shall be under the direct supervision of an individual licensed by the Board under this Chapter. (2008-177, s. 1; 2013-383, s. 8.)

§ 89G-3. Exemptions.

The provisions of this Chapter shall not apply to:

(1)   Any federal or State agency or any political subdivision performing irrigation construction or irrigation contracting work on public property and using its own employees.

(2)   Any property owner who performs irrigation construction work on his or her own property.

(3)   A landscape architect registered under Chapter 89A of the General Statutes.

(4)   A professional engineer licensed under Chapter 89C of the General Statutes.

(5)   Any irrigation construction or irrigation contracting work where the price of all contracts for labor, material, and other items for a given jobsite is less than two thousand five hundred dollars ($2,500).

(6)   Any person performing irrigation construction or irrigation contracting work for temporary irrigation to establish vegetative cover for erosion control.

(7)   Any person performing irrigation construction or irrigation contracting work to control dust on commercial construction sites or mining operations.

(8)   Any person performing irrigation construction or irrigation contracting work for use in agricultural production, farming, or ranching, including land application of animal wastewater.

(9)   Any person performing irrigation construction or irrigation contracting work for use in commercial sod production.

(10)   Any person performing irrigation construction or irrigation contracting work for use in the commercial production of horticultural crops, including nursery and greenhouse operators.

(11)   A general contractor licensed under Article 1 of Chapter 87 of the General Statutes who possesses a classification under G.S. 87-10(b) as a building contractor, a residential contractor, or a public utilities contractor.

(12)   A wastewater contractor certified under Article 5 of Chapter 90A of the General Statutes who performs only the construction of or repair to a wastewater dispersal system.

(13)   Repealed by Session Laws 2013-383, s. 2, effective October 1, 2013.

(14)   A plumbing contractor licensed under Article 2 of Chapter 87 of the General Statutes who performs only the following work: installation, repairs, or maintenance of water mains, water taps, service lines, water meters, or backflow prevention assemblies supplying water for irrigation systems; or repairs to an irrigation system.

(15)   Any person performing irrigation construction or irrigation contracting work for a golf course.

(16)   Any full-time employee of a homeowners association maintaining or repairing an irrigation system owned by the homeowners association of a planned community and located within the planned community's common elements as defined in G.S. 47F-1-103.

(17)   Any person who can document 10 years in business as an irrigation contractor as of January 1, 2009, can document competency in the practice of irrigation construction or irrigation contracting, as determined by the North Carolina Irrigation Contractors' Licensing Board, and meets all other requirements and qualifications for licensure may be issued an irrigation contractor's license under Chapter 89G of the General Statutes, without the requirement of examination, provided that the person submits an application for licensure to the Board prior to October 1, 2012.

(18)   Any unlicensed person or entity who enters into a subcontract with a North Carolina licensed irrigation contractor, where the irrigation work is performed entirely by the North Carolina licensed irrigation contractor in accordance with this Chapter. (2008-177, s. 1; 2012-194, s. 65.8(a); 2013-383, s. 2.)

§ 89G-4. The North Carolina Irrigation Contractors' Licensing Board.

(a)   Composition and Terms. - The North Carolina Irrigation Contractors' Licensing Board is created. The Board shall consist of nine members who shall serve staggered terms. The initial Board shall be selected on or before October 1, 2008, as follows:

(1)   The Commissioner of Agriculture, upon the recommendation of the Carolinas Irrigation Association, shall appoint two irrigation contractors, one to serve a one-year term and one to serve a three-year term.

(2)   The General Assembly, upon the recommendation of the Speaker of the House of Representatives and pursuant to recommendations from the North Carolina Green Industry Council, shall appoint two members, one who is a registered landscape contractor in good standing with the North Carolina Landscape Contractors Registration Board to serve a one-year term and one who is an irrigation contractor to serve a three-year term.

(3)   The General Assembly, upon the recommendation of the President Pro Tempore of the Senate, shall appoint two irrigation contractors, one to serve a one-year term and one to serve a two-year term.

(4)   The President of The University of North Carolina System shall appoint one member from within the ranks of the land grant university community who is knowledgeable in irrigation methods and practices to serve a three-year term. The position is open to both current employees of The University of North Carolina System and persons who have earned emeritus status with The University of North Carolina System.

(5)   The Board of Directors of the North Carolina Chapter of the American Society of Landscape Architects shall appoint one member who is a registered landscape architect to serve a two-year term.

(6)   The Governor shall appoint one public member to serve a two-year term.

Upon the expiration of the terms of the initial Board members, each member shall be appointed by the appointing authorities designated in subdivisions (1) through (6) of this subsection for a three-year term and shall serve until a successor is appointed and qualified. No member may serve more than two consecutive full terms.

(b)   Qualifications. - Members of the Board shall be residents of this State. The irrigation contractor members shall meet the requirements for licensure under this Chapter and remain in good standing with the Board during their terms. The public member of the Board shall not be: (i) trained or experienced in irrigation construction or irrigation contracting; (ii) an agent or employee of a person engaged in the practice of irrigation construction or irrigation contracting; or (iii) the spouse of an individual who may not serve as a public member of the Board.

(c)   Vacancies. - Any vacancy on the Board created by death, resignation, or otherwise shall be filled in the same manner as the original appointment, except that all unexpired terms of Board members appointed by the General Assembly shall be filled in accordance with G.S. 120-122. Appointees to fill vacancies shall serve the remainder of the unexpired term and until their successors are appointed and qualified.

(d)   Removal. - The Board may remove any of its members for neglect of duty, incompetence, or unprofessional conduct. A member subject to disciplinary proceedings in the member's capacity as a licensed irrigation contractor shall be disqualified from participating in the official business of the Board until the charges have been resolved.

(e)   Officers and Meetings. - The Board shall elect annually a chair and other officers as it deems necessary to carry out the purposes of this Chapter and shall hold meetings at least twice a year. A majority of the Board shall constitute a quorum.

(f)   Compensation. - Each member of the Board may receive per diem and reimbursement for travel and subsistence as set forth in G.S. 93B-5.

(g)   Assistance. - The Board shall be entitled to the services of the Attorney General in connection with the affairs of the Board or may, in its discretion, employ an attorney to assist or represent it in the enforcement of this Chapter. (2008-177, s. 1; 2013-383, s. 8.)

§ 89G-5. Powers and duties.

The Board shall have the following powers and duties:

(1)   To administer and enforce the provisions of this Chapter.

(2) To adopt, amend, or repeal rules to carry out the provisions of this Chapter.

(3) To examine and determine the qualifications and fitness of applicants for licensure and licensure renewal.

(4) To issue, renew, deny, restrict, suspend, or revoke licenses.

(5) To reprimand or otherwise discipline licensees under this Chapter.

(6) To receive and investigate complaints from members of the public.

(7) To conduct investigations to determine whether violations of this Chapter exist or constitute grounds for disciplinary action against licensees under this Chapter.

(8) To conduct administrative hearings in accordance with Chapter 150B of the General Statues.

(9) To seek injunctive relief through any court of competent jurisdiction for violations of this Chapter.

(10) To collect fees required by G.S. 89G-10 and other monies permitted by law to be paid to the Board.

(11) To require licensees to file and maintain an adequate surety bond or letter of credit.

(12) To establish and approve continuing educational requirements for persons licensed under this Chapter.

(13) To employ a secretary-treasurer and any other clerical personnel the Board deems necessary to carry out the provisions of this Chapter and to fix compensation for employees.

(14) To maintain a record of all proceedings conducted by the Board and make available to licensees and other concerned parties an annual report of all Board actions.

(15) To adopt and publish a code of professional conduct and practice for all persons licensed under this Chapter. The code shall establish minimum

standards for water conservation in the practice of irrigation construction and contracting.

(16) To publish a list of irrigation best management practices to be followed by licensed irrigation contractors.

(17) To adopt a seal containing the name of the Board for use on licenses and official reports issued by the Board. (2008-177, s. 1; 2013-383, s. 3.)

§ 89G-6. Application; qualifications; examination; issuance.

(a) Upon application to the Board and the payment of the required fees, an applicant may be licensed under this Chapter as an irrigation contractor if the applicant submits evidence that demonstrates his or her qualifications as prescribed in rules adopted by the Board and meets all of the following qualifications:

(1) Is at least 18 years of age.

(2) Is of good moral character as determined by the Board.

(3) Has at least three years of experience in irrigation construction or irrigation contracting or the educational equivalent. Two years of educational training in irrigation construction or irrigation contracting shall be the equivalent of one year of experience.

(4) Files with the Board and maintains a corporate surety bond executed by a company authorized to do business in this State or an irrevocable letter of credit issued by an insured institution. The surety bond or the letter of credit shall be in the amount of ten thousand dollars ($10,000). The surety bond or letter of credit shall be approved by the Board as to form and shall be conditioned upon the obligor's faithfully conforming to and abiding by the provisions of this Chapter. Any person claiming to be injured by an act of a licensed irrigation contractor that constitutes a violation of this Chapter may institute an action to recover against the licensee and the surety.

(b) If the application is satisfactory to the Board, the applicant shall be required to pass an examination administered by the Board. The Board shall establish the scope and subject matter of the examination, and an examination shall be held at least twice a year at a time and place to be determined by the Board. The examination, at a minimum, shall test the applicant's understanding of the following:

(1)   Efficiency of water use and conservation in the practice of irrigation construction and contracting.

(2)   Proper methods of irrigation construction.

(3)   Proper methods for irrigation installation.

(4)   Basic business skills.

(c)   When the Board determines that an applicant has met all the requirements for licensure, the Board shall issue a license to the applicant. (2008-177, s. 1; 2013-383, s. 8.)

§ 89G-6.1. Licensing of business entities, nonresident individuals, and foreign entities.

(a)   The Board may issue a license in the name of a business entity if the business entity pays the license fee required by G.S. 89G-10 and one of the following applies:

(1)   For a corporation, one or more officers or full-time employees empowered to act for the corporation are individuals licensed under this Chapter, and only the individuals licensed under this Chapter execute contracts for irrigation construction and irrigation contracting.

(2)   For a limited liability company, one or more managers or executives as defined in G.S. 57C-1-03 or full-time employees empowered to act for the company are individuals licensed under this Chapter, and only the individuals licensed under this Chapter execute contracts for irrigation construction and irrigation contracting.

(3)   For a partnership, one or more general partners or full-time employees empowered to act for the partnership are individuals licensed under this Chapter, and only the individuals licensed under this Chapter execute contracts for irrigation construction and irrigation contracting.

(4) For a business entity using an assumed name or designated trade name, the owner or one or more full-time employees empowered to act for the owner are individuals licensed under this Chapter, and only the individuals licensed under this Chapter execute contracts for irrigation construction and irrigation contracting.

(b) The Board may issue a license to a nonresident individual who meets the requirements for licensure under this Chapter. A nonresident individual licensed under this Chapter may qualify as the licensed individual under subdivisions (1), (2), and (3) of subsection (a) of this section.

(c) The Board may issue a license in the name of a foreign entity if the following apply:

(1) For a foreign corporation, the corporation has obtained a certificate of authority from the Secretary of State pursuant to Article 15 of Chapter 55 of the General Statutes and complies with the requirements of subdivision (1) of subsection (a) of this section.

(2) For a foreign limited liability company, the company has obtained a certificate of authority from the Secretary of State pursuant to Article 7 of Chapter 57C of the General Statutes and complies with the requirements of subdivision (2) of subsection (a) of this section.

(3) For a foreign partnership, the partnership complies with the requirements of subdivision (3) of subsection (a) of this section.

(d) When the Board issues a license to a business entity or a foreign entity under this section, the Board shall indicate on the license the name and license number of the individual licensee required under subsection (a) of this section. The individual licensee required under subsection (a) of this section shall exercise direct supervision over a contract by a business entity or a foreign entity for irrigation construction or irrigation contracting until the contract is completed.

(e) A business entity or foreign entity licensed under this section shall provide written notice to the Board if the individual licensee required under subsection (a) of this section ceases to be an officer, full-time employee, manager, executive, general partner, or owner of the business entity or foreign entity. The business entity or foreign entity must satisfy the requirements of subsection (a) of this section within 90 days of the effective date of the notice required under this subsection. The Board shall suspend the license of a business entity or foreign entity licensed under this section that fails after 90 days to satisfy the requirements of subsection (a) of this section. (2013-383, s. 4.)

§ 89G-7. Use of seal; posting license.

(a) Upon licensure by the Board, each irrigation contractor shall obtain a seal of the design authorized by the Board and bearing the name of the licensee, the number of the license, and the legend "N.C. Licensed Irrigation Contractor." An irrigation contractor may use the seal only while the license is valid.

(b) Every irrigation contractor issued a license under this Chapter shall display the license conspicuously in the contractor's place of business. (2008-177, s. 1.)

§ 89G-8. Reciprocity.

The Board may issue a license, without examination, to any person who is an irrigation contractor licensed, certified, or registered in another state or country if the requirements for licensure, certification, or registration in the other state or country are substantially equivalent to the requirements for licensure in this State. (2008-177, s. 1.)

§ 89G-9. License renewal and continuing education.

(a) Every license issued under this Chapter shall be renewed on or before December 31 of each year. Any person who desires to continue to practice irrigation contracting or irrigation construction shall apply for license renewal and shall submit the required fees. Licenses that are not renewed shall be automatically revoked. A license may be renewed at any time within one year after its expiration, if: (i) the applicant pays the required renewal fee and late renewal fee; (ii) the Board finds that the applicant has not used the license in a manner inconsistent with the provisions of this Chapter or engaged in the practice of irrigation construction or irrigation contracting after notice of revocation; and (iii) the applicant is otherwise eligible for licensure under the provisions of this Chapter. When necessary, the Board may require a licensee to demonstrate continued competence as a condition of license renewal.

(b)   As a condition of license renewal, an individual licensee shall meet continuing education requirements set by the Board. Each individual licensee shall complete 10 continuing education units per year.

(c)   The Board shall suspend an individual licensee's license for 60 days for failure to obtain continuing education units required by subsection (b) of this section. The Board shall suspend a business entity's or a foreign entity's license for 60 days for failure by the individual licensee required under G.S. 89G-6.1(a) to obtain continuing education units required by subsection (b) of this section. Upon completion of the required continuing education and payment of the reinstatement fee, the Board shall reinstate the license. Failure by an individual licensee to meet the education requirements, to request a reinstatement of the license, or to pay the reinstatement fee within the time provided shall result in the revocation of the license. Upon revocation, an individual shall be required to submit a new application and retake the examination as provided in this Chapter. (2008-177, s. 1; 2013-383, ss. 5, 8.)

§ 89G-10. Expenses and fees.

(a)   The Board may impose the following fees not to exceed the amounts listed below:

(1)	Application fee	$100.00
(2)	Examination fee	200.00
(3)	License renewal	100.00
(3a)	Business entity or foreign entity license fee And business entity or foreign entity license Renewal fee	100.00

(4)	Late renewal fee	50.00
(5)	License by reciprocity	250.00
(6)	Corporate license	100.00
(7)	Duplicate license	25.00.

(b)   When the Board uses a testing service for the preparation, administration, or grading of examinations, the Board may charge the applicant the actual cost of the examination services.

(c)   The Board must annually review the fees set out in this section to determine whether these fees reflect the actual cost of administering this act and seek legislative changes to the fees if necessary. (2008-177, ss. 1, 5; 2013-383, s. 6.)

§ 89G-11. Disciplinary action.

(a)   The Board may deny, restrict, suspend, or revoke a license or refuse to issue or renew a license if a licensee or applicant:

(1)   Employs the use of fraud, deceit, or misrepresentation in obtaining or attempting to obtain a license or the renewal of a license.

(2)   Practices or attempts to practice irrigation construction or irrigation contracting by fraudulent misrepresentation.

(3)   Commits an act of gross malpractice or incompetence as determined by the Board.

(4)   Has been convicted of or pled guilty or no contest to a crime that indicates that the person is unfit or incompetent to practice as an irrigation contractor or that indicates that the person has deceived or defrauded the public.

(5)   Has been declared incompetent by a court of competent jurisdiction.

(6) Has willfully violated any provision in this Chapter or any rules adopted by the Board.

(7) Uses or attempts to use the seal in a fraudulent or unauthorized manner.

(8) Fails to file the required surety bond or letter of credit or to keep the bond or letter of credit in force.

(b) The Board may assess costs, including reasonable attorneys' fees and investigatory costs, in a proceeding under this section against an applicant or licensee found to be in violation of this Chapter. (2008-177, s. 1; 2013-383, ss. 7, 8.)

§ 89G-12. Civil penalties.

(a) In addition to taking any of the actions permitted under G.S. 89G-11, the Board may assess a civil penalty not in excess of two thousand dollars ($2,000) for each violation of any section of this Chapter or the violation of any rules adopted by the Board. The clear proceeds of any civil penalty assessed under this section shall be remitted to the Civil Penalty and Forfeiture Fund in accordance with G.S. 115C-457.2.

(b) Before imposing and assessing a civil penalty and fixing the amount of the penalty, the Board shall, as a part of its deliberations, take into consideration the following factors:

(1) The nature, gravity, and persistence of the particular violation.

(2) The appropriateness of the imposition of a civil penalty when considered alone or in combination with other punishment.

(3) Whether the violation was willful and malicious.

(4) Any other factors that would tend to mitigate or aggravate the violation found to exist.

(c) Schedule of Civil Penalties. - The Board shall establish a schedule of civil penalties for violations of this Chapter and rules adopted by the Board. (2008-177, s. 1.)

§ 89G-13. Injunction to prevent violation; notification of complaints.

(a) If the Board finds that a person who does not have a license issued under this Chapter is engaging in the practice of irrigation construction or irrigation contracting, the Board may appear in its own name in superior court in actions for injunctive relief to prevent any person from violating the provisions of this Chapter or rules adopted by the Board.

(b) A licensed irrigation contractor shall notify the Board by registered mail of any complaints filed against the contractor within 30 days from the date the complaint was filed. (2008-177, s. 1; 2013-383, s. 8.)

Chapter 90.

Medicine and Allied Occupations.

Article 1.

Practice of Medicine.

§ 90-1. North Carolina Medical Society incorporated.

The association of regularly graduated physicians, calling themselves the State Medical Society, is hereby declared to be a body politic and corporate, to be known and distinguished by the name of The Medical Society of the State of North Carolina. The name of the society is now the North Carolina Medical Society. (1858-9, c. 258, s. 1; Code, s. 3121; Rev., s. 4491; C.S., s. 6605; 1981, c. 573, s. 1.)

§ 90-1.1. Definitions.

The following definitions apply in this Article:

(1) Board. - The North Carolina Medical Board.

(2) Hearing officer. - Any current or past member of the Board who is a physician, physician assistant, or nurse practitioner and has an active license or approval to practice medical acts, tasks, or functions issued by the Board, or any current or retired judge of the Office of Administrative Hearings, a State district court, a State superior court, the North Carolina Court of Appeals, the North Carolina Supreme Court, or of the federal judiciary who has an active license to practice law in North Carolina and who is a member in good standing of the North Carolina State Bar.

(3) Integrative medicine. - A diagnostic or therapeutic treatment that may not be considered a conventionally accepted medical treatment and that a licensed physician in the physician's professional opinion believes may be of potential benefit to the patient, so long as the treatment poses no greater risk of harm to the patient than the comparable conventional treatments.

(4) License. - An authorization issued by the Board to a physician or physician assistant to practice medical acts, tasks, or functions.

(4a) Modality. - A method of medical treatment.

(5) The practice of medicine or surgery. - Except as otherwise provided by this subdivision, the practice of medicine or surgery, for purposes of this Article, includes any of the following acts:

a. Advertising, holding out to the public, or representing in any manner that the individual is authorized to practice medicine in this State.

b. Offering or undertaking to prescribe, order, give, or administer any drug or medicine for the use of any other individual.

c. Offering or undertaking to prevent or diagnose, correct, prescribe for, administer to, or treat in any manner or by any means, methods, or devices any disease, illness, pain, wound, fracture, infirmity, defect, or abnormal physical or mental condition of any individual, including the management of pregnancy or parturition.

d. Offering or undertaking to perform any surgical operation on any individual.

e. Using the designation "Doctor," "Doctor of Medicine," "Doctor of Osteopathy," "Doctor of Osteopathic Medicine," "Physician," "Surgeon," "Physician and Surgeon," "Dr.," "M.D.," "D.O.," or any combination thereof in the conduct of any occupation or profession pertaining to the prevention, diagnosis, or treatment of human disease or condition, unless the designation additionally contains the description of or reference to another branch of the healing arts for which the individual holds a valid license in this State or the use of the designation "Doctor" or "Physician" is otherwise specifically permitted by law.

f. The performance of any act, within or without this State, described in this subdivision by use of any electronic or other means, including the Internet or telephone.

The administration of required lethal substances or any assistance whatsoever rendered with an execution under Article 19 of Chapter 15 of the General Statutes does not constitute the practice of medicine or surgery. (2007-346, s. 1; 2009-558, s. 1.1; 2013-154, s. 1(b).)

§ 90-2. Medical Board.

(a) There is established the North Carolina Medical Board to regulate the practice of medicine and surgery for the benefit and protection of the people of North Carolina. The Board shall consist of 12 members.

(1) Seven of the members shall be duly licensed physicians recommended by the Review Panel and appointed by the Governor as set forth in G.S. 90-3.

(2) The remaining five members shall all be appointed by the Governor as follows:

a. One shall be a duly licensed physician who is a doctor of osteopathy or a full-time faculty member of one of the medical schools in North Carolina who utilizes integrative medicine in that person's clinical practice or a member of The Old North State Medical Society. This Board position shall not be subject to recommendations of the Review Panel pursuant to G.S. 90-3.

b. Three shall be public members, and these Board positions shall not be subject to recommendations of the Review Panel pursuant to G.S. 90-3. A public member shall not be a health care provider nor the spouse of a health care provider. For the purpose of Board membership, "health care provider" means any licensed health care professional, agent or employee of a health care institution, health care insurer, health care professional school, or a member of any allied health profession. For purposes of this section, a person enrolled in a program as preparation to be a licensed health care professional or an allied health professional shall be deemed a health care provider. For purposes of this section, any person with significant financial interest in a health service or profession is not a public member.

c. One shall be a physician assistant as defined in G.S. 90-18.1 or a nurse practitioner as defined in G.S. 90-18.2 as recommended by the Review Panel pursuant to G.S. 90-3.

(a1) Each appointing and nominating authority shall endeavor to see, insofar as possible, that its appointees and nominees to the Board reflect the composition of the State with regard to gender, ethnic, racial, and age composition.

(b) No member shall serve more than two complete consecutive three-year terms, except that each member shall serve until a successor is chosen and qualifies.

(c) Repealed by Session Laws 2003-366, s. 1, effective October 1, 2003.

(d) Any member of the Board may be removed from office by the Governor for good cause shown. Any vacancy in the physician, physician assistant, or nurse practitioner membership of the Board shall be filled for the period of the unexpired term by the Governor from a list submitted by the Review Panel pursuant to G.S. 90-3 except as provided in G.S. 90-2(a)(2)a. Any vacancy in the public membership of the Board shall be filled by the Governor for the unexpired term.

(e) The North Carolina Medical Board shall have the power to acquire, hold, rent, encumber, alienate, and otherwise deal with real property in the same manner as any private person or corporation, subject only to approval of the Governor and the Council of State as to the acquisition, rental, encumbering, leasing, and sale of real property. Collateral pledged by the Board for an encumbrance is limited to the assets, income, and revenues of the Board. (1858-9, c. 258, ss. 3, 4; Code, s. 3123; Rev., s. 4492; C.S., s. 6606; Ex. Sess. 1921, c. 44, s. 1; 1981, c. 573, s. 2; 1991 (Reg. Sess., 1992), c. 787, s. 1; 1993,

c. 241, s. 2; 1995, c. 94, s. 1; c. 405, s. 1; 1997-511, s. 1; 2003-366, s. 1; 2007-346, s. 2.)

§ 90-2.1: Repealed by Session Laws 2007-346, s. 3, effective October 1, 2007.

§ 90-3. Review Panel recommends certain Board members; criteria for recommendations.

(a) There is created a Review Panel to review all applicants for the physician positions and the physician assistant or nurse practitioner position on the Board except as provided in G.S. 90-2(a)(2)a. The Review Panel shall consist of nine members, including four from the Medical Society, one from the Old North State Medical Society, one from the North Carolina Osteopathic Medical Association, one from the North Carolina Academy of Physician Assistants, one from the North Carolina Nurses Association Council of Nurse Practitioners, and one public member currently serving on the Board. All physicians, physician assistants, and nurse practitioners serving on the Review Panel shall be actively practicing in North Carolina.

The Review Panel shall contract for the independent administrative services needed to complete its functions and duties. The Board shall provide funds to pay the reasonable cost for the administrative services of the Review Panel. The Board shall convene the initial meeting of the Review Panel. The Review Panel shall elect a chair, and all subsequent meetings shall be convened by the Review Panel.

The Governor shall appoint Board members as provided in G.S. 90-2. The Review Panel shall attempt to make its recommendations to the Governor reflect the composition of the State with regard to gender, ethnic, racial, and age composition.

The Review Panel and its members and staff shall not be held liable in any civil or criminal proceeding for exercising, in good faith, the powers and duties authorized by law.

(b) To be considered qualified for a physician position or the physician assistant or nurse practitioner position on the Board, an applicant shall meet each of the following criteria:

(1) Hold an active, nonlimited license to practice medicine in North Carolina, or in the case of a physician assistant or nurse practitioner, hold an active license or approval to perform medical acts, tasks, and functions in North Carolina.

(2) Have an active clinical or teaching practice. For purposes of this subdivision, the term "active" means patient care, or instruction of students in an accredited medical school or residency, or clinical research program, for 20 hours or more per week.

(3) Have actively practiced in this State for at least five consecutive years immediately preceding the appointment.

(4) Intend to remain in active practice in this State for the duration of the term on the Board.

(5) Submit at least three letters of recommendation, either from individuals or from professional or other societies or organizations.

(6) Have no public disciplinary history with the Board or any other licensing board in this State or another state over the past 10 years before applying for appointment to the Board.

(7) Have no history of felony convictions of any kind.

(8) Have no misdemeanor convictions related to the practice of medicine.

(9) Indicate, in a manner prescribed by the Review Panel, that the applicant: (i) understands that the primary purpose of the Board is to protect the public; (ii) is willing to take appropriate disciplinary action against his or her peers for misconduct or violations of the standards of care or practice of medicine; and (iii) is aware of the time commitment needed to be a constructive member of the Board.

(c) The review panel shall recommend at least two qualified nominees for each open position on the Board. If the Governor chooses not to appoint either of the recommended nominees, the Review Panel shall recommend at least two new qualified nominees.

(d)   Notice of open physician positions or the physician assistant or nurse practitioner position on the Board shall be sent to all physicians currently licensed to practice medicine in North Carolina and all physician assistants and nurse practitioners currently licensed or approved to perform medical acts, tasks, and functions in this State.

(e)   Applicants for positions on the Board shall not be required to be members of any professional association or society, except as provided in G.S. 90-2(a)(2)a. (1858-9, c. 258, s. 9; Code, s. 3126; Rev., s. 4493; C.S., s. 6607; 1981, c. 573, s. 3; 2007-346, s. 4.)

§ 90-4. Board elects officers; quorum.

The North Carolina Medical Board is authorized to elect all officers and adopt all bylaws as may be necessary. A majority of the membership of the Board shall constitute a quorum for the transaction of business. (1858-9, c. 258, s. 11; Code, s. 3128; Rev., s. 4494; C.S., s. 6608; 1981, c. 573, s. 4; 1995, c. 94, s. 7.)

§ 90-5. Meetings of Board.

The North Carolina Medical Board shall assemble once in every year in the City of Raleigh, and shall remain in session from day to day until all applicants who may present themselves for examination within the first two days of this meeting have been examined and disposed of; other meetings in each year may be held at some suitable point in the State if deemed advisable. (Rev., s. 4495; 1915, c. 220, s. 1; C.S., s. 6609; 1935, c. 363; 1981, c. 573, s. 5; 1995, c. 94, s. 8.)

§ 90-5.1. Powers and duties of the Board.

(a)   The Board shall:

(1)   Administer this Article.

(2) Issue interpretations of this Article.

(3) Adopt, amend, or repeal rules as may be necessary to carry out and enforce the provisions of this Article.

(4) Require an applicant or licensee to submit to the Board evidence of the applicant's or licensee's continuing competence in the practice of medicine.

(5) Regulate the retention and disposition of medical records, whether in the possession of a licensee or nonlicensee. In the case of the death of a licensee, the rules may provide for the disposition of the medical records by the estate of the licensee. This subsection shall not apply to records created or maintained by persons licensed under other Articles of this Chapter or to medical records maintained in the normal course of business by licensed health care institutions.

(6) Appoint a temporary or permanent custodian for medical records abandoned by a licensee.

(7) Develop educational programs to facilitate licensee awareness of provisions contained in this Article and public awareness of the role and function of the Board.

(8) Develop and implement methods to identify dyscompetent physicians and physicians who fail to meet acceptable standards of care.

(9) Develop and implement methods to assess and improve physician practice.

(10) Develop and implement methods to ensure the ongoing competence of licensees.

(b) Nothing in subsection (a) of this section shall restrict or otherwise limit powers and duties conferred on the Board in other sections of this Article. (2007-346, s. 5.)

§ 90-5.2. Board to collect and publish certain data.

(a) The Board shall require all physicians and physician assistants to report to the Board certain information, including, but not limited to, the following:

(1)   The names of any schools of medicine or osteopathy attended and the year of graduation.

(2)   Any graduate medical or osteopathic education at any institution approved by the Accreditation Council of Graduate Medical Education, the Committee for the Accreditation of Canadian Medical Schools, the American Osteopathic Association, or the Royal College of Physicians and Surgeons of Canada.

(3)   Any specialty board of certification as approved by the American Board of Medical Specialties, the Bureau of Osteopathic Specialists of American Osteopathic Association, or the Royal College of Physicians and Surgeons of Canada.

(4)   Specialty area of practice.

(5)   Hospital affiliations.

(6)   Address and telephone number of the primary practice setting.

(7)   An e-mail address or facsimile number which shall not be made available to the public and shall be used for the purpose of expediting the dissemination of information about a public health emergency.

(8)   Any final disciplinary order or other action required to be reported to the Board pursuant to G.S. 90-14.13 that results in a suspension or revocation of privileges.

(9)   Any final disciplinary order or action of any regulatory board or agency including other state medical boards, the United States Food and Drug Administration, the United States Drug Enforcement Administration, Medicare, or the North Carolina Medicaid program.

(10)   Conviction of a felony.

(11)   Conviction of certain misdemeanors, occurring within the last 10 years, in accordance with rules adopted by the Board.

(12)   Any medical license, active or inactive, granted by another state or country.

(13) Certain malpractice information received pursuant to G.S. 90-5.3, G.S. 90-14.13, or from other sources in accordance with rules adopted by the Board.

(a1) The Board shall make e-mail addresses and facsimile numbers reported pursuant to G.S. 90-5.2(a)(7) available to the Department of Health and Human Services for use in the North Carolina Controlled Substance Reporting System established by Article 5E of this Chapter.

(b) Except as provided, the Board shall make information collected under G.S. 90-5.2(a) available to the public.

(c) The Board may adopt rules to implement this section.

(d) Failure to provide information as required by this section and in accordance with Board rules or knowingly providing false information may be considered unprofessional conduct as defined in G.S. 90-14(a)(6). (2007-346, s. 6; 2009-217, s. 2; 2013-152, s. 5.)

§ 90-5.3. Reporting and publication of medical judgments, awards, payments, and settlements.

(a) All physicians and physician assistants licensed or applying for licensure by the Board shall report to the Board:

(1) All medical malpractice judgments or awards affecting or involving the physician or physician assistant.

(2) All settlements in the amount of seventy-five thousand dollars ($75,000) or more related to an incident of alleged medical malpractice affecting or involving the physician or physician assistant where the settlement occurred on or after May 1, 2008.

(3) All settlements in the aggregate amount of seventy-five thousand dollars ($75,000) or more related to any one incident of alleged medical malpractice affecting or involving the physician or physician assistant not already reported pursuant to subdivision (2) of this subsection where, instead of a single payment of seventy-five thousand dollars ($75,000) or more occurring on or after May 1, 2008, there is a series of payments made to the same claimant which, in the aggregate, equal or exceed seventy-five thousand dollars ($75,000).

(b) The report required under subsection (a) of this section shall contain the following information:

(1) The date of the judgment, award, payment, or settlement.

(2) The specialty in which the physician or physician assistant was practicing at the time the incident occurred that resulted in the judgment, award, payment, or settlement.

(3) The city, state, and country in which the incident occurred that resulted in the judgment, award, payment, or settlement.

(4) The date the incident occurred that resulted in the judgment, award, payment, or settlement.

(c) The Board shall publish on the Board's Web site or other publication information collected under this section. The Board shall publish this information for seven years from the date of the judgment, award, payment, or settlement. The Board shall not release or publish individually identifiable numeric values of the reported judgment, award, payment, or settlement. The Board shall not release or publish the identity of the patient associated with the judgment, award, payment, or settlement. The Board shall allow the physician or physician assistant to publish a statement explaining the circumstances that led to the judgment, award, payment, or settlement, and whether the case is under appeal. The Board shall ensure these statements:

(1) Conform to the ethics of the medical profession.

(2) Not contain individually identifiable numeric values of the judgment, award, payment, or settlement.

(3) Not contain information that would disclose the patient's identity.

(d) The term "settlement" for the purpose of this section includes a payment made from personal funds, a payment by a third party on behalf of the physician or physician assistant, or a payment from any other source of funds.

(e) Nothing in this section shall limit the Board from collecting information needed to administer this Article. (2009-217, s. 3.)

§ 90-6: Recodified as G.S. 90-8.1 and G.S. 90-8.2, by Session Laws 2007-346, s. 7, effective October 1, 2007.

§ 90-7. Bond of secretary.

The secretary of the North Carolina Medical Board shall give bond with good surety, to the president of the Board, for the safekeeping and proper payment of all moneys that may come into his hands. (1858-9, c. 258, s. 17; Code, s. 3134; Rev., s. 4497; C.S., s. 6611; 1995, c. 94, s. 10.)

§ 90-8. Officers may administer oaths, and subpoena witnesses, records and other materials.

The president and secretary of the Board may administer oaths to all persons appearing before it as the Board may deem necessary to perform its duties, and may summon and issue subpoenas for the appearance of any witnesses deemed necessary to testify concerning any matter to be heard before or inquired into by the Board. The Board may order that any patient records, documents or other material concerning any matter to be heard before or inquired into by the Board shall be produced before the Board or made available for inspection, notwithstanding any other provisions of law providing for the application of any physician-patient privilege with respect to such records, documents or other material. All records, documents, or other material compiled by the Board are subject to the provisions of G.S. 90-16. Notwithstanding the provisions of G.S. 90-16, in any proceeding before the Board, in any record of any hearing before the Board, and in the notice of charges against any licensee, the Board shall withhold from public disclosure the identity of a patient including information relating to dates and places of treatment, or any other information that would tend to identify the patient, unless the patient or the representative of the patient expressly consents to the disclosure. Upon written request, the Board shall revoke a subpoena if, upon a hearing, it finds that the evidence the production of which is required does not relate to a matter in issue, or if the subpoena does not describe with sufficient particularity the evidence the production of which is required, or if for any other reason in law the subpoena is invalid. (1913, c. 20, s. 7; C.S., s. 6612; Ex. Sess. 1921, c. 44, s. 3; 1953, c. 1248, s. 1; 1975, c. 690, s. 1; 1979, c. 107, s. 8; 1987, c. 859, s. 5; 1991, c. 348.)

§ 90-8.1. Rules governing applicants for licensure.

The North Carolina Medical Board is empowered to adopt rules that prescribe additional qualifications for an applicant, including education and examination requirements and application procedures. (C.S., s. 6610; 1921, c. 47, s. 5; Ex. Sess. 1921, c. 44, s. 2; 1973, c. 92, s. 2; 1981, c. 665, s. 1; 1983, c. 53; 1995, c. 94, s. 9; c. 405, s. 2; 1999-290, s. 1; 2007-346, ss. 7, 8.)

§ 90-8.2. Appointment of subcommittees.

(a) The North Carolina Medical Board shall appoint and maintain a subcommittee to work jointly with a subcommittee of the Board of Nursing to develop rules to govern the performance of medical acts by registered nurses, including the determination of reasonable fees to accompany an application for approval not to exceed one hundred dollars ($100.00) and for renewal of approval not to exceed fifty dollars ($50.00). Rules developed by this subcommittee from time to time shall govern the performance of medical acts by registered nurses and shall become effective when adopted by both the North Carolina Medical Board and the Board of Nursing. The North Carolina Medical Board shall have responsibility for securing compliance with these rules.

(b) The North Carolina Medical Board shall appoint and maintain a subcommittee of four licensed physicians to work jointly with a subcommittee of the North Carolina Board of Pharmacy to develop rules to govern the performance of medical acts by clinical pharmacist practitioners, including the determination of reasonable fees to accompany an application for approval not to exceed one hundred dollars ($100.00) and for renewal of approval not to exceed fifty dollars ($50.00). Rules recommended by the subcommittee shall be adopted in accordance with Chapter 150B of the General Statutes by both the North Carolina Medical Board and the North Carolina Board of Pharmacy and shall not become effective until adopted by both Boards. The North Carolina Medical Board shall have responsibility for ensuring compliance with these rules. (C.S., s. 6610; 1921, c. 47, s. 5; Ex. Sess. 1921, c. 44, s. 2; 1973, c. 92, s. 2; 1981, c. 665, s. 1; 1983, c. 53; 1995, c. 94, s. 9; c. 405, s. 2; 1999-290, s. 1; 2007-346, s. 7; 2007-418, s. 3.)

§ 90-9: Repealed by Session Laws 2007-418, s. 2, effective October 1, 2007.

§ 90-9.1. Requirements for licensure as a physician under this Article.

(a) Except as provided in G.S. 90-9.2, to be eligible for licensure as a physician under this Article, an applicant shall submit proof satisfactory to the Board that the applicant:

(1) Has passed each part of an examination described in G.S. 90-10.1;

(2) Is a graduate of:

a. A medical college approved by the Liaison Commission on Medical Education, the Committee for the Accreditation of Canadian Medical Schools, or an osteopathic college approved by the American Osteopathic Association and has successfully completed one year of training in a medical education program approved by the Board after graduation from medical school; or

b. A medical college approved by the Liaison Commission on Medical Education, the Committee for the Accreditation of Canadian Medical Schools, or an osteopathic college approved by the American Osteopathic Association, is a dentist licensed to practice dentistry under Article 2 of Chapter 90 of the General Statutes, and has been certified by the American Board of Oral and Maxillofacial Surgery after having completed a residency in an Oral and Maxillofacial Surgery Residency program approved by the Board before completion of medical school; and

(3) Is of good moral character.

(b) No license may be granted to any applicant who graduated from a medical or osteopathic college that has been disapproved by the Board pursuant to rules adopted by the Board.

(c) The Board may, by rule, require an applicant to comply with other requirements or submit additional information the Board deems appropriate. (2007-346, s. 9.)

§ 90-9.2. Requirements for graduates of foreign medical schools.

(a) To be eligible for licensure under this section, an applicant who is a graduate of a medical school not approved by the Liaison Commission on

Medical Education, the Committee for the Accreditation of Canadian Medical Schools, or the American Osteopathic Association shall submit proof satisfactory to the Board that the applicant:

(1)   Has successfully completed three years of training in a medical education program approved by the Board after graduation from medical school;

(2)   Is of good moral character;

(3)   Has a currently valid standard certificate of Educational Commission for Foreign Medical Graduates (ECFMG); and

(4)   Is able to communicate in English.

(b)   The Board may waive ECFMG certification if the applicant:

(1)   Has passed the ECFMG examination and successfully completed an approved Fifth Pathway Program. The applicant is required to provide the original ECFMG Certification Status Report from the ECFMG; or

(2)   Has been licensed in another state on the basis of written examination before the establishment of ECFMG in 1958.

(c)   The Board may, by rule, require an applicant to comply with other requirements or submit additional information the Board deems appropriate. (2007-346, s. 9.)

§ 90-9.3. Requirements for licensure as a physician assistant.

(a)   To be eligible for licensure as a physician assistant, an applicant shall submit proof satisfactory to the Board that the applicant:

(1)   Has successfully completed an educational program for physician assistants or surgeon assistants accredited by the Committee on Allied Health Education and Accreditation or by the Committee's predecessor or successor entities;

(2)   Holds or previously held a certificate issued by the National Commission on Certification of Physician Assistants; and

(3) Is of good moral character.

(b) Before initiating practice of medical acts, tasks, or functions as a physician assistant, the physician assistant shall provide the Board the name, address, and telephone number of the physician who will supervise the physician assistant in the relevant medical setting.

(c) The Board may, by rule, require an applicant to comply with other requirements or submit additional information the Board deems appropriate. The Board may set fees for physician assistants pursuant to rules adopted by the Board. (2007-346, s. 9.)

§ 90-9.4. Requirements for licensure as an anesthesiologist assistant.

Every applicant for licensure as an anesthesiologist assistant in the State shall meet the following criteria:

(1) Satisfy the North Carolina Medical Board that the applicant is of good moral character.

(2) Submit to the Board proof of completion of a graduate level training program accredited by the Commission of Accreditation of Allied Health Education Programs or its successor organization.

(3) Submit to the Board proof of current certification from the National Commission of Certification of Anesthesiologist Assistants (NCCAA) or its successor organization, including passage of a certification examination administered by the NCCAA. The applicant shall take the certification exam within 12 months after completing training.

(4) Meet any additional qualifications for licensure pursuant to rules adopted by the Board. (2007-346, s. 9.)

§ 90-10: Repealed by Session Laws 2007-418, s. 2, effective October 1, 2007.

§ 90-10.1. Examinations accepted by the Board.

The Board may administer or accept the following examinations for licensure:

(1)   A State Board licensing examination.

(2)   The National Board of Medical Examiners (NBME) examination or its successor.

(3)   The United States Medical Licensing Examination (USMLE) of this section or its successor.

(4)   The Federation Licensing Examination (FLEX) or its successor.

(5)   Other examinations the Board deems equivalent to the examinations described in subdivisions (1) through (3) of this section pursuant to rules adopted by the Board. (2007-346, s. 10.)

§ 90-11. Criminal background checks.

(a)   Repealed by Session Laws 2007-346, s. 11, effective October 1, 2007.

(a1) Repealed by Session Laws 2007-346, s. 9.1, effective October 1, 2007.

(b)   The Department of Justice may provide a criminal record check to the Board for a person who has applied for a license through the Board. The Board shall provide to the Department of Justice, along with the request, the fingerprints of the applicant, any additional information required by the Department of Justice, and a form signed by the applicant consenting to the check of the criminal record and to the use of the fingerprints and other identifying information required by the State or national repositories. The applicant's fingerprints shall be forwarded to the State Bureau of Investigation for a search of the State's criminal history record file, and the State Bureau of Investigation shall forward a set of the fingerprints to the Federal Bureau of Investigation for a national criminal history check. The Board shall keep all information pursuant to this subsection privileged, in accordance with applicable State law and federal guidelines, and the information shall be confidential and shall not be a public record under Chapter 132 of the General Statutes.

The Department of Justice may charge each applicant a fee for conducting the checks of criminal history records authorized by this subsection. (C.S., s. 6615; 1921, c. 47, s. 3; Ex. Sess. 1921, c. 44, s. 5; 1971, c. 1150, s. 3; 1981, c. 573, s. 7; 1995, c. 94, s. 12; 1997-511, s. 2; 2002-147, s. 6; 2007-146, s. 1; 2007-346, ss. 9.1, 11.)

§ 90-12: Repealed by Session Laws 2007-346, s. 12, effective October 1, 2007.

§ 90-12.01. Limited license to practice in a medical education and training program.

(a)   As provided in rules adopted by the Board, the Board may issue a limited license known as a "resident's training license" to a physician not otherwise licensed by the Board who is participating in a graduate medical education training program.

(b)   A resident's training license shall become inactive at the time its holder ceases to be a resident in a training program or obtains any other license to practice medicine issued by the Board. The Board shall retain jurisdiction over the holder of the inactive license. (2007-418, s. 4.)

§ 90-12.1: Recodified as G.S. 90-12.4, by Session Laws 2007-346, s. 7, effective October 1, 2007.

§ 90-12.1A. Limited volunteer license.

(a)   The Board may issue a "limited volunteer license" to an applicant who:

(1)   Has a license to practice medicine and surgery in another state; and

(2)   Produces a letter from the state of licensure indicating the applicant's license is active and in good standing.

(3) Repealed by Session Laws 2011-355, s. 1, effective June 27, 2011.

(b), (c) Repealed by Session Laws 2011-355, s. 1, effective June 27, 2011.

(d) The Board shall issue a limited license under this section within 30 days after an applicant provides the Board with information satisfying the requirements of this section.

(e) The holder of a limited license under this section may practice medicine and surgery only at clinics that specialize in the treatment of indigent patients. The holder of the limited license may not receive compensation for services rendered at clinics specializing in the care of indigent patients.

(e1) The holder of a limited volunteer license shall practice medicine and surgery within this State for no more than 30 days per calendar year.

(f) The holder of a limited license issued pursuant to this section who practices medicine or surgery at places other than clinics that specialize in the treatment of indigent patients shall be guilty of a Class 3 misdemeanor and, upon conviction, shall be fined not less than twenty-five dollars ($25.00) nor more than fifty dollars ($50.00) for each offense. The Board, in its discretion, may revoke the limited license after due notice is given to the holder of the limited license.

(g) The Board may, by rule, require an applicant for a limited license under this section to comply with other requirements or submit additional information the Board deems appropriate. (2007-418, s. 5; 2011-183, s. 54; 2011-355, ss. 1, 8.)

§ 90-12.1B. Retired limited volunteer license.

(a) The Board may issue a "retired limited volunteer license" to an applicant who is a physician and who has allowed his or her license to practice medicine and surgery in this State or another state to become inactive.

(b) A physician holding a limited license under this section shall comply with the continuing medical education requirements pursuant to rules adopted by the Board.

(c) The holder of a limited license under this section may practice medicine and surgery only at clinics that specialize in the treatment of indigent patients. The holder of the limited license may not receive compensation for services rendered at clinics specializing in the care of indigent patients.

(d) The Board shall issue a limited license under this section within 30 days after an applicant provides the Board with information satisfying the requirements of this section.

(e) The holder of a limited license issued pursuant to this section who practices medicine or surgery at places other than clinics that specialize in the treatment of indigent patients shall be guilty of a Class 3 misdemeanor and, upon conviction, shall be fined not less than twenty-five dollars ($25.00) nor more than fifty dollars ($50.00) for each offense. The Board, in its discretion, may revoke the limited license after due notice is given to the holder of the limited license.

(f) The Board may, by rule, require an applicant for a limited license under this section to comply with other requirements or submit additional information the Board deems appropriate. (2011-355, s. 2.)

§ 90-12.2: Recodified as G.S. 90-12.5, by Session Laws 2007-346, s. 7, effective October 1, 2007.

§ 90-12.2A. Special purpose license.

(a) The Board may issue a special purpose license to practice medicine to an applicant who:

(1) Holds a full and unrestricted license to practice in at least one other jurisdiction; and

(2) Does not have any current or pending disciplinary or other action against him or her by any medical licensing agency in any state or other jurisdiction.

(b) The holder of the special purpose license practicing medicine or surgery beyond the limitations of the license shall be guilty of a Class 3 misdemeanor and, upon conviction, shall be fined not less than twenty-five dollars ($25.00) nor more than fifty dollars ($50.00) for each offense. The Board, at its discretion, may revoke the special license after due notice is given to the holder of the special purpose license.

(c) The Board may adopt rules and set fees as appropriate to implement the provisions of this section. (2007-418, s. 6.)

§ 90-12.3. Medical school faculty license.

(a) The Board may issue a medical school faculty license to practice medicine and surgery to a physician who:

(1) Holds a full-time appointment as either a lecturer, assistant professor, associate professor, or full professor at one of the following medical schools:

a. Duke University School of Medicine;

b. The University of North Carolina at Chapel Hill School of Medicine;

c. Wake Forest University School of Medicine; or

d. East Carolina University School of Medicine; and

(2) Is not subject to disciplinary order or other action by any medical licensing agency in any state or other jurisdiction.

(b) The holder of the medical school faculty license issued under this section shall not practice medicine or surgery outside the confines of the medical school or an affiliate of the medical school. The holder of the medical school faculty license practicing medicine or surgery beyond the limitations of the license shall be guilty of a Class 3 misdemeanor and, upon conviction, shall be fined not less than twenty-five dollars ($25.00) nor more than fifty dollars ($50.00) for each offense. The Board, at its discretion, may revoke the special license after due notice is given to the holder of the medical school faculty license.

(c) The Board may adopt rules and set fees related to issuing medical school faculty licenses. The Board may, by rule, set a time limit for the term of a medical school faculty license. (2007-418, s. 7.)

§ 90-12.4. Physician assistant limited volunteer license.

(a) The Board shall issue a limited volunteer license to an applicant who:

(1) Holds a current license or registration in another state; and

(2) Produces a letter from the state of licensure indicating the applicant's license or registration is active and in good standing.

(b) The Board shall issue a limited license under this section within 30 days after the applicant provides the Board with information satisfying the requirements of this section.

(c) The holder of a limited license may perform medical acts, tasks, or functions as a physician assistant only at clinics that specialize in the treatment of indigent patients. The holder of a limited license may not receive payment or other compensation for services rendered at clinics specializing in the care of indigent patients. The holder of a limited volunteer license shall practice as a physician assistant within this State for no more than 30 days per calendar year.

(d) Before initiating the performance of medical acts, tasks, or functions as a physician assistant licensed under this section, the physician assistant shall provide the Board the name, address, and telephone number of the physician licensed under this Article who will supervise the physician assistant in the clinic specializing in the care of indigent patients.

(e) The holder of a limited license issued pursuant to this section who practices as a physician assistant at places other than clinics that specialize in the treatment of indigent patients shall be guilty of a Class 3 misdemeanor and, upon conviction, shall be fined not less than twenty-five dollars ($25.00) nor more than fifty dollars ($50.00) for each offense. The Board, in its discretion, may revoke the limited license after due notice is given to the holder of the limited license.

(f) The Board may, by rule, require an applicant for a limited license under this section to comply with other requirements or submit additional information the Board deems appropriate. (1997-511, s. 3; 2007-346, s. 7; 2011-355, s. 3.)

§ 90-12.4A. Reserved for future codification purposes.

§ 90-12.4B. Physician Assistant retired limited volunteer license.

(a) The Board may issue a "retired limited volunteer license" to an applicant who is a physician assistant and who has allowed his or her license to become inactive.

(b) A physician assistant holding a retired limited volunteer license under this section shall comply with the continuing medical education requirements pursuant to rules adopted by the Board.

(c) The holder of a retired limited volunteer license under this section may perform medical acts, tasks, or functions as a physician assistant only at clinics that specialize in the treatment of indigent patients. The holder of a retired limited volunteer license may not receive compensation for services rendered at clinics specializing in the care of indigent patients.

(d) The Board shall issue a retired limited volunteer license under this section within 30 days after an applicant provides the Board with information satisfying the requirements of this section.

(e) The holder of a retired limited volunteer license issued pursuant to this section who practices as a physician assistant at places other than clinics that specialize in the treatment of indigent patients shall be guilty of a Class 3 misdemeanor and, upon conviction, shall be fined not less than twenty-five dollars ($25.00) nor more than fifty dollars ($50.00) for each offense. The Board, in its discretion, may revoke the limited license after due notice is given to the holder of the limited license.

(f) The Board may, by rule, require an applicant for a retired limited volunteer license under this section to comply with other requirements or submit additional information the Board deems appropriate. (2011-355, s. 4.)

§ 90-12.5. Disasters and emergencies.

In the event of an occurrence which the Governor of the State of North Carolina has declared a state of emergency, or in the event of an occurrence for which a county or municipality has enacted an ordinance to deal with states of emergency under G.S. 166A-19.31, or to protect the public health, safety, or welfare of its citizens under Article 22 of Chapter 130A of the General Statutes, G.S. 160A-174(a) or G.S. 153A-121(a), as applicable, the Board may waive the requirements of this Article in order to permit the provision of emergency health services to the public. (2002-179, s. 20(a); 2007-346, s. 7; 2012-12, s. 2(ff).)

§ 90-13: Repealed by Session Laws 2007-418, s. 2, effective October 1, 2007.

§ 90-13.1. License fees.

(a)   Each applicant for a license to practice medicine and surgery in this State under either G.S. 90-9.1 or G.S. 90-9.2 shall pay to the North Carolina Medical Board an application fee of three hundred fifty dollars ($350.00).

(b)   Each applicant for a limited license to practice in a medical education and training program under G.S. 90-12.01 shall pay to the Board a fee of one hundred dollars ($100.00).

(c)   An applicant for a limited volunteer license under G.S. 90-12.1A or G.S. 90-12.1B shall not pay a fee.

(d)   A fee of twenty-five dollars ($25.00) shall be paid for the issuance of a duplicate license.

(e)   All fees shall be paid in advance to the North Carolina Medical Board, to be held in a fund for the use of the Board.

(f)   For the initial and annual licensure of an anesthesiologist assistant, the Board may require the payment of a fee not to exceed one hundred fifty dollars ($150.00). (1858-9, c. 258, s. 13; Code, s. 3130; Rev., s. 4501; 1913, c. 20, ss. 4, 5; C.S., s. 6619; 1921, c. 47, s. 5; Ex. Sess. 1921, c. 44, s. 7; 1953, c. 187; 1969, c. 929, s. 4; 1971, c. 817, s. 2; c. 1150, s. 5; 1977, c. 838, s. 4; 1979, c.

196, s. 1; 1981, c. 573, s. 15; 1983 (Reg. Sess., 1984), c. 1063, s. 1; 1985, c. 362, ss. 1-3; 1987, c. 859, ss. 13, 14; 1993 (Reg. Sess., 1994), c. 566, s. 2; 1995, c. 94, s. 15; c. 509, s. 37; 2000-5, s. 2; 2005-402, s. 5; 2007-146, s. 2; 2007-346, ss. 7, 13(a); 2007-418, s. 8; 2011-355, s. 5.)

§ 90-13.2. Registration every year with Board.

(a)   Every person licensed to practice medicine by the North Carolina Medical Board shall register annually with the Board within 30 days of the person's birthday.

(b)   A person who registers with the Board shall report to the Board the person's name and office and residence address and any other information required by the Board, and shall pay an annual registration fee of one hundred seventy-five dollars ($175.00), except those who have a limited license to practice in a medical education and training program approved by the Board for the purpose of education or training shall pay a registration fee of one hundred twenty-five dollars ($125.00), those who have a retired limited volunteer license pursuant to G.S. 90-12.1B shall pay an annual registration fee of twenty-five dollars ($25.00), and those who have a limited volunteer license pursuant to G.S. 90-12.1A shall pay no annual registration fee. However, licensees who have a limited license to practice for the purpose of education and training under G.S. 90-12.01 shall not be required to pay more than one annual registration fee for each year of training.

(c)   A physician who is not actively engaged in the practice of medicine in North Carolina and who does not wish to register the license may direct the Board to place the license on inactive status.

(d)   A physician who is not actively engaged in the practice of medicine in North Carolina and who does not wish to register the license may direct the Board to place the license on inactive status.

(e)   A physician who fails to register as required by this section shall pay an additional fee of fifty dollars ($50.00) to the Board. The license of any physician who fails to register and who remains unregistered for a period of 30 days after certified notice of the failure is automatically inactive. The Board shall retain jurisdiction over the holder of the inactive license.

(f) Except as provided in G.S. 90-12.1B, a person whose license is inactive shall not practice medicine in North Carolina nor be required to pay the annual registration fee.

(g) Upon payment of all accumulated fees and penalties, the license of the physician may be reinstated, subject to the Board requiring the physician to appear before the Board for an interview and to comply with other licensing requirements. The penalty may not exceed the maximum fee for a license under G.S. 90-13.1. (1957, c. 597; 1969, c. 929, s. 5; 1979, c. 196, s. 2; 1983 (Reg. Sess., 1984), c. 1063, s. 2; 1987, c. 859, s. 12; 1993 (Reg. Sess., 1994), c. 566, s. 1; 1995, c. 94, s. 16; 1995 (Reg. Sess., 1996), c. 634, s. 1(a); 1997-481, s. 3; 2000-5, s. 3; 2001-493, s. 3; 2005-402, s. 6; 2007-346, s. 7; 2007-418, s. 9; 2011-355, s. 6.)

§ 90-13.3. Salaries, fees, expenses of the Board.

(a) The compensation and expenses of the members and officers of the Board and all expenses proper and necessary in the opinion of the Board to the discharge of its duties under and to enforce the laws regulating the practice of medicine or surgery shall be paid out of the fund, upon the warrant of the Board.

(b) The per diem compensation of Board members shall not exceed two hundred dollars ($200.00) per member for time spent in the performance and discharge of duties as a member. Any unexpended sum of money remaining in the treasury of the Board at the expiration of the terms of office of the members of the Board shall be paid over to their successors in office. (2007-346, s. 13(b).)

§ 90-14. Disciplinary Authority.

(a) The Board shall have the power to place on probation with or without conditions, impose limitations and conditions on, publicly reprimand, assess monetary redress, issue public letters of concern, mandate free medical services, require satisfactory completion of treatment programs or remedial or educational training, fine, deny, annul, suspend, or revoke a license, or other authority to practice medicine in this State, issued by the Board to any person who has been found by the Board to have committed any of the following acts or conduct, or for any of the following reasons:

(1)   Immoral or dishonorable conduct.

(2)   Producing or attempting to produce an abortion contrary to law.

(3)   Made false statements or representations to the Board, or willfully concealed from the Board material information in connection with an application for a license, an application, request or petition for reinstatement or reactivation of a license, an annual registration of a license, or an investigation or inquiry by the Board.

(4)   Repealed by Session Laws 1977, c. 838, s. 3.

(5)   Being unable to practice medicine with reasonable skill and safety to patients by reason of illness, drunkenness, excessive use of alcohol, drugs, chemicals, or any other type of material or by reason of any physical or mental abnormality. The Board is empowered and authorized to require a physician licensed by it to submit to a mental or physical examination by physicians designated by the Board before or after charges may be presented against the physician, and the results of the examination shall be admissible in evidence in a hearing before the Board.

(6)   Unprofessional conduct, including, but not limited to, departure from, or the failure to conform to, the standards of acceptable and prevailing medical practice, or the ethics of the medical profession, irrespective of whether or not a patient is injured thereby, or the committing of any act contrary to honesty, justice, or good morals, whether the same is committed in the course of the licensee's practice or otherwise, and whether committed within or without North Carolina. The Board shall not revoke the license of or deny a license to a person, or discipline a licensee in any manner, solely because of that person's practice of a therapy that is experimental, nontraditional, or that departs from acceptable and prevailing medical practices unless, by competent evidence, the Board can establish that the treatment has a safety risk greater than the prevailing treatment or that the treatment is generally not effective.

(7)   Conviction in any court of a crime involving moral turpitude, or the violation of a law involving the practice of medicine, or a conviction of a felony; provided that a felony conviction shall be treated as provided in subsection (c) of this section.

(8) By false representations has obtained or attempted to obtain practice, money or anything of value.

(9) Has advertised or publicly professed to treat human ailments under a system or school of treatment or practice other than that for which the physician has been educated.

(10) Adjudication of mental incompetency, which shall automatically suspend a license unless the Board orders otherwise.

(11) Lack of professional competence to practice medicine with a reasonable degree of skill and safety for patients or failing to maintain acceptable standards of one or more areas of professional physician practice. In this connection the Board may consider repeated acts of a physician indicating the physician's failure to properly treat a patient. The Board may, upon reasonable grounds, require a physician to submit to inquiries or examinations, written or oral, as the Board deems necessary to determine the professional qualifications of such licensee. In order to annul, suspend, deny, or revoke a license of an accused person, the Board shall find by the greater weight of the evidence that the care provided was not in accordance with the standards of practice for the procedures or treatments administered.

(11a) Not actively practiced medicine or practiced as a physician assistant, or having not maintained continued competency, as determined by the Board, for the two-year period immediately preceding the filing of an application for an initial license from the Board or a request, petition, motion, or application to reactivate an inactive, suspended, or revoked license previously issued by the Board. The Board is authorized to adopt any rules or regulations it deems necessary to carry out the provisions of this subdivision.

(12) Promotion of the sale of drugs, devices, appliances or goods for a patient, or providing services to a patient, in such a manner as to exploit the patient, and upon a finding of the exploitation, the Board may order restitution be made to the payer of the bill, whether the patient or the insurer, by the physician; provided that a determination of the amount of restitution shall be based on credible testimony in the record.

(13) Having a license to practice medicine or the authority to practice medicine revoked, suspended, restricted, or acted against or having a license to practice medicine denied by the licensing authority of any jurisdiction. For

purposes of this subdivision, the licensing authority's acceptance of a license to practice medicine voluntarily relinquished by a physician or relinquished by stipulation, consent order, or other settlement in response to or in anticipation of the filing of administrative charges against the physician's license, is an action against a license to practice medicine.

(14)   The failure to respond, within a reasonable period of time and in a reasonable manner as determined by the Board, to inquiries from the Board concerning any matter affecting the license to practice medicine.

(15)   The failure to complete an amount not to exceed 150 hours of continuing medical education during any three consecutive calendar years pursuant to rules adopted by the Board.

The Board may, in its discretion and upon such terms and conditions and for such period of time as it may prescribe, restore a license so revoked or otherwise acted upon, except that no license that has been revoked shall be restored for a period of two years following the date of revocation.

(b)   The Board shall refer to the North Carolina Physicians Health Program all licensees whose health and effectiveness have been significantly impaired by alcohol, drug addiction or mental illness. Sexual misconduct shall not constitute mental illness for purposes of this subsection.

(c)   A felony conviction shall result in the automatic revocation of a license issued by the Board, unless the Board orders otherwise or receives a request for a hearing from the person within 60 days of receiving notice from the Board, after the conviction, of the provisions of this subsection. If the Board receives a timely request for a hearing in such a case, the provisions of G.S. 90-14.2 shall be followed.

(d)   Repealed by Session Laws 2006-144, s. 4, effective October 1, 2006, and applicable to acts or omissions that occur on or after that date.

(e)   The Board and its members and staff shall not be held liable in any civil or criminal proceeding for exercising, in good faith, the powers and duties authorized by law.

(f)   A person, partnership, firm, corporation, association, authority, or other entity acting in good faith without fraud or malice shall be immune from civil liability for (i) reporting, investigating, assessing, monitoring, or providing an expert medical opinion to the Board regarding the acts or omissions of a licensee or applicant that violate the provisions of subsection (a) of this section or any other provision of law relating to the fitness of a licensee or applicant to practice medicine and (ii) initiating or conducting proceedings against a licensee or applicant if a complaint is made or action is taken in good faith without fraud or malice. A person shall not be held liable in any civil proceeding for testifying before the Board in good faith and without fraud or malice in any proceeding involving a violation of subsection (a) of this section or any other law relating to the fitness of an applicant or licensee to practice medicine, or for making a recommendation to the Board in the nature of peer review, in good faith and without fraud and malice.

(g)   Prior to taking action against any licensee for providing care not in accordance with the standards of practice for the procedures or treatments administered, the Board shall whenever practical consult with a licensee who routinely utilizes or is familiar with the same modalities and who has an understanding of the standards of practice for the modality administered. Information obtained as result of the consultation shall be available to the licensee at the informal nonpublic precharge conference.

(h)   No investigation of a licensee shall be initiated upon the direction of a single member of the Board without another Board member concurring. A Board member shall not serve as an expert in determining the basis for the initiation of an investigation.

(i)   At the time of first communication from the Board or agent of the Board to a licensee regarding a complaint or investigation, the Board shall provide notice in writing to the licensee that informs the licensee: (i) of the existence of any complaint or other information forming the basis for the initiation of an investigation; (ii) that the licensee may retain counsel; (iii) how the Board will communicate with the licensee regarding the investigation or disciplinary proceeding in accordance with subsections (m) and (n) of this section; (iv) that the licensee has a duty to respond to inquiries from the Board concerning any matter affecting the license, and all information supplied to the Board and its staff will be considered by the Board in making a determination with regard to the matter under investigation; (v) that the Board will complete its investigation within six months or provide an explanation as to why it must be extended; and (vi) that if the Board makes a decision to initiate public disciplinary proceedings, the licensee may request in writing an informal nonpublic precharge conference.

(j)   After the Board has made a nonpublic determination to initiate disciplinary proceedings, but before public charges have been issued, the licensee requesting so in writing, shall be entitled to an informal nonpublic precharge conference. At least five days prior to the informal nonpublic precharge conference, the Board will provide to the licensee the following: (i) all relevant information obtained during an investigation, including exculpatory evidence except for information that would identify an anonymous complainant; (ii) the substance of any written expert opinion that the Board relied upon, not including information that would identify an anonymous complainant or expert reviewer; (iii) notice that the licensee may retain counsel, and if the licensee retains counsel all communications from the Board or agent of the Board regarding the disciplinary proceeding will be made through the licensee's counsel; (iv) notice that if a Board member initiated the investigation then that Board member will not participate in the adjudication of the matter before the Board or hearing committee; (v) notice that the Board may use an administrative law judge or designate hearing officers to conduct hearings as a hearing committee to take evidence; (vi) notice that the hearing shall proceed in the manner prescribed in Article 3A of Chapter 150B of the General Statutes and as otherwise provided in this Article; and (vii) any Board member who serves as a hearing officer in this capacity shall not serve as part of the quorum that determines the final agency decision.

(k)   Unless the conditions specified in G.S. 150B-3(c) exist, the Board shall not seek to require of a licensee the taking of any action adversely impacting the licensee's medical practice or license without first giving notice of the proposed action, the basis for the proposed action, and information required under subsection (i) of this section.

(l)   The Board shall complete any investigation initiated pursuant to this section no later than six months from the date of first communication required under subsection (i) of this section, unless the Board provides to the licensee a written explanation of the circumstances and reasons for extending the investigation.

(m)   If a licensee retains counsel to represent the licensee in any matter related to a complaint, investigation, or proceeding, the Board shall communicate to the licensee through the licensee's counsel.

(n)   Notwithstanding subsection (m) of this section, if the licensee has retained counsel and the Board has not made a nonpublic determination to initiate disciplinary proceedings, the Board may serve orders to produce, orders to appear, or provide notice that the Board will not be taking any further action against a licensee to both the licensee and the licensee's counsel. (C.S., s. 6618; 1921, c. 47, s. 4; Ex. Sess. 1921, c. 44, s. 6; 1933, c. 32; 1953, c. 1248, s. 2; 1969, c. 612, s. 4; c. 929, s. 6; 1975, c. 690, s. 4; 1977, c. 838, s. 3; 1981, c. 573, ss. 9, 10; 1987, c. 859, ss. 6-10; 1993, c. 241, s. 1; 1995, c. 405, s. 4; 1997-443, s. 11A.118(a); 1997-481, s. 1; 2000-184, s. 5; 2003-366, ss. 3, 4; 2006-144, s. 4; 2007-346, s. 14; 2009-363, ss. 2, 3; 2009-558, ss. 1.2, 1.3, 1.4.)

§ 90-14.1. Judicial review of Board's decision denying issuance of a license.

Whenever the North Carolina Medical Board has determined that a person who has duly made application to take an examination to be given by the Board showing his education, training and other qualifications required by said Board, or that a person who has taken and passed an examination given by the Board, has failed to satisfy the Board of his qualifications to be examined or to be issued a license, for any cause other than failure to pass an examination, the Board shall immediately notify such person of its decision, and indicate in what respect the applicant has so failed to satisfy the Board. Such applicant shall be given a formal hearing before the Board upon request of such applicant filed with or mailed by registered mail to the secretary of the Board at Raleigh, North Carolina, within 10 days after receipt of the Board's decision, stating the reasons for such request. The Board shall within 20 days of receipt of such request notify such applicant of the time and place of a public hearing, which shall be held within a reasonable time. The burden of satisfying the Board of his qualifications for licensure shall be upon the applicant. Following such hearing, the Board shall determine whether the applicant is qualified to be examined or is entitled to be licensed as the case may be. Any such decision of the Board shall be subject to judicial review upon appeal to the Superior Court of Wake County upon the filing with the Board of a written notice of appeal with exceptions taken to the decision of the Board within 20 days after service of notice of the Board's final decision. Within 30 days after receipt of notice of appeal, the secretary of the Board shall certify to the clerk of the Superior Court of Wake County the record of the case which shall include a copy of the notice of hearing, a transcript of the testimony and evidence received at the hearing, a copy of the decision of the Board, and a copy of the notice of appeal and exceptions. Upon appeal the case shall be heard by the judge without a jury, upon the record, except that in cases of alleged omissions or errors in the record, testimony may be taken by the court. The decision of the Board shall be upheld unless the substantial rights of the applicant have been prejudiced because the decision of the Board is in violation of law or is not supported by any evidence admissible under this Article, or is arbitrary or capricious. Each party to the review proceeding may appeal to the Supreme Court as hereinafter provided in G.S. 90-14.11. (1953, c. 1248, s. 3; 1995, c. 94, s. 14.)

§ 90-14.2. Hearing before disciplinary action.

(a) Before the Board shall take disciplinary action against any license granted by it, the licensee shall be given a written notice indicating the charges made against the licensee, which notice may be prepared by a committee or one or more members of the Board designated by the Board, and stating that the licensee will be given an opportunity to be heard concerning the charges at a time and place stated in the notice, or at a time and place to be thereafter designated by the Board, and the Board shall hold a public hearing not less than 30 days from the date of the service of notice upon the licensee, at which the licensee may appear personally and through counsel, may cross examine witnesses and present evidence in the licensee's own behalf. A licensee who is mentally incompetent shall be represented at such hearing and shall be served with notice as herein provided by and through a guardian ad litem appointed by the clerk of the court of the county in which the licensee resides. The licensee may file written answers to the charges within 30 days after the service of the notice, which answer shall become a part of the record but shall not constitute evidence in the case.

(b) Once charges have been issued, neither counsel for the Board nor counsel for the respondent shall communicate ex parte, directly or indirectly, pertaining to a matter that is an issue of fact or a question of law with a hearing officer or Board member who is permitted to participate in a final decision in a disciplinary proceeding. In conducting hearings, the Board shall retain independent counsel to provide advice to the Board or any hearing committee constituted under G.S. 90-14.5(a) concerning contested matters of procedure and evidence. (1953, c. 1248, s. 3; 1975, c. 690, s. 5; 2007-346, s. 15; 2009-558, s. 2.)

§ 90-14.3. Service of notices.

Any notice required by this Chapter may be served either personally by an employee of the Board or by an officer authorized by law to serve process, or by registered or certified mail, return receipt requested, directed to the licensee or applicant at his last known address as shown by the records of the Board. If notice is served personally, it shall be deemed to have been served at the time when the officer or employee of the Board delivers the notice to the person addressed or delivers the notice at the licensee's or applicant's last known address as shown by records of the Board with a person of suitable age and discretion then residing therein. Where notice is served by registered or certified mail, it shall be deemed to have been served on the date borne by the return receipt showing delivery of the notice to the licensee's or applicant's last known address as shown by the records of the Board, regardless of whether the notice was actually received or whether the notice was unclaimed or undeliverable for any reason. (1953, c. 1248, s. 3; 1995, c. 405, s. 5; 2007-346, s. 16.)

§ 90-14.4: Repealed by Session Laws 2007-346, s. 17, effective October 1, 2007.

§ 90-14.5. Use of hearing committee and depositions; appointment of hearing officers.

(a) Except as provided in subsection (a1) of this section, the Board, in its discretion, may designate in writing three or more hearing officers to conduct hearings as a hearing committee to take evidence. A majority of hearing officers participating in a hearing committee shall be licensees of the Board. The Board shall make a reasonable effort to include on the panel at least one physician licensed in the same or similar specialty as the licensee against whom the complaint has been filed. If a current or retired judge as described in G.S. 90-1.1(2) who is not a current or past Board member participates as a hearing officer, the Board may elect not to retain independent counsel for the hearing committee.

(a1) The Board may use an administrative law judge consistent with Article 3A of Chapter 150B of the General Statutes in lieu of a hearing committee so long as the Board has not alleged that the licensee failed to meet an applicable standard of medical care.

(b)   Evidence and testimony may be presented at hearings before the Board or a hearing committee in the form of depositions before any person authorized to administer oaths in accordance with the procedure for the taking of depositions in civil actions in the superior court.

(c)   The hearing committee shall submit a recommended decision that contains findings of fact and conclusions of law to the Board. Before the Board makes a final decision, it shall give each party an opportunity to file written exceptions to the recommended decision made by the hearing committee and to present oral arguments to the Board. A quorum of the Board will issue a final decision. No member of the Board who served as a member of the hearing committee described in subsection (a) of this section may participate as a member of the quorum of the Board that issues a final agency decision.

(d)   Hearing officers are entitled to receive per diem compensation and reimbursement for expenses as authorized by the Board. The per diem compensation shall not exceed the amount allowed by G.S. 90-13.3. (1953, c. 1248, s. 3; 2006-144, s. 5; 2007-346, s. 18; 2009-558, s. 3.)

§ 90-14.6. Evidence admissible.

(a)   Except as otherwise provided in proceedings held pursuant to this Article the Board shall admit and hear evidence in the same manner and form as prescribed by law for civil actions. A complete record of such evidence shall be made, together with the other proceedings incident to the hearing.

(b)   Subject to the North Carolina Rules of Civil Procedure and Rules of Evidence, in proceedings held pursuant to this Article, the individual under investigation may call witnesses, including medical practitioners licensed in the United States with training and experience in the same field of practice as the individual under investigation and familiar with the standard of care among members of the same health care profession in North Carolina. Witnesses shall not be restricted to experts certified by the American Board of Medical Specialties. A Board member shall not testify as an expert witness.

(c)   Subject to the North Carolina Rules of Civil Procedure and Rules of Evidence, statements contained in medical or scientific literature shall be competent evidence in proceedings held pursuant to this Article. Documentary evidence may be received in the form of a copy or excerpt or may be incorporated by reference, if the materials so incorporated are available for examination by the parties. Upon timely request, a party shall be given an opportunity to compare the copy with the original if available.

(d)   When evidence is not reasonably available under the Rules of Civil Procedure and Rules of Evidence to show relevant facts, then the most reliable and substantial evidence available shall be admitted.

(e)   Any final agency decision of the Board shall be based upon a preponderance of the evidence admitted in the hearing. (1953, c. 1248, s. 3; 2003-366, s. 5; 2007-346, s. 19; 2009-558, s. 4.)

§ 90-14.7. Procedure where person fails to request or appear for hearing.

If a person who has requested a hearing does not appear, and no continuance has been granted, the Board or its trial examiner or committee may hear the evidence of such witnesses as may have appeared, and the Board may proceed to consider the matter and dispose of it on the basis of the evidence before it. For good cause, the Board may reopen any case for further hearing. (1953, c. 1248, s. 3.)

§ 90-14.8. Appeal from Board's decision taking disciplinary action on a license.

(a)   A licensee against whom the Board imposes any public disciplinary sanction, as authorized under G.S. 90-14(a), may appeal such action.

(b)   A licensee against whom any public disciplinary sanction is imposed by the Board may obtain a review of the decision of the Board in the Superior Court of Wake County, or the county in which the licensee resides, upon filing with the secretary of the Board a written notice of appeal within 30 days after the date of the service of the decision of the Board, stating all exceptions taken to the decision of the Board and indicating the court in which the appeal is to be heard. The court shall schedule and hear the case within six months of the filing of the appeal.

(c)   Within 30 days after the receipt of a notice of appeal as herein provided, the Board shall prepare, certify and file with the clerk of the Superior Court in the county where the notice of appeal has been filed the record of the case comprising a copy of the charges, notice of hearing, transcript of testimony, and copies of documents or other written evidence produced at the hearing, decision of the Board, and notice of appeal containing exceptions to the decision of the Board. (1953, c. 1248, s. 3; 1981, c. 573, s. 12; 2007-346, s. 20; 2009-558, s. 5.)

§ 90-14.9. Appeal bond; stay of Board order.

(a) The person seeking the review shall file with the clerk of the reviewing court a copy of the notice of appeal and an appeal bond of two hundred dollars ($200.00) at the same time the notice of appeal is filed with the Board. Subject to subsection (b) of this section, at any time before or during the review proceeding the aggrieved person may apply to the reviewing court for an order staying the operation of the Board decision pending the outcome of the review, which the court may grant or deny in its discretion.

(b) No stay shall be granted under this section unless the Board is given prior notice and an opportunity to be heard in response to the application for an order staying the operation of the Board decision. (1953, c. 1248, s. 3; 1995, c. 405, s. 6.)

§ 90-14.10. Scope of review.

Upon the review of the Board's decision taking disciplinary action on a license, the case shall be heard by the judge without a jury, upon the record, except that in cases of alleged omissions or errors in the record, testimony thereon may be taken by the court. The court may affirm the decision of the Board or remand the case for further proceedings; or it may reverse or modify the decision if the substantial rights of the accused physician have been prejudiced because the findings or decisions of the Board are in violation of substantive or procedural law, or are not supported by competent, material, and substantial evidence admissible under this Article, or are arbitrary or capricious. At any time after the notice of appeal has been filed, the court may remand the case to the Board for the hearing of any additional evidence which is material and is not cumulative and which could not reasonably have been presented at the hearing before the Board. (1953, c. 1248, s. 3; 2007-346, s. 21.)

§ 90-14.11. Appeal; appeal bond.

(a) Any party to the review proceeding, including the Board, may appeal from the decision of the superior court under rules of procedure applicable in other civil cases. No appeal bond shall be required of the Board. Subject to subsection (b) of this section, the appealing party may apply to the superior court for a stay of that court's decision or a stay of the Board's decision, whichever shall be appropriate, pending the outcome of the appeal.

(b) No stay shall be granted unless all parties are given prior notice and an opportunity to be heard in response to the application for an order staying the operation of the Board decision. (1953, c. 1248, s. 3; 1989, c. 770, s. 75.1; 1995, c. 405, s. 7.)

§ 90-14.12. Injunctions.

The Board may appear in its own name in the superior courts in an action for injunctive relief to prevent violation of this Article and the superior courts shall have power to grant such injunctions regardless of whether criminal prosecution has been or may be instituted as a result of such violations. Actions under this section shall be commenced in the superior court district or set of districts as defined in G.S. 7A-41.1 in which the respondent resides or has his principal place of business or in which the alleged acts occurred, or in the case of an action against a nonresident, in the district where the Board resides. (1953, c. 1248, s. 3; 1981, c. 573, s. 13; 1987 (Reg. Sess., 1988), c. 1037, s. 100; 2001-27, s. 1.)

§ 90-14.13. Reports of disciplinary action by health care institutions; reports of professional liability insurance awards or settlements; immunity from liability.

(a) The chief administrative officer of every licensed hospital or other health care institution, including Health Maintenance Organizations, as defined in G.S. 58-67-5, preferred providers, as defined in G.S. 58-50-56, and all other provider organizations that issue credentials to physicians who practice medicine in the

State, shall, after consultation with the chief of staff of that institution, report to the Board the following actions involving a physician's privileges to practice in that institution within 30 days of the date that the action takes effect:

(1) A summary revocation, summary suspension, or summary limitation of privileges, regardless of whether the action has been finally determined.

(2) A revocation, suspension, or limitation of privileges that has been finally determined by the governing body of the institution.

(3) A resignation from practice or voluntary reduction of privileges.

(4) Any action reportable pursuant to Title IV of P.L. 99-660, the Health Care Quality Improvement Act of 1986, as amended, not otherwise reportable under subdivisions (1), (2), or (3) of this subsection.

(a1) A hospital is not required to report:

(1) The suspension or limitation of a physician's privileges for failure to timely complete medical records unless the suspension or limitation is the third within the calendar year for failure to timely complete medical records. Upon reporting the third suspension or limitation, the hospital shall also report the previous two suspensions or limitations.

(2) A resignation from practice due solely to the physician's completion of a medical residency, internship, or fellowship.

(a2) The Board shall report all violations of subsection (a) of this section known to it to the licensing agency for the institution involved. The licensing agency for the institution involved is authorized to order the payment of a civil penalty of two hundred fifty dollars ($250.00) for a first violation and five hundred dollars ($500.00) for each subsequent violation if the institution fails to report as required under subsection (a) of this section.

(b) Any licensed physician who does not possess professional liability insurance shall report to the Board any award of damages or any settlement of any malpractice complaint affecting his or her practice within 30 days of the award or settlement.

(c) The chief administrative officer of each insurance company providing professional liability insurance for physicians who practice medicine in North

Carolina, the administrative officer of the Liability Insurance Trust Fund Council created by G.S. 116-220, and the administrative officer of any trust fund or other fund operated or administered by a hospital authority, group, or provider shall report to the Board within 30 days any of the following:

(1)   Any award of damages or settlement of any claim or lawsuit affecting or involving a person licensed under this Article that it insures.

(2)   Any cancellation or nonrenewal of its professional liability coverage of a physician, if the cancellation or nonrenewal was for cause.

(3)   A malpractice payment that is reportable pursuant to Title IV of P.L. 99-660, the Health Care Quality Improvement Act of 1986, as amended, not otherwise reportable under subdivision (1) or (2) of this subsection.

(d)   The Board shall report all violations of this section to the Commissioner of Insurance. The Commissioner of Insurance is authorized to order the payment of a civil penalty of two hundred fifty dollars ($250.00) for a first violation and five hundred dollars ($500.00) for each subsequent violation against an insurer for failure to report as required under this section.

(e)   The Board may request details about any action covered by this section, and the licensees or officers shall promptly furnish the requested information. The reports required by this section are privileged, not open to the public, confidential and are not subject to discovery, subpoena, or other means of legal compulsion for release to anyone other than the Board or its employees or agents involved in application for license or discipline, except as provided in G.S. 90-16. Any officer making a report required by this section, providing additional information required by the Board, or testifying in any proceeding as a result of the report or required information shall be immune from any criminal prosecution or civil liability resulting therefrom unless such person knew the report was false or acted in reckless disregard of whether the report was false. (1981, c. 573, s. 14; 1987, c. 859, s. 11; 1995, c. 405, s. 8; 1997-481, s. 2; 1997-519, s. 3.14; 2006-144, s. 6.)

§ 90-15: Recodified as G.S. 90-13.1, by Session Laws 2007-346, s. 7, effective October 1, 2007.

§ 90-15.1: Recodified as G.S. 90-13.2, by Session Laws 2007-346, s. 7, effective October 1, 2007.

§ 90-16. Self-reporting requirements; confidentiality of Board investigative information; cooperation with law enforcement; patient protection; Board to keep public records.

(a) The North Carolina Medical Board shall keep a regular record of its proceedings with the names of the members of the Board present, the names of the applicants for license, and other information as to its actions. The North Carolina Medical Board shall publish the names of those licensed within 30 days after granting the license.

(b) The Board may in a closed session receive evidence involving or concerning the treatment of a patient who has not expressly or impliedly consented to the public disclosure of such treatment as may be necessary for the protection of the rights of such patient or of the accused physician and the full presentation of relevant evidence.

(c) All records, papers, investigative files, investigative reports, other investigative information and other documents containing information in the possession of or received or gathered by the Board, or its members or employees or consultants as a result of investigations, inquiries, assessments, or interviews conducted in connection with a licensing, complaint, assessment, potential impairment matter, disciplinary matter, or report of professional liability insurance awards or settlements pursuant to G.S. 90-14.13, shall not be considered public records within the meaning of Chapter 132 of the General Statutes and are privileged, confidential, and not subject to discovery, subpoena, or other means of legal compulsion for release to any person other than the Board, its employees or consultants involved in the application for license, impairment assessment, or discipline of a license holder, except as provided in subsections (d) and (e1) of this section. For purposes of this subsection, investigative information includes information relating to the identity of, and a report made by, a physician or other person performing an expert review for the Board and transcripts of any deposition taken by Board counsel in preparation for or anticipation of a hearing held pursuant to this Article but not admitted into evidence at the hearing.

(d) The Board shall provide the licensee or applicant with access to all information in its possession that the Board intends to offer into evidence in presenting its case in chief at the contested hearing on the matter, subject to any privilege or restriction set forth by rule, statute, or legal precedent, upon written request from a licensee or applicant who is the subject of a complaint or investigation, or from the licensee's or applicant's counsel, unless good cause is shown for delay. The Board is not required to provide any of the following:

(1) A Board investigative report.

(2) The identity of a non-testifying complainant.

(3) Attorney-client communications, attorney work product, or other materials covered by a privilege recognized by the Rules of Civil Procedure or the Rules of Evidence.

(e) Information furnished to a licensee or applicant, or counsel for a licensee or applicant, under subsection (d) of this section shall be subject to discovery or subpoena between and among the parties in a civil case in which the licensee is a party.

(e1) When the Board receives a complaint regarding the care of a patient, the Board shall provide the licensee with a copy of the complaint as soon as practical and inform the complainant of the disposition of the Board's inquiry into the complaint and the Board's basis for that disposition. If providing a copy of the complaint identifies an anonymous complainant or compromises the integrity of an investigation, the Board shall provide the licensee with a summary of all substantial elements of the complaint. Upon written request of a patient, the Board may provide the patient a licensee's written response to a complaint filed by the patient with the Board regarding the patient's care. Upon written request of a complainant, who is not the patient but is authorized by State and federal law to receive protected health information about the patient, the Board may provide the complainant a licensee's written response to a complaint filed with the Board regarding the patient's care. Any information furnished to the patient or complainant pursuant to this subsection shall be inadmissible in evidence in any civil proceeding. However, information, documents, or records otherwise available are not immune from discovery or use in a civil action merely because they were included in the Board's review or were the subject of information furnished to the patient or complainant pursuant to this subsection.

(f) Any notice or statement of charges against any licensee, or any notice to any licensee of a hearing in any proceeding shall be a public record within the meaning of Chapter 132 of the General Statutes, notwithstanding that it may contain information collected and compiled as a result of any such investigation, inquiry or interview; and provided, further, that if any such record, paper or other document containing information theretofore collected and compiled by the Board, as hereinbefore provided, is received and admitted in evidence in any hearing before the Board, it shall thereupon be a public record within the meaning of Chapter 132 of the General Statutes.

(g) In any proceeding before the Board, in any record of any hearing before the Board, and in the notice of the charges against any licensee (notwithstanding any provision herein to the contrary) the Board may withhold from public disclosure the identity of a patient who has not expressly or impliedly consented to the public disclosure of treatment by the accused physician.

(h) If investigative information in the possession of the Board, its employees, or agents indicates that a crime may have been committed, the Board may report the information to the appropriate law enforcement agency or district attorney of the district in which the offense was committed.

(i) The Board shall cooperate with and assist a law enforcement agency or district attorney conducting a criminal investigation or prosecution of a licensee by providing information that is relevant to the criminal investigation or prosecution to the investigating agency or district attorney. Information disclosed by the Board to an investigative agency or district attorney remains confidential and may not be disclosed by the investigating agency except as necessary to further the investigation.

(j) All persons licensed under this Article shall self-report to the Board within 30 days of arrest or indictment any of the following:

(1) Any felony arrest or indictment.

(2) Any arrest for driving while impaired or driving under the influence.

(3) Any arrest or indictment for the possession, use, or sale of any controlled substance.

(k) The Board, its members and staff, may release confidential or nonpublic information to any health care licensure board in this State or another state or authorized Department of Health and Human Services personnel with enforcement or investigative responsibilities about the issuance, denial, annulment, suspension, or revocation of a license, or the voluntary surrender of a license by a licensee of the Board, including the reasons for the action, or an investigative report made by the Board. The Board shall notify the licensee within 60 days after the information is transmitted. A summary of the information that is being transmitted shall be furnished to the licensee. If the licensee requests in writing within 30 days after being notified that the information has been transmitted, the licensee shall be furnished a copy of all information so transmitted. The notice or copies of the information shall not be provided if the information relates to an ongoing criminal investigation by any law enforcement agency or authorized Department of Health and Human Services personnel with enforcement or investigative responsibilities. (1858-9, c. 258, s. 12; Code, s. 3129; Rev., s. 4500; C.S., s. 6620; 1921, c. 47, s. 6; 1977, c. 838, s. 5; 1993 (Reg. Sess., 1994), c. 570, s. 6; 1995, c. 94, s. 17; 1997-481, s. 4; 2006-144, s. 7; 2007-346, s. 22; 2009-363, s. 4; 2009-558, s. 6.)

§ 90-17. Repealed by Session Laws 1967, c. 691, s. 59.

§ 90-18. Practicing without license; penalties.

(a) No person shall perform any act constituting the practice of medicine or surgery, as defined in this Article, or any of the branches thereof, unless the person shall have been first licensed and registered so to do in the manner provided in this Article. Any person who practices medicine or surgery without being duly licensed and registered, as provided in this Article, shall not be allowed to maintain any action to collect any fee for such services. Any person so practicing without being duly licensed and registered in this State shall be guilty of a Class 1 misdemeanor. Any person so practicing without being duly licensed and registered in this State and who is falsely representing himself or herself in a manner as being licensed or registered under this Article or any Article of this Chapter shall be guilty of a Class I felony. Any person so practicing without being duly licensed and registered in this State and who is an out-of-state practitioner shall be guilty of a Class I felony. Any person who has a license or approval under this Article that is inactive due solely to the failure to complete annual registration in a timely fashion as required by this Article or any person who is licensed, registered, and practicing under any other Article of this Chapter shall be guilty of a Class 1 misdemeanor.

(b)   Repealed by Session Laws 2007-346, s. 23, effective October 1, 2007.

(c)   The following shall not constitute practicing medicine or surgery as defined in this Article:

(1)   The administration of domestic or family remedies.

(2)   The practice of dentistry by any legally licensed dentist engaged in the practice of dentistry and dental surgery.

(3)   The practice of pharmacy by any legally licensed pharmacist engaged in the practice of pharmacy.

(3a)   The provision of drug therapy management by a licensed pharmacist engaged in the practice of pharmacy pursuant to an agreement that is physician, pharmacist, patient, and disease specific when performed in accordance with rules and rules developed by a joint subcommittee of the North Carolina Medical Board and the North Carolina Board of Pharmacy and approved by both Boards. Drug therapy management shall be defined as: (i) the implementation of predetermined drug therapy which includes diagnosis and product selection by the patient's physician; (ii) modification of prescribed drug dosages, dosage forms, and dosage schedules; and (iii) ordering tests; (i), (ii), and (iii) shall be pursuant to an agreement that is physician, pharmacist, patient, and disease specific.

(4)   The practice of medicine and surgery by any surgeon or physician of the United States Army, Navy, or Public Health Service in the discharge of his official duties.

(5)   The treatment of the sick or suffering by mental or spiritual means without the use of any drugs or other material means.

(6)   The practice of optometry by any legally licensed optometrist engaged in the practice of optometry.

(7)   The practice of midwifery as defined in G.S. 90-178.2.

(8) The practice of podiatric medicine and surgery by any legally licensed podiatric physician when engaged in the practice of podiatry as defined in Article 12A of this Chapter.

(9) The practice of osteopathy by any legally licensed osteopath when engaged in the practice of osteopathy as defined by law, and especially G.S. 90-129.

(10) The practice of chiropractic by any legally licensed chiropractor when engaged in the practice of chiropractic as defined by law, and without the use of any drug or surgery.

(11) The practice of medicine or surgery by any nonregistered reputable physician or surgeon who comes into this State, either in person or by use of any electronic or other mediums, on an irregular basis, to consult with a resident registered physician or to consult with personnel at a medical school about educational or medical training. This proviso shall not apply to physicians resident in a neighboring state and regularly practicing in this State.

(11a) The practice of medicine or surgery by any physician who comes into this State to practice medicine or surgery so long as:

a. The physician or surgeon has an oral or written agreement with a sports team to provide general or emergency medical care to the team members, coaching staff, or families traveling with the team for a specific sporting event taking place in this State; and

b. The physician or surgeon does not provide care or consultation to any person residing in this State other than an individual described in sub-subdivision a. of this subdivision.

The exemption shall remain in force while the physician or surgeon is traveling with the team. The exemption shall not exceed 10 days per individual sporting event. However, the executive director of the Board may grant a physician or surgeon additional time for exemption of up to 20 additional days per individual sporting event.

(12) Any person practicing radiology as hereinafter defined shall be deemed to be engaged in the practice of medicine within the meaning of this Article. "Radiology" shall be defined as, that method of medical practice in which demonstration and examination of the normal and abnormal structures, parts or

functions of the human body are made by use of X ray. Any person shall be regarded as engaged in the practice of radiology who makes or offers to make, for a consideration, a demonstration or examination of a human being or a part or parts of a human body by means of fluoroscopic exhibition or by the shadow imagery registered with photographic materials and the use of X rays; or holds himself out to diagnose or able to make or makes any interpretation or explanation by word of mouth, writing or otherwise of the meaning of such fluoroscopic or registered shadow imagery of any part of the human body by use of X rays; or who treats any disease or condition of the human body by the application of X rays or radium. Nothing in this subdivision shall prevent the practice of radiology by any person licensed under the provisions of Articles 2, 7, 8, and 12A of this Chapter.

(13) The performance of any medical acts, tasks, and functions by a licensed physician assistant at the direction or under the supervision of a physician in accordance with rules adopted by the Board. This subdivision shall not limit or prevent any physician from delegating to a qualified person any acts, tasks, and functions that are otherwise permitted by law or established by custom. The Board shall authorize physician assistants licensed in this State or another state to perform specific medical acts, tasks, and functions during a disaster.

(14) The practice of nursing by a registered nurse engaged in the practice of nursing and the performance of acts otherwise constituting medical practice by a registered nurse when performed in accordance with rules and regulations developed by a joint subcommittee of the North Carolina Medical Board and the Board of Nursing and adopted by both boards.

(15) The practice of dietetics/nutrition by a licensed dietitian/nutritionist under the provisions of Article 25 of this Chapter.

(16) The practice of acupuncture by a licensed acupuncturist in accordance with the provisions of Article 30 of this Chapter.

(17) The use of an automated external defibrillator as provided in G.S. 90-21.15.

(18) The practice of medicine by any nonregistered physician residing in another state or foreign country who is contacted by one of the physician's regular patients for treatment by use of the Internet or a toll-free telephone number while the physician's patient is temporarily in this State.

(19) The practice of medicine or surgery by any physician who comes into this State to practice medicine or surgery at a camp that specializes in providing therapeutic recreation for individuals with chronic illnesses, as long as all the following conditions are satisfied:

a. The physician provides documentation to the medical director of the camp that the physician is licensed and in good standing to practice medicine in another state.

b. The physician provides services only at the camp or in connection with camp events or camp activities that occur off the grounds of the camp.

c. The physician receives no compensation for the services.

d. The physician provides those services within this State for no more than 30 days per calendar year.

e. The camp has a medical director who holds an unrestricted license to practice medicine and surgery issued under this Article.

(20) The provision of anesthesia services by a licensed anesthesiologist assistant under the supervision of an anesthesiologist licensed under Article 1 of this Chapter in accordance with rules adopted by the Board. (1858-9, c. 258, s. 2; Code, s. 3122; 1885, c. 117, s. 2; c. 261; 1889, c. 181, ss. 1, 2; Rev., ss. 3645, 4502; C.S., s. 6622; 1921, c. 47, s. 7; Ex. Sess. 1921, c. 44, s. 8; 1941, c. 163; 1967, c. 263, s. 1; 1969, c. 612, s. 5; c. 929, s. 3; 1971, c. 817, s. 1; c. 1150, s. 6; 1973, c. 92, s. 1; 1983, c. 897, s. 2; 1993, c. 303, s. 2; c. 539, s. 615; 1994, Ex. Sess., c. 24, s. 14(c); 1995, c. 94, ss. 18, 19; 1997-511, s. 4; 1997-514, s. 1; 1999-290, s. 2; 2000-113, s. 2; 2001-27, s. 2; 2003-109, s. 1; 2005-415, s. 2; 2007-146, s. 3; 2007-346, s. 23; 2011-183, s. 127(b); 2011-194, s. 1.)

§ 90-18.1. Limitations on physician assistants.

(a) Any person who is licensed under the provisions of G.S. 90-9.3 to perform medical acts, tasks, and functions as an assistant to a physician may use the title "physician assistant". Any other person who uses the title in any form or holds out to be a physician assistant or to be so licensed, shall be deemed to be in violation of this Article.

(b)   Physician assistants are authorized to write prescriptions for drugs under the following conditions:

(1)   The North Carolina Medical Board has adopted regulations governing the approval of individual physician assistants to write prescriptions with such limitations as the Board may determine to be in the best interest of patient health and safety.

(2)   The physician assistant holds a current license issued by the Board.

(3)   The North Carolina Medical Board has assigned an identification number to the physician assistant which is shown on the written prescription.

(4)   The supervising physician has provided to the physician assistant written instructions about indications and contraindications for prescribing drugs and a written policy for periodic review by the physician of the drugs prescribed.

(c)   Physician assistants are authorized to compound and dispense drugs under the following conditions:

(1)   The function is performed under the supervision of a licensed pharmacist.

(2)   Rules and regulations of the North Carolina Board of Pharmacy governing this function are complied with.

(3)   The physician assistant holds a current license issued by the Board.

(d)   Physician assistants are authorized to order medications, tests and treatments in hospitals, clinics, nursing homes, and other health facilities under the following conditions:

(1)   The North Carolina Medical Board has adopted regulations governing the approval of individual physician assistants to order medications, tests, and treatments with such limitations as the Board may determine to be in the best interest of patient health and safety.

(2)   The physician assistant holds a current license issued by the Board.

(3)   The supervising physician has provided to the physician assistant written instructions about ordering medications, tests, and treatments, and when

appropriate, specific oral or written instructions for an individual patient, with provision for review by the physician of the order within a reasonable time, as determined by the Board, after the medication, test, or treatment is ordered.

(4)   The hospital or other health facility has adopted a written policy, approved by the medical staff after consultation with the nursing administration, about ordering medications, tests, and treatments, including procedures for verification of the physician assistants' orders by nurses and other facility employees and such other procedures as are in the interest of patient health and safety.

(e)   Any prescription written by a physician assistant or order given by a physician assistant for medications, tests, or treatments shall be deemed to have been authorized by the physician approved by the Board as the supervisor of the physician assistant and the supervising physician shall be responsible for authorizing the prescription or order.

(e1)   Any medical certification completed by a physician assistant for a death certificate shall be deemed to have been authorized by the physician approved by the Board as the supervisor of the physician assistant, and the supervising physician shall be responsible for authorizing the completion of the medical certification.

(f)   Any registered nurse or licensed practical nurse who receives an order from a physician assistant for medications, tests, or treatments is authorized to perform that order in the same manner as if it were received from a licensed physician.

(g)   Any person who is licensed under G.S. 90-9.3 to perform medical acts, tasks, and functions as an assistant to a physician shall comply with each of the following:

(1)   Maintain a current and active license to practice in this State.

(2)   Maintain an active registration with the Board.

(3)   Have a current Intent to Practice form filed with the Board.

(h)   A physician assistant serving active duty in the Armed Forces of the United States is exempt from the requirements of subdivision (g)(3) of this section.

(i)   A physician assistant's license shall become inactive any time the holder fails to comply with the requirements of subsection (g) of this section. A physician assistant with an inactive license shall not practice medical acts, tasks, or functions. The Board shall retain jurisdiction over the holder of the inactive license. (1975, c. 627; 1977, c. 904, s. 1; 1977, 2nd Sess., c. 1194, s. 1; 1995, c. 94, s. 20; 1997-511, s. 5; 2007-346, ss. 24, 25; 2011-183, s. 56; 2011-197, s. 1.)

§ 90-18.2. Limitations on nurse practitioners.

(a)   Any nurse approved under the provisions of G.S. 90-18(14) to perform medical acts, tasks or functions may use the title "nurse practitioner." Any other person who uses the title in any form or holds out to be a nurse practitioner or to be so approved, shall be deemed to be in violation of this Article.

(b)   Nurse practitioners are authorized to write prescriptions for drugs under the following conditions:

(1)   The North Carolina Medical Board and Board of Nursing have adopted regulations developed by a joint subcommittee governing the approval of individual nurse practitioners to write prescriptions with such limitations as the boards may determine to be in the best interest of patient health and safety;

(2)   The nurse practitioner has current approval from the boards;

(3)   The North Carolina Medical Board has assigned an identification number to the nurse practitioner which is shown on the written prescription; and

(4)   The supervising physician has provided to the nurse practitioner written instructions about indications and contraindications for prescribing drugs and a written policy for periodic review by the physician of the drugs prescribed.

(c)   Nurse practitioners are authorized to compound and dispense drugs under the following conditions:

(1)   The function is performed under the supervision of a licensed pharmacist; and

(2) Rules and regulations of the North Carolina Board of Pharmacy governing this function are complied with.

(d) Nurse practitioners are authorized to order medications, tests and treatments in hospitals, clinics, nursing homes and other health facilities under the following conditions:

(1) The North Carolina Medical Board and Board of Nursing have adopted regulations developed by a joint subcommittee governing the approval of individual nurse practitioners to order medications, tests and treatments with such limitations as the boards may determine to be in the best interest of patient health and safety;

(2) The nurse practitioner has current approval from the boards;

(3) The supervising physician has provided to the nurse practitioner written instructions about ordering medications, tests and treatments, and when appropriate, specific oral or written instructions for an individual patient, with provision for review by the physician of the order within a reasonable time, as determined by the Board, after the medication, test or treatment is ordered; and

(4) The hospital or other health facility has adopted a written policy, approved by the medical staff after consultation with the nursing administration, about ordering medications, tests and treatments, including procedures for verification of the nurse practitioners' orders by nurses and other facility employees and such other procedures as are in the interest of patient health and safety.

(e) Any prescription written by a nurse practitioner or order given by a nurse practitioner for medications, tests or treatments shall be deemed to have been authorized by the physician approved by the boards as the supervisor of the nurse practitioner and such supervising physician shall be responsible for authorizing such prescription or order.

(e1) Any medical certification completed by a nurse practitioner for a death certificate shall be deemed to have been authorized by the physician approved by the boards as the supervisor of the nurse practitioner, and the supervising physician shall be responsible for authorizing the completion of the medical certification.

(f) Any registered nurse or licensed practical nurse who receives an order from a nurse practitioner for medications, tests or treatments is authorized to perform that order in the same manner as if it were received from a licensed physician. (1977, 2nd Sess., c. 1194, s. 2; 1995, c. 94, s. 21; 2011-197, s. 2.)

§ 90-18.2A. Physician assistants receiving, prescribing, or dispensing prescription drugs without charge or fee.

The North Carolina Medical Board shall have sole jurisdiction to regulate and license physician assistants receiving, prescribing, or dispensing prescription drugs under the supervision of a licensed physician without charge or fee to the patient. The provisions of G.S. 90-18.1(c)(1), (c)(2), and G.S. 90-85.21(b), shall not apply to the receiving, prescribing, or dispensing of prescription drugs without charge or fee to the patient. (2004-124, s. 10.2E(a).)

§ 90-18.3. Physical examination by nurse practitioners and physician assistants.

(a) Whenever a statute or State agency rule requires that a physical examination shall be conducted by a physician, the examination may be conducted and the form signed by a nurse practitioner or a physician's assistant, and a physician need not be present. Nothing in this section shall otherwise change the scope of practice of a nurse practitioner or a physician's assistant, as defined by G.S. 90-18.1 and G.S. 90-18.2, respectively.

(b) This section shall not apply to physical examinations conducted pursuant to G.S. 1A-1, Rule 35; G.S. 15B-12; G.S. 90-14 unless those statutes or rules are amended to make the provisions of this section applicable. (1999-226, s. 1; 2004-124, s. 18.2(f).)

§ 90-18.4. Limitations on clinical pharmacist practitioners.

(a) Any pharmacist who is approved under the provisions of G.S. 90-18(c)(3a) to perform medical acts, tasks, and functions may use the title "clinical pharmacist practitioner". Any other person who uses the title in any form or holds himself or herself out to be a clinical pharmacist practitioner or to be so licensed shall be deemed to be in violation of this Article.

(b) Clinical pharmacist practitioners are authorized to implement predetermined drug therapy, which includes diagnosis and product selection by the patient's physician, modify prescribed drug dosages, dosage forms, and dosage schedules, and to order laboratory tests pursuant to a drug therapy management agreement that is physician, pharmacist, patient, and disease specific under the following conditions:

(1) The North Carolina Medical Board and the North Carolina Board of Pharmacy have adopted rules developed by a joint subcommittee governing the approval of individual clinical pharmacist practitioners to practice drug therapy management with such limitations that the Boards determine to be in the best interest of patient health and safety.

(2) The clinical pharmacist practitioner has current approval from both Boards.

(3) The North Carolina Medical Board has assigned an identification number to the clinical pharmacist practitioner which is shown on written prescriptions written by the clinical pharmacist practitioner.

(4) The drug therapy management agreement prohibits the substitution of a chemically dissimilar drug product by the pharmacist for the product prescribed by the physician without the explicit consent of the physician and includes a policy for periodic review by the physician of the drugs modified pursuant to the agreement or changed with the consent of the physician.

(c) Clinical pharmacist practitioners in hospitals and other health facilities that have an established pharmacy and therapeutics committee or similar group that determines the prescription drug formulary or other list of drugs to be utilized in the facility and determines procedures to be followed when considering a drug for inclusion on the formulary and procedures to acquire a nonformulary drug for a patient may order medications and tests under the following conditions:

(1) The North Carolina Medical Board and the North Carolina Board of Pharmacy have adopted rules governing the approval of individual clinical pharmacist practitioners to order medications and tests with such limitations as the Boards determine to be in the best interest of patient health and safety.

(2) The clinical pharmacist practitioner has current approval from both Boards.

(3) The supervising physician has provided to the clinical pharmacist practitioner written instructions for ordering, changing, or substituting drugs, or ordering tests with provision for review of the order by the physician within a reasonable time, as determined by the Boards, after the medication or tests are ordered.

(4) The hospital or health facility has adopted a written policy, approved by the medical staff after consultation with nursing administrators, concerning the ordering of medications and tests, including procedures for verification of the clinical pharmacist practitioner's orders by nurses and other facility employees and such other procedures that are in the best interest of patient health and safety.

(5) Any drug therapy order written by a clinical pharmacist practitioner or order for medications or tests shall be deemed to have been authorized by the physician approved by the Boards as the supervisor of the clinical pharmacist practitioner and the supervising physician shall be responsible for authorizing the prescription order.

(d) Any registered nurse or licensed practical nurse who receives a drug therapy order from a clinical pharmacist practitioner for medications or tests is authorized to perform that order in the same manner as if the order was received from a licensed physician. (1999-290, s. 3.)

§ 90-18.5. Limitations on anesthesiologist assistants.

(a) Any person who is licensed to provide anesthesia services as an assistant to an anesthesiologist licensed under Article 1 of this Chapter may use the title "anesthesiologist assistant." Any other person who uses the title in any form or holds himself or herself out to be an anesthesiologist assistant or to be so licensed without first obtaining a license shall be deemed in violation of this Article. A student in any anesthesiologist assistant training program shall be identified as a "student anesthesiologist assistant" or an "anesthesiologist assistant student," but under no circumstances shall the student use or permit to be used on the student's behalf the terms "intern," "resident," or "fellow."

(b) Anesthesiologist assistants are authorized to provide anesthesia services under the supervision of an anesthesiologist licensed under Article 1 of this Chapter under the following conditions:

(1) The North Carolina Medical Board has adopted rules governing the provision of anesthesia services by an anesthesiologist assistant consistent with the requirements of subsection (c) of this section.

(2) The anesthesiologist assistant holds a current license issued by the Board or is a student anesthesiologist assistant participating in a training program leading to certification by the National Commission for Certification of Anesthesiologist Assistants and licensure as an anesthesiologist assistant under G.S. 90-9.4.

(c) The North Carolina Medical Board shall adopt rules to implement this section that include requirements and limitations on the provision of anesthesia services by an anesthesiologist assistant as determined by the Board to be in the best interests of patient health and safety. Rules adopted by the Board pursuant to this section shall include the following requirements:

(1) That an anesthesiologist assistant be supervised by an anesthesiologist licensed under this Article who is actively engaged in clinical practice and immediately available on-site to provide assistance to the anesthesiologist assistant.

(2) That an anesthesiologist may supervise no more than two anesthesiologist assistants or student anesthesiologist assistants at one time. The limitation on the number of anesthesiologist assistants and student anesthesiologist assistants that an anesthesiologist may supervise in no way restricts the number of other qualified anesthesia providers an anesthesiologist may concurrently supervise. After January 1, 2010, the Board may allow an anesthesiologist to supervise up to four licensed anesthesiologist assistants concurrently and may revise the supervision limitations of student anesthesiologist assistants such that the supervision requirements for student anesthesiologist assistants are similar to the supervision requirements for student nurse anesthetists.

(3) That anesthesiologist assistants comply with all continuing education requirements and recertification requirements of the National Commission for Certification of Anesthesiologist Assistants or its successor organization.

(d) Nothing in this section shall limit or expand the scope of practice of physician assistants under existing law. (2007-146, s. 4; 2008-187, s. 14.)

§ 90-18.6. Requirements for certain nicotine replacement therapy programs.

The Health and Wellness Trust Fund ("Trust Fund") or the Department of Health and Human Services ("Department") may contract for the operation of a tobacco-use cessation program through which the Trust Fund or the Department, as applicable, may engage agents or contractors for the purpose of (i) recommending to individuals over-the-counter nicotine replacement therapy products and supplying the products free of charge to the individual and (ii) discussing with the individual contraindications and all other aspects of over-the-counter nicotine replacement therapy. All medical aspects of the nicotine replacement therapy programs shall be supervised by a physician who is licensed under this Article to practice medicine and who is under contract to or employed by the Trust Fund or the Department, as applicable, for the purpose of supervising nicotine replacement therapy programs. The physician under contract with or employed by the Trust Fund or the Department, as applicable, shall be responsible for supervision of all agents or contractors of nicotine replacement therapy programs that provide nicotine replacement therapy services to members of the public. The Trust Fund or the Department, as contracting entity, shall report the name of the supervising physician to the North Carolina Medical Board. (2008-107, s. 10.4B.)

§ 90-18.7. Coordination of rules on pathological materials.

The North Carolina Medical Board (Board) shall adopt rules governing the procedures regarding the request for and release of pathological materials made to clinical laboratories within the jurisdiction of the Board. These rules shall be consistent with the North Carolina Hospital Association Best Practices Principles and the College of American Pathologists 2003 Professional Relations Manual and shall be developed in consultation with the Division of Health Service Regulation, Department of Health and Human Services, to ensure consistency in procedures governing pathological materials. (2013-43, s. 2.)

§§ 90-19 through 90-20. Repealed by Session Laws 1967, c. 691, s. 59.

§ 90-21: Repealed by Session Laws 2007-346, s. 26, effective October 1, 2007.

Article 1A.

Treatment of Minors.

Part 1. General Provisions.

§ 90-21.1. When physician may treat minor without consent of parent, guardian or person in loco parentis.

It shall be lawful for any physician licensed to practice medicine in North Carolina to render treatment to any minor without first obtaining the consent and approval of either the father or mother of said child, or any person acting as guardian, or any person standing in loco parentis to said child where:

(1) The parent or parents, the guardian, or a person standing in loco parentis to said child cannot be located or contacted with reasonable diligence during the time within which said minor needs to receive the treatment herein authorized, or

(2) Where the identity of the child is unknown, or where the necessity for immediate treatment is so apparent that any effort to secure approval would delay the treatment so long as to endanger the life of said minor, or

(3) Where an effort to contact a parent, guardian, or person standing in loco parentis would result in a delay that would seriously worsen the physical condition of said minor, or

(4) Where the parents refuse to consent to a procedure, and the necessity for immediate treatment is so apparent that the delay required to obtain a court

order would endanger the life or seriously worsen the physical condition of the child. No treatment shall be administered to a child over the parent's objection as herein authorized unless the physician shall first obtain the opinion of another physician licensed to practice medicine in the State of North Carolina that such procedure is necessary to prevent immediate harm to the child.

Provided, however, that the refusal of a physician to use, perform or render treatment to a minor without the consent of the minor's parent, guardian, or person standing in the position of loco parentis, in accordance with this Article, shall not constitute grounds for a civil action or criminal proceedings against such physician. (1965, c. 810, s. 1; 1977, c. 625, s. 1.)

§ 90-21.2. "Treatment" defined.

The word "treatment" as used in G.S. 90-21.1 is hereby defined to mean any medical procedure or treatment, including X rays, the administration of drugs, blood transfusions, use of anesthetics, and laboratory or other diagnostic procedures employed by or ordered by a physician licensed to practice medicine in the State of North Carolina that is used, employed, or ordered to be used or employed commensurate with the exercise of reasonable care and equal to the standards of medical practice normally employed in the community where said physician administers treatment to said minor. (1965, c. 810, s. 2.)

§ 90-21.3. Performance of surgery on minor; obtaining second opinion as to necessity.

The word "treatment" as defined in G.S. 90-21.2 shall also include any surgical procedure which in the opinion of the attending physician is necessary under the terms and conditions set out in G.S. 90-21.1; provided, however, no surgery shall be conducted upon a minor as herein authorized unless the surgeon shall first obtain the opinion of another physician licensed to practice medicine in the State of North Carolina that said surgery is necessary under the conditions set forth in G.S. 90-21.1; provided further, that in any emergency situation that shall arise in a rural community, or in a community where it is impossible for the surgeon to contact any other physician for the purpose of obtaining his opinion as to the necessity for immediate surgery, it shall not be necessary for the surgeon to obtain approval from another physician before performing such surgery as is necessary under the terms and conditions set forth in G.S. 90-21.1. (1965, c. 810, s. 3.)

§ 90-21.4. Responsibility, liability and immunity of physicians.

(a) Any physician licensed to practice medicine in North Carolina providing health services to a minor under the terms, conditions and circumstances of this Article shall not be held liable in any civil or criminal action for providing such services without having obtained permission from the minor's parent, legal guardian, person standing in loco parentis, or a legal custodian other than a parent when granted specific authority in a custody order to consent to medical or psychiatric treatment. The physician shall not be relieved on the basis of this Article from liability for negligence in the diagnosis and treatment of a minor.

(b) The physician shall not notify a parent, legal guardian, person standing in loco parentis, or a legal custodian other than a parent when granted specific authority in a custody order to consent to medical or psychiatric treatment, without the permission of the minor, concerning the medical health services set out in G.S. 90-21.5(a), unless the situation in the opinion of the attending physician indicates that notification is essential to the life or health of the minor. If a parent, legal guardian[,] person standing in loco parentis, or a legal custodian other than a parent when granted specific authority in a custody order to consent to medical or psychiatric treatment contacts the physician concerning the treatment or medical services being provided to the minor, the physician may give information. (1965, c. 810, s. 4; 1977, c. 582, s. 1; 1985, c. 589, s. 30.)

§ 90-21.5. Minor's consent sufficient for certain medical health services.

(a) Any minor may give effective consent to a physician licensed to practice medicine in North Carolina for medical health services for the prevention, diagnosis and treatment of (i) venereal disease and other diseases reportable under G.S. 130A-135, (ii) pregnancy, (iii) abuse of controlled substances or alcohol, and (iv) emotional disturbance. This section does not authorize the inducing of an abortion, performance of a sterilization operation, or admission to a 24-hour facility licensed under Article 2 of Chapter 122C of the General Statutes except as provided in G.S. 122C-223. This section does not prohibit the admission of a minor to a treatment facility upon his own written application in an emergency situation as authorized by G.S. 122C-223.

(b)   Any minor who is emancipated may consent to any medical treatment, dental and health services for himself or for his child. (1971, c. 35; 1977, c. 582, s. 2; 1983, c. 302, s. 2; 1985, c. 589, s. 31; 1985 (Reg. Sess., 1986), c. 863, s. 4; 2009-570, s. 10.)

Part 2. Parental or Judicial Consent for Abortion.

§ 90-21.6. Definitions.

For the purposes of Part 2 only of this Article, unless the context clearly requires otherwise:

(1)   "Unemancipated minor" or "minor" means any person under the age of 18 who has not been married or has not been emancipated pursuant to Article 35 of Chapter 7B of the General Statutes.

(2)   "Abortion" means the use or prescription of any instrument, medicine, drug, or any other substance or device with intent to terminate the pregnancy of a woman known to be pregnant, for reasons other than to save the life or preserve the health of an unborn child, to remove a dead unborn child, or to deliver an unborn child prematurely, by accepted medical procedures in order to preserve the health of both the mother and the unborn child. (1995, c. 462, s. 1; 1998-202, s. 13(t).)

§ 90-21.7. Parental consent required.

(a)   No physician licensed to practice medicine in North Carolina shall perform an abortion upon an unemancipated minor unless the physician or agent thereof or another physician or agent thereof first obtains the written consent of the minor and of:

(1)   A parent with custody of the minor; or

(2)   The legal guardian or legal custodian of the minor; or

(3)   A parent with whom the minor is living; or

(4)   A grandparent with whom the minor has been living for at least six months immediately preceding the date of the minor's written consent.

(b)   The pregnant minor may petition, on her own behalf or by guardian ad litem, the district court judge assigned to the juvenile proceedings in the district court where the minor resides or where she is physically present for a waiver of the parental consent requirement if:

(1)   None of the persons from whom consent must be obtained pursuant to this section is available to the physician performing the abortion or the physician's agent or the referring physician or the agent thereof within a reasonable time or manner; or

(2)   All of the persons from whom consent must be obtained pursuant to this section refuse to consent to the performance of an abortion; or

(3)   The minor elects not to seek consent of the person from whom consent is required. (1995, c. 462, s. 1.)

§ 90-21.8. Procedure for waiver of parental consent.

(a)   The requirements and procedures under Part 2 of this Article are available and apply to unemancipated minors seeking treatment in this State.

(b)   The court shall ensure that the minor or her guardian ad litem is given assistance in preparing and filing the petition and shall ensure that the minor's identity is kept confidential.

(c)   The minor may participate in proceedings in the court on her own behalf or through a guardian ad litem. The court shall advise her that she has a right to appointed counsel, and counsel shall be provided upon her request in accordance with rules adopted by the Office of Indigent Defense Services.

(d)   Court proceedings under this section shall be confidential and shall be given precedence over other pending matters necessary to ensure that the court may reach a decision promptly. In no case shall the court fail to rule within seven days of the time of filing the application. This time limitation may be extended at the request of the minor. At the hearing, the court shall hear evidence relating to the emotional development, maturity, intellect, and understanding of the minor; the nature, possible consequences, and alternatives to the abortion; and any other evidence that the court may find useful in determining whether the parental consent requirement shall be waived.

(e)　The parental consent requirement shall be waived if the court finds:

(1)　That the minor is mature and well-informed enough to make the abortion decision on her own; or

(2)　That it would be in the minor's best interests that parental consent not be required; or

(3)　That the minor is a victim of rape or of felonious incest under G.S. 14-178.

(f)　The court shall make written findings of fact and conclusions of law supporting its decision and shall order that a confidential record of the evidence be maintained. If the court finds that the minor has been a victim of incest, whether felonious or misdemeanor, it shall advise the Director of the Department of Social Services of its findings for further action pursuant to Article 3 of Chapter 7B of the General Statutes.

(g)　If the female petitioner so requests in her petition, no summons or other notice may be served upon the parents, guardian, or custodian of the minor female.

(h)　The minor may appeal an order issued in accordance with this section. The appeal shall be a de novo hearing in superior court. The notice of appeal shall be filed within 24 hours from the date of issuance of the district court order. The de novo hearing may be held out of district and out of session and shall be held as soon as possible within seven days of the filing of the notice of appeal. The record of the de novo hearing is a confidential record and shall not be open for general public inspection. The Chief Justice of the North Carolina Supreme Court shall adopt rules necessary to implement this subsection.

(i)　No court costs shall be required of any minor who avails herself of the procedures provided by this section. (1995, c. 462, s. 1; 1998-202, s. 13(u); 2000-144, s. 35.)

§ 90-21.9. Medical emergency exception.

The requirements of parental consent prescribed by G.S. 90-21.7(a) shall not apply when, in the best medical judgment of the physician based on the facts of the case before the physician, a medical emergency exists that so complicates the pregnancy as to require an immediate abortion, or when the conditions prescribed by G.S. 90-21.1(4) are met. (1995, c. 462, s. 1.)

§ 90-21.10. Penalty.

Any person who intentionally performs an abortion with knowledge that, or with reckless disregard as to whether, the person upon whom the abortion is to be performed is an unemancipated minor, and who intentionally or knowingly fails to conform to any requirement of Part 2 of this Article shall be guilty of a Class 1 misdemeanor. (1995, c. 462, s. 1.)

Article 1B.

Medical Malpractice Actions.

§ 90-21.11. Definitions.

The following definitions apply in this Article:

(1)   Health care provider. - Without limitation, any of the following:

a.   A person who pursuant to the provisions of Chapter 90 of the General Statutes is licensed, or is otherwise registered or certified to engage in the practice of or otherwise performs duties associated with any of the following: medicine, surgery, dentistry, pharmacy, optometry, midwifery, osteopathy, podiatry, chiropractic, radiology, nursing, physiotherapy, pathology, anesthesiology, anesthesia, laboratory analysis, rendering assistance to a physician, dental hygiene, psychiatry, or psychology.

b. A hospital, a nursing home licensed under Chapter 131E of the General Statutes, or an adult care home licensed under Chapter 131D of the General Statutes.

c. Any other person who is legally responsible for the negligence of a person described by sub-subdivision a. of this subdivision, a hospital, a nursing home licensed under Chapter 131E of the General Statutes, or an adult care home licensed under Chapter 131D of the General Statutes.

d. Any other person acting at the direction or under the supervision of a person described by sub-subdivision a. of this subdivision, a hospital, a nursing home licensed under Chapter 131E of the General Statutes, or an adult care home licensed under Chapter 131D of the General Statutes.

(2) Medical malpractice action. - Either of the following:

a. A civil action for damages for personal injury or death arising out of the furnishing or failure to furnish professional services in the performance of medical, dental, or other health care by a health care provider.

b. A civil action against a hospital, a nursing home licensed under Chapter 131E of the General Statutes, or an adult care home licensed under Chapter 131D of the General Statutes for damages for personal injury or death, when the civil action (i) alleges a breach of administrative or corporate duties to the patient, including, but not limited to, allegations of negligent credentialing or negligent monitoring and supervision and (ii) arises from the same facts or circumstances as a claim under sub-subdivision a. of this subdivision. (1975, 2nd Sess., c. 977, s. 4; 1987, c. 859, s. 1; 1995, c. 509, s. 135.2(o); 2011-400, s. 5.)

§ 90-21.12. Standard of health care.

(a) Except as provided in subsection (b) of this section, in any medical malpractice action as defined in G.S. 90-21.11(2)(a), the defendant health care provider shall not be liable for the payment of damages unless the trier of fact finds by the greater weight of the evidence that the care of such health care provider was not in accordance with the standards of practice among members of the same health care profession with similar training and experience situated in the same or similar communities under the same or similar circumstances at the time of the alleged act giving rise to the cause of action; or in the case of a medical malpractice action as defined in G.S. 90-21.11(2)(b), the defendant health care provider shall not be liable for the payment of damages unless the trier of fact finds by the greater weight of the evidence that the action or inaction of such health care provider was not in accordance with the standards of practice among similar health care providers situated in the same or similar communities under the same or similar circumstances at the time of the alleged act giving rise to the cause of action.

(b)   In any medical malpractice action arising out of the furnishing or the failure to furnish professional services in the treatment of an emergency medical condition, as the term "emergency medical condition" is defined in 42 U.S.C. § 1395dd(e)(1)(A), the claimant must prove a violation of the standards of practice set forth in subsection (a) of this section by clear and convincing evidence. (1975, 2nd Sess., c. 977, s. 4; 2011-283, s. 4.1(a); 2011-400, s. 6.)

§ 90-21.12A. Nonresident physicians.

A patient may bring a medical malpractice claim in the courts of this State against a nonresident physician who practices medicine or surgery by use of any electronic or other media in this State. (1997-514, s. 2.)

§ 90-21.13. Informed consent to health care treatment or procedure.

(a)   No recovery shall be allowed against any health care provider upon the grounds that the health care treatment was rendered without the informed consent of the patient or other person authorized to give consent for the patient where:

(1)   The action of the health care provider in obtaining the consent of the patient or other person authorized to give consent for the patient was in accordance with the standards of practice among members of the same health care profession with similar training and experience situated in the same or similar communities; and

(2)   A reasonable person, from the information provided by the health care provider under the circumstances, would have a general understanding of the

procedures or treatments and of the usual and most frequent risks and hazards inherent in the proposed procedures or treatments which are recognized and followed by other health care providers engaged in the same field of practice in the same or similar communities; or

(3)   A reasonable person, under all the surrounding circumstances, would have undergone such treatment or procedure had he been advised by the health care provider in accordance with the provisions of subdivisions (1) and (2) of this subsection.

(b)   A consent which is evidenced in writing and which meets the foregoing standards, and which is signed by the patient or other authorized person, shall be presumed to be a valid consent. This presumption, however, may be subject to rebuttal only upon proof that such consent was obtained by fraud, deception or misrepresentation of a material fact. A consent that meets the foregoing standards, that is given by a patient, or other authorized person, who under all the surrounding circumstances has capacity to make and communicate health care decisions, is a valid consent.

(c)   The following persons, in the order indicated, are authorized to consent to medical treatment on behalf of a patient who is comatose or otherwise lacks capacity to make or communicate health care decisions:

(1)   A guardian of the patient's person, or a general guardian with powers over the patient's person, appointed by a court of competent jurisdiction pursuant to Article 5 of Chapter 35A of the General Statutes; provided that, if the patient has a health care agent appointed pursuant to a valid health care power of attorney, the health care agent shall have the right to exercise the authority to the extent granted in the health care power of attorney and to the extent provided in G.S. 32A-19(a) unless the Clerk has suspended the authority of that health care agent in accordance with G.S. 35A-1208(a);

(2)   A health care agent appointed pursuant to a valid health care power of attorney, to the extent of the authority granted;

(3)   An attorney-in-fact, with powers to make health care decisions for the patient, appointed by the patient pursuant to Article 1 or Article 2 of Chapter 32A of the General Statutes, to the extent of the authority granted;

(4)   The patient's spouse;

(5) A majority of the patient's reasonably available parents and children who are at least 18 years of age;

(6) A majority of the patient's reasonably available siblings who are at least 18 years of age; or

(7) An individual who has an established relationship with the patient, who is acting in good faith on behalf of the patient, and who can reliably convey the patient's wishes.

(c1) If none of the persons listed under subsection (c) of this section is reasonably available, then the patient's attending physician, in the attending physician's discretion, may provide health care treatment without the consent of the patient or other person authorized to consent for the patient if there is confirmation by a physician other than the patient's attending physician of the patient's condition and the necessity for treatment; provided, however, that confirmation of the patient's condition and the necessity for treatment are not required if the delay in obtaining the confirmation would endanger the life or seriously worsen the condition of the patient.

(d) No action may be maintained against any health care provider upon any guarantee, warranty or assurance as to the result of any medical, surgical or diagnostic procedure or treatment unless the guarantee, warranty or assurance, or some note or memorandum thereof, shall be in writing and signed by the provider or by some other person authorized to act for or on behalf of such provider.

(e) In the event of any conflict between the provisions of this section and those of G.S. 35A-1245, 90-21.17, and 90-322, Articles 1A and 19 of Chapter 90, and Article 3 of Chapter 122C of the General Statutes, the provisions of those sections and Articles shall control and continue in full force and effect. (1975, 2nd Sess., c. 977, s. 4; 2003-13, s. 5; 2007-502, s. 13; 2008-187, s. 37(b).)

§ 90-21.14. First aid or emergency treatment; liability limitation.

(a) Any person, including a volunteer medical or health care provider at a facility of a local health department as defined in G.S. 130A-2 or at a nonprofit community health center or a volunteer member of a rescue squad, who receives no compensation for his services as an emergency medical care provider, who renders first aid or emergency health care treatment to a person who is unconscious, ill or injured,

(1)   When the reasonably apparent circumstances require prompt decisions and actions in medical or other health care, and

(2)   When the necessity of immediate health care treatment is so reasonably apparent that any delay in the rendering of the treatment would seriously worsen the physical condition or endanger the life of the person,

shall not be liable for damages for injuries alleged to have been sustained by the person or for damages for the death of the person alleged to have occurred by reason of an act or omission in the rendering of the treatment unless it is established that the injuries were or the death was caused by gross negligence, wanton conduct or intentional wrongdoing on the part of the person rendering the treatment. The immunity conferred in this section also applies to any person who uses an automated external defibrillator (AED) and otherwise meets the requirements of this section.

(a1)   Recodified as G.S. 90-21.16 by Session Laws 2001-230, s. 1(a), effective October 1, 2001.

(b)   Nothing in this section shall be deemed or construed to relieve any person from liability for damages for injury or death caused by an act or omission on the part of such person while rendering health care services in the normal and ordinary course of his business or profession. Services provided by a volunteer health care provider who receives no compensation for his services and who renders first aid or emergency treatment to members of athletic teams are deemed not to be in the normal and ordinary course of the volunteer health care provider's business or profession.

(c)   In the event of any conflict between the provisions of this section and those of G.S. 20-166(d), the provisions of G.S. 20-166(d) shall control and continue in full force and effect. (1975, 2nd Sess., c. 977, s. 4; 1985, c. 611, s. 2; 1989, cc. 498, 655; 1991, c. 655, s. 1; 1993, c. 439, s. 1; 1995, c. 85, s. 1; 2000-5, s. 4; 2001-230, ss. 1(a), 2; 2009-424, s. 1.)

§ 90-21.15. Emergency treatment using automated external defibrillator; immunity.

(a) It is the intent of the General Assembly that, when used in accordance with this section, an automated external defibrillator may be used during an emergency for the purpose of attempting to save the life of another person who is in or who appears to be in cardiac arrest.

(b) For purposes of this section:

(1) "Automated external defibrillator" means a device, heart monitor, and defibrillator that meets all of the following requirements:

a. The device has received approval from the United States Food and Drug Administration of its premarket notification filed pursuant to 21 U.S.C. § 360(k), as amended.

b. The device is capable of recognizing the presence or absence of ventricular fibrillation or rapid ventricular tachycardia and is capable of determining, without intervention by an operator, whether defibrillation should be performed.

c. Upon determining that defibrillation should be performed, the device automatically charges and requests delivery of, or delivers, an electrical impulse to an individual's heart.

(2) "Person" means an individual, corporation, limited liability company, partnership, association, unit of government, or other legal entity.

(3) "Training" means a nationally recognized course or training program in cardiopulmonary resuscitation (CPR) and automated external defibrillator use including the programs approved and provided by the:

a. American Heart Association.

b. American Red Cross.

(c) The use of an automated external defibrillator when used to attempt to save or to save a life shall constitute "first-aid or emergency health care treatment" under G.S. 90-21.14(a).

(d) The person who provides the cardiopulmonary resuscitation and automated external defibrillator training to a person using an automated external defibrillator, the person responsible for the site where the automated external defibrillator is located when the person has provided for a program of training, and a North Carolina licensed physician writing a prescription without compensation for an automated external defibrillator whether or not required by any federal or state law, shall be immune from civil liability arising from the use of an automated external defibrillator used in accordance with subsection (c) of this section.

(e) The immunity from civil liability otherwise existing under law shall not be diminished by the provisions of this section.

(f) Nothing in this section requires the purchase, placement, or use of automated external defibrillators by any person, entity, or agency of State, county, or local government. Nothing in this section applies to a product's liability claim against a manufacturer or seller as defined in G.S. 99B-1.

(g) In order to enhance public health and safety, a seller of an automated external defibrillator shall notify the North Carolina Department of Health and Human Services, Division of Health Service Regulation, Office of Emergency Medical Services of the existence, location, and type of automated external defibrillator. (2000-113, s. 1; 2007-182, s. 1.1.)

§ 90-21.16. Volunteer health care professionals; liability limitation.

(a) This section applies as follows:

(1) Any volunteer medical or health care provider at a facility of a local health department or at a nonprofit community health center,

(2) Any volunteer medical or health care provider rendering services to a patient referred by a local health department as defined in G.S. 130A-2(5), nonprofit community health center, or nonprofit community health referral service at the provider's place of employment,

(3) Any volunteer medical or health care provider serving as medical director of an emergency medical services (EMS) agency, or

(4) Repealed by Session Laws 2011-355, s. 7, effective June 27, 2011.

(5) Any volunteer medical or health care provider licensed or certified in this State who provides services within the scope of the provider's license or certification at a free clinic facility, who receives no compensation for medical services or other related services rendered at the facility, center, agency, or clinic, or who neither charges nor receives a fee for medical services rendered to the patient referred by a local health department, nonprofit community health center, or nonprofit community health referral service at the provider's place of employment shall not be liable for damages for injuries or death alleged to have occurred by reason of an act or omission in the rendering of the services unless it is established that the injuries or death were caused by gross negligence, wanton conduct, or intentional wrongdoing on the part of the person rendering the services. The free clinic, local health department facility, nonprofit community health center, nonprofit community health referral service, or agency shall use due care in the selection of volunteer medical or health care providers, and this subsection shall not excuse the free clinic, health department facility, community health center, or agency for the failure of the volunteer medical or health care provider to use ordinary care in the provision of medical services to its patients.

(b) Nothing in this section shall be deemed or construed to relieve any person from liability for damages for injury or death caused by an act or omission on the part of such person while rendering health care services in the normal and ordinary course of his or her business or profession. Services provided by a medical or health care provider who receives no compensation for his or her services and who voluntarily renders such services at the provider's place of employment, facilities of free clinics, local health departments as defined in G.S. 130A-2, nonprofit community health centers, or as a volunteer medical director of an emergency medical services (EMS) agency, are deemed not to be in the normal and ordinary course of the volunteer medical or health care provider's business or profession.

(c) As used in this section, a "free clinic" is a nonprofit, 501(c)(3) tax-exempt organization organized for the purpose of providing health care services without charge or for a minimum fee to cover administrative costs.

(c1) For a volunteer medical or health care provider who provides services at a free clinic to receive the protection from liability provided in this section, the free clinic shall provide the following notice to the patient, or person authorized to give consent for treatment, for the patient's retention prior to the delivery of health care services:

"NOTICE

Under North Carolina law, a volunteer medical or health care provider shall not be liable for damages for injuries or death alleged to have occurred by reason of an act or omission in the medical or health care provider's voluntary provision of health care services unless it is established that the injuries or death were caused by gross negligence, wanton conduct, or intentional wrongdoing on the part of the volunteer medical or health care provider."

(d)   A nonprofit community health referral service that refers low-income patients to medical or health care providers for free services is not liable for the acts or omissions of the medical or health care providers in rendering service to that patient if the nonprofit community health referral service maintains liability insurance covering the acts and omissions of the nonprofit health referral service and any liability pursuant to subsection (a) of this section.

(e)   As used in this section, a "nonprofit community health referral service" is a nonprofit, 501(c)(3) tax-exempt organization organized to provide for no charge the referral of low-income, uninsured patients to volunteer health care providers who provide health care services without charge to patients. (1991, c. 655, s. 1,; 1993, c. 439, s. 1; 1995, c. 85, s. 1; 2000-5, s. 4; 2001-230, ss. 1(a), 1(b); 2009-435, s. 1; 2011-355, s. 7; 2013-49, s. 1.)

§ 90-21.17. Portable do not resuscitate order and Medical Order for Scope of Treatment.

(a)   It is the intent of this section to recognize a patient's desire and right to withhold cardiopulmonary resuscitation and other life-prolonging measures to avoid loss of dignity and unnecessary pain and suffering through the use of a portable do not resuscitate ("DNR") order or a Medical Order for Scope of Treatment (MOST).

This section establishes an optional and nonexclusive procedure by which a patient or the patient's representative may exercise this right.

(b)   A physician may issue a portable DNR order or MOST for a patient:

(1) With the consent of the patient;

(2) If the patient is a minor, with the consent of the patient's parent or guardian; or

(3) If the patient is not a minor but is incapable of making an informed decision regarding consent for the order, with the consent of the patient's representative.

The physician shall document the basis for the DNR order or MOST in the patient's medical record. When the order is a MOST, the patient or the patient's representative must sign the form, provided, however, that if it is not practicable for the patient's representative to sign the original MOST form, the patient's representative shall sign a copy of the completed form and return it to the health care professional completing the form. The copy of the form with the signature of the patient's representative, whether in paper or electronic form, shall be placed in the patient's medical record. When the signature of the patient's representative is on a separate copy of the MOST form, the original MOST form must indicate in the appropriate signature field that the signature is "on file".

(c) The Department of Health and Human Services shall develop a portable DNR order form and a MOST form. The official DNR form shall include fields for the name of the patient; the name, address, and telephone number of the physician; the signature of the physician; and other relevant information. At a minimum, the official MOST form shall include fields for: the name of the patient; an advisory that a patient is not required to have a MOST; the name, telephone number, and signature of the physician, physician assistant, or nurse practitioner authorizing the order; the name and contact information of the health care professional who prepared the form with the patient or the patient's representative; information on who agreed (i.e., the patient or the patient's representative) to the options selected on the MOST form; a range of options for cardiopulmonary resuscitation, medical interventions, antibiotics, medically administered fluids and nutrition; patient or patient representative's name, contact information, and signature; effective date of the form and review dates; a prominent advisory that directions in a MOST form may suspend, while those MOST directions are in effect, any conflicting directions in a patient's previously executed declaration of an advance directive for a natural death ("living will"), health care power of attorney, or other legally authorized instrument; and an advisory that the MOST may be revoked by the patient or the patient's representative. The official MOST form shall also include the following statement written in boldface type directly above the signature line: "You are not required to sign this form to receive treatment." The form may be approved by reference to a standard form that meets the requirements of this subsection. For purposes of this section, the "patient's representative" means an individual from the list of persons authorized to consent to the withholding of life-prolonging measures pursuant to G.S. 90-322.

(d)   No physician, emergency medical professional, hospice provider, or other health care provider shall be subject to criminal prosecution, civil liability, or disciplinary action by any professional licensing or certification agency for withholding cardiopulmonary resuscitation or other life-prolonging measures from a patient in good faith reliance on an original DNR order or MOST form adopted pursuant to subsection (c) of this section, provided that (i) there are no reasonable grounds for doubting the validity of the order or the identity of the patient, and (ii) the provider does not have actual knowledge of the revocation of the portable DNR order or MOST. No physician, emergency medical professional, hospice provider, or other health care provider shall be subject to criminal prosecution, civil liability, or disciplinary action by any professional licensing or certification agency for failure to follow a DNR order or MOST form adopted pursuant to subsection (c) of this section if the provider had no actual knowledge of the existence of the DNR order or MOST.

(e)   A health care facility may develop policies and procedures that authorize the facility's provider to accept a portable DNR order or MOST as if it were an order of the medical staff of that facility. This section does not prohibit a physician in a health care facility from issuing a written order, other than a portable DNR order or MOST not to resuscitate a patient in the event of cardiac or respiratory arrest, or to use, withhold, or withdraw additional medical interventions as provided in the MOST, in accordance with acceptable medical practice and the facility's policies.

(f)   Nothing in this section shall affect the validity of portable DNR order or MOST forms in existence prior to the effective date of this section. (2001-445, s. 1; 2007-502, s. 14.)

§ 90-21.18. Medical directors; liability limitation.

A medical director of a licensed nursing home shall not be named a defendant in an action pursuant to this Article except under any of the following circumstances:

(1) Where allegations involve a patient under the direct care of the medical director.

(2) Where allegations involve willful or intentional misconduct, recklessness, or gross negligence in connection with the failure to supervise, or other acts performed or failed to be performed, by the medical director in a supervisory or consulting role. (2004-149, s. 2.9.)

§ 90-21.19. Liability limit for noneconomic damages.

(a) Except as otherwise provided in subsection (b) of this section, in any medical malpractice action in which the plaintiff is entitled to an award of noneconomic damages, the total amount of noneconomic damages for which judgment is entered against all defendants shall not exceed five hundred thousand dollars ($500,000). Judgment shall not be entered against any defendant for noneconomic damages in excess of five hundred thousand dollars ($500,000) for all claims brought by all parties arising out of the same professional services. On January 1 of every third year, beginning with January 1, 2014, the Administrative Office of the Courts shall reset the limitation on damages for noneconomic loss set forth in this subsection to be equal to five hundred thousand dollars ($500,000) times the ratio of the Consumer Price Index for November of the prior year to the Consumer Price Index for November 2011. The Administrative Office of the Courts shall inform the Revisor of Statutes of the reset limitation. The Revisor of Statutes shall publish this reset limitation as an editor's note to this section. In the event that any verdict or award of noneconomic damages stated pursuant to G.S. 90-21.19B exceeds these limits, the court shall modify the judgment as necessary to conform to the requirements of this subsection.

(b) Notwithstanding subsection (a) of this section, there shall be no limit on the amount of noneconomic damages for which judgment may be entered against a defendant if the trier of fact finds both of the following:

(1) The plaintiff suffered disfigurement, loss of use of part of the body, permanent injury or death.

(2) The defendant's acts or failures, which are the proximate cause of the plaintiff's injuries, were committed in reckless disregard of the rights of others, grossly negligent, fraudulent, intentional or with malice.

(c) The following definitions apply in this section:

(1) Consumer Price Index. - The Consumer Price Index - All Urban Consumers, for the South urban area, as published by the Bureau of Labor Statistics of the United States Department of Labor.

(2) Noneconomic damages. - Damages to compensate for pain, suffering, emotional distress, loss of consortium, inconvenience, and any other nonpecuniary compensatory damage. "Noneconomic damages" does not include punitive damages as defined in G.S. 1D-5.

(3) Same professional services. - The transactions, occurrences, or series of transactions or occurrences alleged to have caused injury to the health care provider's patient.

(d) Any award of damages in a medical malpractice action shall be stated in accordance with G.S. 90-21.19B. If a jury is determining the facts, the court shall not instruct the jury with respect to the limit of noneconomic damages under subsection (a) of this section, and neither the attorney for any party nor a witness shall inform the jury or potential members of the jury panel of that limit. (2011-400, s. 7.)

§ 90-21.19A: Reserved for future codification purposes.

§ 90-21.19B. Verdicts and awards of damages in medical malpractice actions; form.

In any malpractice action, any verdict or award of damages, if supported by the evidence, shall indicate specifically what amount, if any, is awarded for noneconomic damages. If applicable, the court shall instruct the jury on the definition of noneconomic damages under G.S. 90-21.19(b). (2011-400, s. 8.)

Article 1C.

Physicians and Hospital Reports.

§ 90-21.20. Reporting by physicians and hospitals of wounds, injuries and illnesses.

(a)   Such cases of wounds, injuries or illnesses as are enumerated in subsection (b) shall be reported as soon as it becomes practicable before, during or after completion of treatment of a person suffering such wounds, injuries, or illnesses. If such case is treated in a hospital, sanitarium or other medical institution or facility, such report shall be made by the Director, Administrator, or other person designated by the Director or Administrator, or if such case is treated elsewhere, such report shall be made by the physician or surgeon treating the case, to the chief of police or the police authorities of the city or town of this State in which the hospital or other institution, or place of treatment is located. If such hospital or other institution or place of treatment is located outside the corporate limits of a city or town, then the report shall be made by the proper person in the manner set forth above to the sheriff of the respective county or to one of his deputies.

(b)   Cases of wounds, injuries or illnesses which shall be reported by physicians, and hospitals include every case of a bullet wound, gunshot wound, powder burn or any other injury arising from or caused by, or appearing to arise from or be caused by, the discharge of a gun or firearm, every case of illness apparently caused by poisoning, every case of a wound or injury caused, or apparently caused, by a knife or sharp or pointed instrument if it appears to the physician or surgeon treating the case that a criminal act was involved, and every case of a wound, injury or illness in which there is grave bodily harm or grave illness if it appears to the physician or surgeon treating the case that the wound, injury or illness resulted from a criminal act of violence.

(c)   Each report made pursuant to subsections (a) and (b) above shall state the name of the wounded, ill or injured person, if known, and the age, sex, race, residence or present location, if known, and the character and extent of his injuries.

(c1) In addition to the reporting requirements of subsection (b) of this section, cases involving recurrent illness or serious physical injury to any child under the age of 18 years where the illness or injury appears, in the physician's professional judgment, to be the result of non-accidental trauma shall be reported by the physician as soon as it becomes practicable before, during, or after completion of treatment. If the case is treated in a hospital, sanitarium, or other medical institution or facility, the report shall be made by the Director, Administrator, or other person designated by the Director or Administrator of the medical institution or facility, or if the case is treated elsewhere, the report shall be made by the physician or surgeon treating the case to the chief of police or the police authorities of the city or town in this State in which the hospital or other institution or place of treatment is located. If the hospital or other institution or place of treatment is located outside the corporate limits of a city or town, then the report shall be made by the proper person in the manner set forth above to the sheriff of the respective county or to one of the sheriff's deputies. This reporting requirement is in addition to the duty set forth in G.S. 7B-301 to report child abuse, neglect, dependence, or the death of any juvenile as the result of maltreatment to the director of the department of social services in the county where the juvenile resides or is found.

(d) Any hospital, sanitarium, or other like institution or Director, Administrator, or other designated person, or physician or surgeon participating in good faith in the making of a report pursuant to this section shall have immunity from any liability, civil or criminal, that might otherwise be incurred or imposed as the result of the making of such report. (1971, c. 4; 1977, c. 31; c. 843, s. 2; 2008-179, s. 1.)

§ 90-21.20A. Reporting by physicians of pilots' mental or physical disabilities or infirmities.

(a) A physician who reports to a government agency responsible for pilots' licenses or certificates or a government agency responsible for air safety that a pilot or an applicant for a pilot's license or certificate suffers from or probably suffers from a physical disability or infirmity that the physician believes will or reasonably could affect the person's ability to safely operate an aircraft shall have immunity, civil or criminal, that might otherwise be incurred or imposed as the result of making such a report.

(b) A physician who gives testimony about a pilot's or an applicant's mental or physical disability or infirmity in any administrative hearing or other proceeding held to consider the issuance, renewal, revocation, or suspension of a pilot's license or certificate shall have immunity from any liability, civil or criminal, that might otherwise be incurred or imposed as the result of such testimony. (1997-464, s. 2.)

§ 90-21.20B. Access to and disclosure of medical information for certain purposes.

(a) Notwithstanding G.S. 8-53 or any other provision of law, a health care provider may disclose to a law enforcement officer protected health information only to the extent that the information may be disclosed under the federal Standards for Privacy of Individually Identifiable Health Information, 45 C.F.R. § 164.512(f) and is not specifically prohibited from disclosure by other state or federal law.

(a1) Notwithstanding any other provision of law, if a person is involved in a vehicle crash:

(1) Any health care provider who is providing medical treatment to the person shall, upon request, disclose to any law enforcement officer investigating the crash the following information about the person: name, current location, and whether the person appears to be impaired by alcohol, drugs, or another substance.

(2) Law enforcement officers shall be provided access to visit and interview the person upon request, except when the health care provider requests temporary privacy for medical reasons.

(3) A health care provider shall disclose a certified copy of all identifiable health information related to that person as specified in a search warrant or an order issued by a judicial official.

(b) A prosecutor or law enforcement officer receiving identifiable health information under this section shall not disclose this information to others except as necessary to the investigation or otherwise allowed by law.

(c) A certified copy of identifiable health information, if relevant, shall be admissible in any hearing or trial without further authentication.

(d) As used in this section, "health care provider" has the same meaning as in G.S. 90-21.11.

(e) Notwithstanding G.S. 8-53 or any other provision of law, a health care provider may disclose protected health information for purposes of treatment, payment, or health care operations to the extent that disclosure is permitted under 45 C.F.R. § 164.506 and is not specifically prohibited by other state or federal law. As used in this subsection, "treatment, payment, or health care operations" are as defined in the Standards for Privacy of Individually Identifiable Health Information. (2006-253, s. 17; 2007-115, s. 3.)

§ 90-21.21: Repealed by Session Laws 1979, c. 529, s. 1.

Article 1D.

Peer Review.

§ 90-21.22. Peer review agreements.

(a) The North Carolina Medical Board may, under rules adopted by the Board in compliance with Chapter 150B of the General Statutes, enter into agreements with the North Carolina Medical Society and its local medical society components, and with the North Carolina Academy of Physician Assistants for the purpose of conducting peer review activities. Peer review activities to be covered by such agreements shall include investigation, review, and evaluation of records, reports, complaints, litigation and other information about the practices and practice patterns of physicians licensed by the Board, and of physician assistants approved by the Board, and shall include programs for impaired physicians and impaired physician assistants. Agreements between the Academy and the Board shall be limited to programs for impaired physicians and physician assistants and shall not include any other peer review activities.

(b) Peer review agreements shall include provisions for the society and for the Academy to receive relevant information from the Board and other sources, conduct the investigation and review in an expeditious manner, provide assurance of confidentiality of nonpublic information and of the review process, make reports of investigations and evaluations to the Board, and to do other related activities for promoting a coordinated and effective peer review process. Peer review agreements shall include provisions assuring due process.

(c)   Each society which enters a peer review agreement with the Board shall establish and maintain a program for impaired physicians licensed by the Board. The Academy, after entering a peer review agreement with the Board, shall either enter an agreement with the North Carolina Medical Society for the inclusion of physician assistants in the Society's program for impaired physicians, or shall establish and maintain the Academy's own program for impaired physician assistants. The purpose of the programs shall be to identify, review, and evaluate the ability of those physicians and physician assistants to function in their professional capacity and to provide programs for treatment and rehabilitation. The Board may provide funds for the administration of impaired physician and impaired physician assistant programs and shall adopt rules with provisions for definitions of impairment; guidelines for program elements; procedures for receipt and use of information of suspected impairment; procedures for intervention and referral; monitoring treatment, rehabilitation, post-treatment support and performance; reports of individual cases to the Board; periodic reporting of statistical information; assurance of confidentiality of nonpublic information and of the review process.

(d)   Upon investigation and review of a physician licensed by the Board, or a physician assistant approved by the Board, or upon receipt of a complaint or other information, a society which enters a peer review agreement with the Board, or the Academy if it has a peer review agreement with the Board, as appropriate, shall report immediately to the Board detailed information about any physician or physician assistant licensed or approved by the Board if:

(1)   The physician or physician assistant constitutes an imminent danger to the public or to himself by reason of impairment, mental illness, physical illness, the commission of professional sexual boundary violations, or any other reason;

(2)   The physician or physician assistant refuses to cooperate with the program, refuses to submit to treatment, or is still impaired after treatment and exhibits professional incompetence; or

(3)   It reasonably appears that there are other grounds for disciplinary action.

(e) Any confidential patient information and other nonpublic information acquired, created, or used in good faith by the Academy or a society pursuant to this section shall remain confidential and shall not be subject to discovery or subpoena in a civil case. No person participating in good faith in the peer review or impaired physician or impaired physician assistant programs of this section shall be required in a civil case to disclose any information acquired or opinions, recommendations, or evaluations acquired or developed solely in the course of participating in any agreements pursuant to this section.

(f) Peer review activities conducted in good faith pursuant to any agreement under this section shall not be grounds for civil action under the laws of this State and are deemed to be State directed and sanctioned and shall constitute State action for the purposes of application of antitrust laws. (1987, c. 859, s. 15; 1993, c. 176, s. 1; 1995, c. 94, s. 23; 2006-144, s. 8.)

§ 90-21.22A. Medical review and quality assurance committees.

(a) As used in this section, the following terms mean:

(1) "Medical review committee." - A committee composed of health care providers licensed under this Chapter that is formed for the purpose of evaluating the quality of, cost of, or necessity for health care services, including provider credentialing. "Medical review committee" does not mean a medical review committee established under G.S. 131E-95.

(2) "Quality assurance committee." - Risk management employees of an insurer licensed to write medical professional liability insurance in this State, who work in collaboration with health care providers licensed under this Chapter, and insured by that insurer, to evaluate and improve the quality of health care services.

(b) A member of a duly appointed medical review or quality assurance committee who acts without malice or fraud shall not be subject to liability for damages in any civil action on account of any act, statement, or proceeding undertaken, made, or performed within the scope of the functions of the committee.

(c) The proceedings of a medical review or quality assurance committee, the records and materials it produces, and the materials it considers shall be confidential and not considered public records within the meaning of G.S. 132-1, 131E-309, or 58-2-100; and shall not be subject to discovery or introduction into evidence in any civil action against a provider of health care services who directly provides services and is licensed under this Chapter, a PSO licensed under Article 17 of Chapter 131E of the General Statutes, an ambulatory surgical facility licensed under Chapter 131E of the General Statutes, or a hospital licensed under Chapter 122C or Chapter 131E of the General Statutes or that is owned or operated by the State, which civil action results from matters that are the subject of evaluation and review by the committee. No person who was in attendance at a meeting of the committee shall be required to testify in any civil action as to any evidence or other matters produced or presented during the proceedings of the committee or as to any findings, recommendations, evaluations, opinions, or other actions of the committee or its members. However, information, documents, or records otherwise available are not immune from discovery or use in a civil action merely because they were presented during proceedings of the committee. Documents otherwise available as public records within the meaning of G.S. 132-1 do not lose their status as public records merely because they were presented or considered during proceedings of the committee. A member of the committee may testify in a civil action but cannot be asked about the person's testimony before the committee or any opinions formed as a result of the committee hearings.

(d) This section applies to a medical review committee, including a medical review committee appointed by one of the entities licensed under Articles 1 through 67 of Chapter 58 of the General Statutes.

(e) Subsection (c) of this section does not apply to proceedings initiated under G.S. 58-50-61 or G.S. 58-50-62. (1997-519, s. 4.3; 1998-227, s. 3; 2002-179, s. 18; 2004-149, s. 2.6.)

§ 90-21.23. Election by State.

For the purpose of making applicable in the State the early opt-in provisions of Title 4 of the "Health Care Quality Improvement Act of 1986," P.L. 99-660, the State elects to exercise on October 1, 1987, the provisions of Title 4, Section 411(c)(2)(A) of that act to promote good faith professional review activities. (1987, c. 859, s. 19.)

Article 1E.

Certificate of Public Advantage.

§ 90-21.24. Findings.

The General Assembly of North Carolina makes the following findings:

(1)   That technological and scientific developments in health care have enhanced the prospects for further improvement in the quality of care provided to North Carolina citizens.

(2)   That the cost of improved technology and improved scientific methods for the provision of health care contributes substantially to the increasing cost of health care. Cost increases make it increasingly difficult for physicians in rural areas of North Carolina to offer care.

(3)   That cooperative agreements among physicians, hospitals, and others for the provision of health care services may foster improvements in the quality of health care for North Carolina citizens, moderate increases in cost, and improve access to needed services in rural areas of North Carolina.

(4)   That physicians are often in the best position to identify and structure cooperative arrangements that enhance quality of care, improve access, and achieve cost-efficiency in the provision of care.

(5)   That federal and State antitrust laws may prohibit or discourage cooperative arrangements that are beneficial to North Carolina citizens, despite their potential for or actual reduction in competition, and that such agreements should be permitted and encouraged.

(6)   That competition as currently mandated by federal and State antitrust laws should be supplanted by a regulatory program to permit and encourage cooperative agreements between physicians or between physicians, hospitals, and others, that are beneficial to North Carolina citizens when the benefits of cooperative agreements outweigh their disadvantages caused by their potential or actual adverse effects on competition.

(7)   That regulatory as well as judicial oversight of cooperative agreements should be provided to ensure that the benefits of cooperative agreements permitted and encouraged in North Carolina outweigh any disadvantages attributable to any reduction in competition likely to result from the agreements. (1995, c. 395, s. 2.)

§ 90-21.25. Definitions.

As used in this Article, the following terms have the meanings specified:

(1)   "Attorney General" means the Attorney General of the State of North Carolina, or any attorney to whom the Attorney General delegates authority and responsibility to act pursuant to this Article.

(2)   "Cooperative agreement" means an agreement among two or more physicians, or between a physician, hospital, or any other person or persons, for the sharing, allocation, or referral of patients, personnel, instructional programs, support services and facilities, or medical, diagnostic, or laboratory facilities or equipment, or procedures or other services traditionally offered by physicians. Cooperative agreement shall not include any agreement that would permit self-referrals of patients by a health care provider that is otherwise prohibited by law.

(3)   "Department" means the North Carolina Department of Health and Human Services.

(4)   "Federal or State antitrust laws" means any and all federal or State laws prohibiting monopolies or agreements in restraint of trade, including, but not limited to, the federal Sherman Act, Clayton Act, and Federal Trade Commission Act, and the North Carolina laws codified in Chapter 75 of the General Statutes.

(5)   "Hospital" means any hospital required to be licensed under Chapter 131E or 122C of the General Statutes.

(6)   "Person" means any individual, firm, partnership, corporation, association, public or private institution, political subdivision, or government agency.

(7) "Physician" means an individual licensed to practice medicine pursuant to Article 1 of this Chapter. (1995, c. 395, s. 2; 1997-443, s. 11A.118(a).)

§ 90-21.26. Certificate of public advantage; application.

(a) A physician and any person who is a party to a cooperative agreement with a physician may negotiate, enter into, and conduct business pursuant to a cooperative agreement without being subject to damages, liability, or scrutiny under any State antitrust law if a certificate of public advantage is issued for the cooperative agreement, or in the case of activities to negotiate or enter into a cooperative agreement, if an application for a certificate of public advantage is filed in good faith. It is the intention of the General Assembly that immunity from federal antitrust laws shall also be conferred by this statute and the State regulatory program that it establishes.

(b) Parties to a cooperative agreement may apply to the Department for a certificate of public advantage governing that cooperative agreement. The application must include an executed written copy of the cooperative agreement or letter of intent with respect to the agreement, a description of the nature and scope of the activities and cooperation in the agreement, any consideration passing to any party under the agreement, and any additional materials necessary to fully explain the agreement and its likely effects. A copy of the application and all additional related materials shall be submitted to the Attorney General at the same time the application is made to the Department. (1995, c. 395, s. 2.)

§ 90-21.27. Procedure for review; standards for review.

(a) The Department shall review the application in accordance with the standards set forth in subsection (b) of this section and shall hold a public hearing with the opportunity for the submission of oral and written public comments in accordance with rules adopted by the Department. The Department shall determine whether the application should be granted or denied within 90 days of the date of filing of an application. Provided, however, that the Department may extend the review period for a specified period of time upon notice to the parties.

(b) The Department shall determine that a certificate of public advantage should be issued for a cooperative agreement, if it determines that the applicant has demonstrated by clear and convincing evidence that the benefits likely to result from the agreement outweigh the disadvantages likely to result from a reduction in competition from the agreement.

(1) In evaluating the potential benefits of a cooperative agreement, the Department shall consider whether one or more of the following benefits may result from the cooperative agreement:

a. Enhancement of the quality of health care provided to North Carolina citizens;

b. Preservation of other health care facilities in geographical proximity to the communities traditionally served by those facilities;

c. Lower costs of, or gains in the efficiency of delivering, health care services;

d. Improvements in the utilization of health care resources and equipment;

e. Avoidance of duplication of health care resources; and

f. The extent to which medically underserved populations are expected to utilize the proposed services.

(2) In evaluating the potential disadvantages of a cooperative agreement, the Department shall consider whether one or more of the following disadvantages may result from the cooperative agreement:

a. The extent to which the agreement may increase the costs or prices of health care at the locations of parties to the cooperative agreement;

b. The extent to which the agreement may have an adverse impact on patients in the quality, availability, and price of health care services;

c. The extent to which the agreement may reduce competition among the parties to the agreement and the likely effects thereof;

d. The extent to which the agreement may have an adverse impact on the ability of health maintenance organizations, preferred provider organizations, managed health care service agents, or other health care payors to negotiate optimal payment and service arrangements with hospitals, physicians, allied health care professionals, or other health care providers;

e. The extent to which the agreement may result in a reduction in competition among physicians, allied health professionals, other health care providers, or other persons furnishing health care services; and

f. The availability of arrangements that are less restrictive to competition and achieve the same benefits or a more favorable balance of benefits over disadvantages attributable to any reduction in competition.

(3) In making its determination, the Department may consider other benefits or disadvantages that may be identified. (1995, c. 395, s. 2; 1997-456, s. 27.)

§ 90-21.28. Issuance of a certificate.

If the Department determines that the likely benefits of a cooperative agreement outweigh the likely disadvantages attributable to reduction of competition as a result of the agreement by clear and convincing evidence, and the Attorney General has not stated any objection to issuance of a certificate during the review period, the Department shall issue a certificate of public advantage for the cooperative agreement at the conclusion of the review period. Such certificate shall include any conditions of operation under the agreement that the Department, in consultation with the Attorney General, determines to be appropriate in order to ensure that the cooperative agreement and activities engaged in pursuant thereto are consistent with this Article and its purpose to limit health care costs. The Department shall include conditions to control prices of health care services provided under the cooperative agreement. Consideration shall be given to assure that access to health care is provided to all areas of the State. The Department shall publish its decisions on applications for certificates of public advantage in the North Carolina Register. (1995, c. 395, s. 2.)

§ 90-21.29. Objection by Attorney General.

If the Attorney General is not persuaded that the applicant has demonstrated by clear and convincing evidence that the benefits likely to result from the agreement outweigh the likely disadvantages of any reduction of competition to result from the agreement as set forth in G.S. 90-21.27, the Attorney General may, within the review period, state an objection to the issuance of a certificate of public advantage and may extend the review period for a specified period of time. Notice of the objection and any extension of the review period shall be provided in writing to the applicant, together with a general explanation of the concerns of the Attorney General. The parties may attempt to reach agreement with the Attorney General on modifications to the agreement or to conditions in the certificate so that the Attorney General no longer objects to issuance of a certificate. If the Attorney General withdraws the objection and the Department maintains its determination that a certificate should be issued, the Department shall issue a certificate of public advantage with any appropriate conditions as soon as practicable following withdrawal of the objection. If the Attorney General does not withdraw the objection, a certificate shall not be issued. (1995, c. 395, s. 2.)

§ 90-21.30. Record keeping.

The Department shall maintain on file all cooperative agreements for which certificates of public advantage are in effect and a copy of the certificate, including any conditions imposed. Any party to a cooperative agreement who terminates an agreement shall file a notice of termination with the Department within 30 days after termination. These files shall be public records as set forth in Chapter 132 of the General Statutes. (1995, c. 395, s. 2.)

§ 90-21.31. Review after issuance of certificate.

If at any time following the issuance of a certificate of public advantage, the Department or the Attorney General has questions concerning whether the parties to the cooperative agreement have complied with any condition of the certificate or whether the benefits or likely benefits resulting from a cooperative agreement may no longer outweigh the disadvantages or likely disadvantages attributable to a reduction in competition resulting from the agreement, the Department or the Attorney General shall advise the parties to the agreement and either the Department or the Attorney General shall request any information necessary to complete a review of the matter. (1995, c. 395, s. 2.)

§ 90-21.32. Periodic reports.

(a)   During the time that a certificate is in effect, a report of activities pursuant to the cooperative agreement must be filed every two years with the Department on or by the anniversary day on which the certificate was issued. A copy of the periodic report shall be submitted to the Attorney General at the same time it is filed with the Department. A report shall include all of the following:

(1)   A description of the activities conducted pursuant to the agreement.

(2)   Price and cost information.

(3)   The nature and scope of the activities pursuant to the agreement anticipated for the next two years and the likely effect of those activities.

(4)   A signed certificate by each party to the agreement that the benefits or likely benefits of the cooperative agreement as conditioned continue to outweigh the disadvantages or likely disadvantages of any reduction in competition from the agreement as conditioned.

(5)   Any additional information requested by the Department or the Attorney General.

The Department shall give public notice in the North Carolina Register that a report has been received. After notice is given, the public shall have 30 days to file written comments on the report and on the benefits and disadvantages of continuing the certificate of public advantage. Periodic reports, public comments, and information submitted in response to a request shall be public records as set forth in Chapter 132 of the General Statutes.

(b)   Failure to file a periodic report required by this section after notice of default, or failure to provide information requested pursuant to a review under G.S. 90-21.31 are grounds for revocation of the certificate by the Attorney General or the Department.

(c) The Department shall review each periodic report, public comments, and information submitted in response to a request under G.S. 90-21.31 to determine whether the advantages or likely advantages of the cooperative agreement continue to outweigh the disadvantages or likely disadvantages of any reduction in competition from the agreement, and to determine what, if any, changes in the conditions of the certificate should be made. In the review the Department shall consider the benefits and disadvantages set forth in G.S. 90-21.27. Within 60 days of the filing of a periodic report, the Department shall determine whether the certificate should remain in effect and whether any changes to the conditions in the certificate should be made. Provided, however, that the Department may extend the review period an additional 30 days. If the Department or Attorney General determines that the parties to the cooperative agreement have not complied with any condition of the certificate, the Department or the Attorney General shall revoke the certificate and the parties shall be notified. If the certificate is revoked, the parties shall be entitled to no benefits under this Article, beginning on the date of revocation. If the Department determines that the certificate should remain in effect and the Attorney General has not stated any objection to the certificate remaining in effect during the review period, the certificate shall remain in effect subject to any changes in the conditions of the certificate imposed by the Department. The parties shall be notified in writing of the Department's decision and of any changes in the conditions of the certificate. The Department shall publish its decision and any changes in the conditions in the North Carolina Register.

If the Department determines that the benefits or likely benefits of the agreement and the unavoidable costs of terminating the agreement do not continue to outweigh the disadvantages or likely disadvantages of any reduction in competition from the agreement, or if the Attorney General objects to the certificate remaining in effect based upon a review of the benefits and disadvantages set forth in G.S. 90-21.27, the Department shall notify the parties to the agreement in writing of its determination or the objections of the Attorney General and shall provide a summary of any concerns of the Department or Attorney General to the parties. (1995, c. 395, s. 2.)

§ 90-21.33. Right to judicial action.

(a) Any applicant or other person aggrieved by a decision to issue or not issue a certificate of public advantage is entitled to judicial review of the action or inaction in superior court. Suit for judicial review under this subsection shall be filed within 30 days of public notice of the decision to issue or deny issuance of the certificate. To prevail in any action for judicial review brought under this subsection, the plaintiff or petitioner must establish that the determination by the Department or the Attorney General was arbitrary or capricious.

(b) Any party or other person aggrieved by a decision to allow the certificate to remain in effect or to make changes in the conditions of the certificate is entitled to judicial review of the decision in superior court. Suit for judicial review under this subsection shall be filed within 30 days of public notice of the decision to allow the certificate to remain in effect or to make changes in the conditions of the certificate. To prevail in any action for judicial review brought under this subsection, the plaintiff or petitioner must establish that the determination by the Department or the Attorney General was arbitrary or capricious.

(c) If the Department or the Attorney General determines the certificate should not remain in effect, the Attorney General may bring suit in the Superior Court of Wake County on behalf of the Department or on its own behalf to seek an order to authorize the cancellation of the certificate. To prevail in the action, the Attorney General must establish that the benefits resulting from the agreement are outweighed by the disadvantages attributable to reduction in competition resulting from the agreement.

(d) In any action instituted under this section, the work product of the Department or the Attorney General or his staff is not a public record under Chapter 132 of the General Statutes and shall not be discoverable or admissible, nor shall the Attorney General or any member of the Attorney General's staff be compelled to be a witness, whether in discovery or at any hearing or trial. (1995, c. 395, s. 2.)

§ 90-21.34. Fees for applications and periodic reports.

(a) The Department and the Attorney General shall establish and collect administrative fees for filing of an application for a certificate of public advantage based on the total cost of the project for which the application is made, in an amount not to exceed fifteen thousand dollars ($15,000), and an administrative fee for filing each periodic report required to be filed in an amount not to exceed two thousand five hundred dollars ($2,500). The fee schedule established should generate sufficient revenue to offset the costs of the program. An application filing fee must be paid to the Department at the time an application for a certificate of public advantage is submitted pursuant to G.S. 90-21.26. A periodic report filing fee must be paid to the Department at the time a periodic report is submitted to it pursuant to G.S. 90-21.32.

(b)   If the Department or the Attorney General determines that consultants are needed to complete a review of an application, an additional application fee may be established by prior agreement with the applicants before the application is considered. The amount of the additional fee may not exceed the costs of contracting with the necessary consultants. The additional fee shall not be considered in determining whether an application fee exceeds the maximum application fee amount set in subsection (a) of this section. (1995, c. 395, s. 2.)

§ 90-21.35. Department and Attorney General authority.

The Department and Attorney General shall adopt rules to conduct review of applications for certificates of public advantage and of periodic reports filed in connection therewith and to bring actions in the Superior Court of Wake County as required under G.S. 90-21.33. This Article shall not limit the authority of the Attorney General under federal or State antitrust laws. (1995, c. 395, s. 2.)

§ 90-21.36. Effects of certificate of public advantage; other laws.

(a)   Activities conducted pursuant to a cooperative agreement for which a certificate of public advantage has been issued are immunized from challenge or scrutiny under State antitrust laws. In addition, conduct in negotiating and entering into a cooperative agreement for which an application for a certificate of public advantage is filed in good faith shall be immune from challenge or scrutiny under State antitrust laws, regardless of whether a certificate is issued. It is the intention of the General Assembly that this Article shall also immunize covered activities from challenge or scrutiny under any noncompetition provisions of the federal antitrust law.

(b)   Nothing in this Article shall exempt physicians or others from compliance with State or federal laws governing certificate of need, licensure, or other regulatory requirements.

(c) Any dispute among the parties to cooperative agreement concerning its meaning or terms is governed by normal principles of contract law. (1995, c. 395, s. 2.)

§§ 90-21.37 through 90-21.40. Reserved for future codification purposes.

Article 1F.

Psychotherapy Patient/Client Sexual Exploitation Act.

§ 90-21.41. Definitions.

The following definitions apply in this Article:

(1) Client. - A person who may also be called patient or counselee who seeks or obtains psychotherapy, whether or not the person is charged for the service. The term "client" includes a former client.

(2) Psychotherapist. - A psychiatrist licensed in accordance with Article 1 of Chapter 90 of the General Statutes, a psychologist as defined in G.S. 90-270.2(9), a licensed professional counselor as defined in G.S. 90-330(a)(2), a substance abuse professional as defined in G.S. 90-113.31(8), a social worker engaged in a clinical social work practice as defined in G.S. 90B-3(6), a fee-based pastoral counselor as defined in G.S. 90-382(4), a licensed marriage and family therapist as defined in G.S. 90-270.47(3), or a mental health service provider, who performs or purports to perform psychotherapy.

(3) Psychotherapy. - The professional treatment or professional counseling of a mental or emotional condition that includes revelation by the client of intimate details of thoughts and emotions of a very personal nature to assist the client in modifying behavior, thoughts and emotions that are maladjustive or contribute to difficulties in living.

(4) Sexual exploitation. - Either of the following, whether or not it occurred with the consent of a client or during any treatment, consultation, evaluation, interview, or examination:

a. Sexual contact which includes any of the following actions:

1. Sexual intercourse, cunnilingus, fellatio, anal intercourse, or any intrusion, however slight, into the oral, genital, or anal openings of the client's body by any part of the psychotherapist's body or by any object used by the psychotherapist for the purpose of sexual stimulation or gratification of either the psychotherapist or the client; or any intrusion, however slight, into the oral, genital, or anal openings of the psychotherapist's body by any part of the client's body or by any object used by the client for the purpose of sexual stimulation or gratification of either the psychotherapist or the client, if agreed to, or not resisted by the psychotherapist.

2. Kissing of, or the intentional touching by the psychotherapist of, the client's lips, genital area, groin, inner thigh, buttocks, or breast, or of the clothing covering any of these body parts, for the purpose of sexual stimulation or gratification of either the psychotherapist or the client, or kissing of, or the intentional touching by the client of, the psychotherapist's lips, genital area, groin, inner thigh, buttocks, or breast, or of the clothing covering any of these body parts, if agreed to or not resisted by the psychotherapist, for the purpose of sexual stimulation or gratification to either the psychotherapist or the client.

b. Any act done or statement made by the psychotherapist for the purpose of sexual stimulation or gratification of the client or psychotherapist which includes any of the following actions:

1. The psychotherapist's relating to the client the psychotherapist's own sexual fantasies or the details of the psychotherapist's own sexual life.

2. The uncovering or display of breasts or genitals of the psychotherapist to the client.

3. The showing of sexually graphic pictures to the client for purposes other than diagnosis or treatment.

4. Statements containing sexual innuendo, sexual threats, or sexual suggestions regarding the relationship between the psychotherapist and the client.

(5) Sexual history. - Sexual activity of the client other than that conduct alleged by the client to constitute sexual exploitation in an action pursuant to this Article.

(6) Therapeutic deception. - A representation by a psychotherapist that sexual contact with the psychotherapist is consistent with or part of the client's treatment. (1998-213, s. 1.)

§ 90-21.42. Action for sexual exploitation.

Any client who is sexually exploited by the client's psychotherapist shall have remedy by civil action for sexual exploitation if the sexual exploitation occurred:

(1) At any time between and including the first date and last date the client was receiving psychotherapy from the psychotherapist;

(2) Within three years after the termination of the psychotherapy; or

(3) By means of therapeutic deception. (1998-213, s. 1.)

§ 90-21.43. Remedies.

A person found to have been sexually exploited as provided under this Article may recover from the psychotherapist actual or nominal damages, and reasonable attorneys' fees as the court may allow. The trier of fact may award punitive damages in accordance with the provisions of Chapter 1D of the General Statutes. (1998-213, s. 1.)

§ 90-21.44. Scope of discovery.

(a) In an action under this Article, evidence of the client's sexual history is not subject to discovery, except under the following conditions:

(1) The client claims impairment of sexual functioning.

(2) The psychotherapist requests a hearing prior to conducting discovery and makes an offer of proof of the relevancy of the evidence, and the court finds

that the information is relevant and that the probative value of the history outweighs its prejudicial effect.

(b)   The court shall allow the discovery only of specific information or examples of the client's conduct that are determined by the court to be relevant. The court order shall detail the information or conduct that is subject to discovery. (1998-213, s. 1.)

§ 90-21.45. Admissibility of evidence of sexual history.

(a)   At the trial of an action under this Article, evidence of the client's sexual history is not admissible unless:

(1)   The psychotherapist requests a hearing prior to trial and makes an offer of proof of the relevancy of the sexual history; and

(2)   The court finds that, in the interest of justice, the evidence is relevant and that the probative value of the evidence substantially outweighs its prejudicial effect.

(b)   The court shall allow the admission only of specific information or examples of instances of the client's conduct that are determined by the court to be relevant. The court's order shall detail the conduct that is admissible, and no other such evidence may be introduced.

(c)   Sexual history otherwise admissible pursuant to this section may not be proved by reputation or opinion. (1998-213, s. 1.)

§ 90-21.46. Prohibited defense.

It shall not be a defense in any action brought pursuant to this Article that the client consented to the sexual exploitation or that the sexual contact with a client occurred outside a therapy or treatment session or that it occurred off the premises regularly used by the psychotherapist for therapy or treatment sessions. (1998-213, s. 1.)

§ 90-21.47. Statute of limitations.

An action for sexual exploitation must be commenced within three years after the cause of action accrues. A cause of action for sexual exploitation accrues at the later of either:

(1) The last act of the psychotherapist giving rise to the cause of action.

(2) At the time the client discovers or reasonably should discover that the sexual exploitation occurred; however, no cause of action shall be commenced more than 10 years from the last act of the psychotherapist giving rise to the cause of action. (1998-213, s. 1.)

§ 90-21.48. Agreements to not pursue complaint before licensing entity void.

Any provision of a settlement agreement of a claim based in whole or part on an allegation of sexual exploitation as defined in this Article, which prohibits a party from initiating or pursuing a complaint before the regulatory entity responsible for overseeing the conduct or licensing of the psychotherapist, is void. (1998-213, s. 1.)

§ 90-21.49. Reserved for future codification purposes.

Article 1G.

Health Care Liability.

§ 90-21.50. Definitions.

As used in this Article, unless the context clearly indicates otherwise, the term:

(1) "Health benefit plan" means an accident and health insurance policy or certificate; a nonprofit hospital or medical service corporation contract; a health maintenance organization subscriber contract; a self-insured indemnity program

or prepaid hospital and medical benefits plan offered under the State Health Plan for Teachers and State Employees and subject to the requirements of Article 3 of Chapter 135 of the General Statutes, a plan provided by a multiple employer welfare arrangement; or a plan provided by another benefit arrangement, to the extent permitted by the Employee Retirement Income Security Act of 1974, as amended, or by any waiver of or other exception to that act provided under federal law or regulation. Except for the Health Insurance Program for Children established under Part 8 of Article 2 of Chapter 108A of the General Statutes, "Health benefit plan" does not mean any plan implemented or administered by the North Carolina or United States Department of Health and Human Services, or any successor agency, or its representatives. "Health benefit plan" does not mean any of the following kinds of insurance:

a. Accident.

b. Credit.

c. Disability income.

d. Long-term or nursing home care.

e. Medicare supplement.

f. Specified disease.

g. Dental or vision.

h. Coverage issued as a supplement to liability insurance.

i. Workers' compensation.

j. Medical payments under automobile or homeowners.

k. Hospital income or indemnity.

l. Insurance under which benefits are payable with or without regard to fault and that is statutorily required to be contained in any liability policy or equivalent self-insurance.

m. Short-term limited duration health insurance policies as defined in Part 144 of Title 45 of the Code of Federal Regulations.

(2) "Health care decision" means a determination that is made by a managed care entity and is subject to external review under Part 4 of Article 50 of Chapter 58 of the General Statutes and is also a determination that:

a. Is a noncertification, as defined in G.S. 58-50-61, of a prospective or concurrent request for health care services, and

b. Affects the quality of the diagnosis, care, or treatment provided to an enrollee or insured of the health benefit plan.

(3) "Health care provider" means:

a. An individual who is licensed, certified, or otherwise authorized under this Chapter to provide health care services in the ordinary course of business or practice of a profession or in an approved education or training program; or

b. A health care facility, licensed under Chapters 131E or 122C of the General Statutes, where health care services are provided to patients;

"Health care provider" includes: (i) an agent or employee of a health care facility that is licensed, certified, or otherwise authorized to provide health care services; (ii) the officers and directors of a health care facility; and (iii) an agent or employee of a health care provider who is licensed, certified, or otherwise authorized to provide health care services.

(4) "Health care service" means a health or medical procedure or service rendered by a health care provider that:

a. Provides testing, diagnosis, or treatment of a health condition, illness, injury, or disease; or

b. Dispenses drugs, medical devices, medical appliances, or medical goods for the treatment of a health condition, illness, injury, or disease.

(5) "Insured or enrollee" means a person that is insured by or enrolled in a health benefit plan under a policy, plan, certificate, or contract issued or delivered in this State by an insurer.

(6) "Insurer" means an entity that writes a health benefit plan and that is an insurance company subject to Chapter 58 of the General Statutes, a service corporation organized under Article 65 of Chapter 58 of the General Statutes, a health maintenance organization organized under Article 67 of Chapter 58 of the General Statutes, a self-insured health maintenance organization or managed care entity operated or administered by or under contract with the Executive Administrator and Board of Trustees of the State Health Plan for Teachers and State Employees pursuant to Article 3 of Chapter 135 of the General Statutes, a multiple employer welfare arrangement subject to Article 49 of Chapter 58 of the General Statutes, or the State Health Plan for Teachers and State Employees.

(7) "Managed care entity" means an insurer that:

a. Delivers, administers, or undertakes to provide for, arrange for, or reimburse for health care services or assumes the risk for the delivery of health care services; and

b. Has a system or technique to control or influence the quality, accessibility, utilization, or costs and prices of health care services delivered or to be delivered to a defined enrollee population.

Except for the State Health Plan for Teachers and State Employees and the Health Insurance Program for Children, "managed care entity" does not include: (i) an employer purchasing coverage or acting on behalf of its employees or the employees of one or more subsidiaries or affiliated corporations of the employer, or (ii) a health care provider.

(8) "Ordinary care" means that degree of care that, under the same or similar circumstances, a managed care entity of ordinary prudence would have used at the time the managed care entity made the health care decision.

(9) "Physician" means:

a. An individual licensed to practice medicine in this State;

b. A professional association or corporation organized under Chapter 55B of the General Statutes; or

c. A person or entity wholly owned by physicians.

(10) "Successor external review process" means an external review process equivalent in all respects to G.S. 58-50-75 through G.S. 58-50-95 that is approved by the Department and implemented by a health benefit plan in the event that G.S. 58-50-75 through G.S. 58-50-95 are found by a court of competent jurisdiction to be void, unenforceable, or preempted by federal law, in whole or in part. (2001-446, s. 4.7; 2007-323, s. 28.22A(o); 2007-345, s. 12.)

§ 90-21.51. Duty to exercise ordinary care; liability for damages for harm.

(a) Each managed care entity for a health benefit plan has the duty to exercise ordinary care when making health care decisions and is liable for damages for harm to an insured or enrollee proximately caused by its failure to exercise ordinary care.

(b) In addition to the duty imposed under subsection (a) of this section, each managed care entity for a health benefit plan is liable for damages for harm to an insured or enrollee proximately caused by decisions regarding whether or when the insured or enrollee would receive a health care service made by:

(1) Its agents or employees; or

(2) Representatives that are acting on its behalf and over whom it has exercised sufficient influence or control to reasonably affect the actual care and treatment of the insured or enrollee which results in the failure to exercise ordinary care.

(c) It shall be a defense to any action brought under this section against a managed care entity for a health benefit plan that:

(1) The managed care entity and its agents or employees, or representatives for whom the managed care entity is liable under subsection (b) of this section, did not control or influence or advocate for the decision regarding whether or when the insured or enrollee would receive a health care service; or

(2) The managed care entity did not deny or delay payment for any health care service or treatment prescribed or recommended by a physician or health care provider to the insured or enrollee.

(d) In an action brought under this Article against a managed care entity, a finding that a physician or health care provider is an agent or employee of the managed care entity may not be based solely on proof that the physician or health care provider appears in a listing of approved physicians or health care providers made available to insureds or enrollees under the managed care entity's health benefit plan.

(e) An action brought under this Article is not a medical malpractice action as defined in Article 1B of this Chapter. A managed care entity may not use as a defense in an action brought under this Article any law that prohibits the corporate practice of medicine.

(f) A managed care entity shall not be liable for the independent actions of a health care provider, who is not an agent or employee of the managed care entity, when that health care provider fails to exercise the standard of care required by G.S. 90-21.12. A health care provider shall not be liable for the independent actions of a managed care entity when the managed care entity fails to exercise the standard of care required by this Article.

(g) Nothing in this Article shall be construed to create an obligation on the part of a managed care entity to provide to an insured or enrollee a health care service or treatment that is not covered under its health benefit plan.

(h) A managed care entity shall not enter into a contract with a health care provider, or with an employer or employer group organization, that includes an indemnification or hold harmless clause for the acts or conduct of the managed care entity. Any such indemnification or hold harmless clause is void and unenforceable to the extent of the restriction. (2001-446, s. 4.7.)

§ 90-21.52. No liability under this Article on the part of an employer or employer group organization that purchases coverage or assumes risk on behalf of its employees or a physician or health care provider; liability of State Health Plan under State Tort Claims Act.

(a) Except as otherwise provided in subsection (b) of this section, this Article does not create any liability on the part of an employer or employer group purchasing organization that purchases health care coverage or assumes risk on behalf of its employees.

(b)   Liability in tort of the State Health Plan for Teachers and State Employees for its health care decisions shall be under Article 31 of Chapter 143 of the General Statutes.

(c)   This Article does not create any liability on the part of a physician or health care provider in addition to that otherwise imposed under existing law. No managed care entity held liable under this Article shall be entitled to contribution under Chapter 1B of the General Statutes. No managed care entity held liable under this Article shall have a right to indemnity against physicians, health care providers, or entities wholly owned by physicians or health care providers or any combination thereof, except when:

(1)   The liability of the managed care entity is based on an administrative decision to approve or disapprove payment or reimbursement for, or denial, reduction, or termination of coverage, for a health care service and the physician organizations, health care providers, or entities wholly owned by physicians or health care providers or any combination thereof, which have made the decision at issue, have agreed explicitly, in a written addendum or agreement separate from the managed care organization's standard professional service agreement, to assume responsibility for making noncertification decisions under G.S. 58-50-61(13) with respect to certain insureds or enrollees; and

(2)   The managed care entity has not controlled or influenced or advocated for the decision regarding whether or when payment or reimbursement should be made or whether or when the insured or enrollee should receive a health care service.

The right to indemnity set forth herein shall not apply to professional medical or health care services provided by a physician or health care provider, and shall only apply where the agreement to assume responsibility for making noncertification decisions for the managed care entity is shown to have been undertaken voluntarily and the managed care organization has not adversely affected the terms and conditions of the relationship with the health care provider based upon the willingness to execute or refusal to execute an agreement under G.S. 58-50-61(13). (2001-446, s. 4.7; 2001-508, s. 2; 2007-323, s. 28.22A(o); 2007-345, s. 12.)

§ 90-21.53. Separate trial required.

Upon motion of any party in an action that includes a claim brought pursuant to this Article involving a managed care entity, the court shall order separate discovery and a separate trial of any claim, cross-claim, counterclaim, or third-party claim against any physician or other health care provider. (2001-446, s. 4.7.)

§ 90-21.54. Exhaustion of administrative remedies and appeals.

No action may be commenced under this Article until the plaintiff has exhausted all administrative remedies and appeals, including those internal remedies and appeals established under G.S. 58-50-61 through G.S. 58-50-62, and G.S. 58-50-75 through G.S. 58-50-95, and including those established under any successor external review process. (2001-446, s. 4.7.)

§ 90-21.55. External review decision.

(a)   Either the insured or enrollee or the personal representative of the insured or enrollee or the managed care entity may use an external review decision made in accordance with G.S. 58-50-75 through G.S. 58-50-95, or made in accordance with any successor external review process, as evidence in any cause of action which includes an action brought under this Part, provided that an adequate foundation is laid for the introduction of the external review decision into evidence and the testimony is subject to cross-examination.

(b)   Any information, documents, or other records or materials considered by the Independent Review Organization licensed under Part 4 of Article 50 of Chapter 58 of the General Statutes, or the successor review process, in conducting its review shall be admissible in any action commenced under this Article in accordance with Chapter 8 of the General Statutes and the North Carolina Rules of Evidence. (2001-446, s. 4.7.)

§ 90-21.56. Remedies.

(a) Except as provided in G.S. 90-21.52(b), an insured or enrollee who has been found to have been harmed by the managed care entity pursuant to an action brought under this Article may recover actual or nominal damages and, subject to the provisions and limitations of Chapter 1D of the General Statutes, punitive damages.

(b) This Article does not limit a plaintiff from pursuing any other remedy existing under the law or seeking any other relief that may be available outside of the cause of action and relief provided under this Article.

(c) The rights conferred under this Article as well as any rights conferred by the Constitution of North Carolina or the Constitution of the United States may not be waived, deferred, or lost pursuant to any contract between the insured or enrollee and the managed care entity that relates to a dispute involving a health care decision. Arbitration or mediation may be used to settle the controversy if, after the controversy arises, the insured or enrollee, or the estate of the insured or enrollee, voluntarily and knowingly consents in writing to use arbitration or mediation to settle the controversy. (2001-446, s. 4.7.)

Article 1H.

Voluntary Arbitration of Negligent Health Care Claims.

§ 90-21.60. Voluntary arbitration; prior agreements to arbitration void.

(a) Application of Article. - This Article applies to all claims for damages for personal injury or wrongful death based on alleged negligence in the provision of health care by a health care provider as defined in G.S. 90-21.11 where all parties have agreed to submit the dispute to arbitration under this Article in accordance with the requirements of G.S. 90-21.61.

(b) When Agreement Is Void. - Except as provided in G.S. 90-21.61(a), any contract provision or other agreement entered into prior to the commencement of an action that purports to require a party to elect arbitration under this Article is void and unenforceable. This Article does not impair the enforceability of any arbitration provision that does not specifically require arbitration under this Article. (2007-541, s. 1.)

§ 90-21.61. Requirements for submitting to arbitration.

(a) Before Action Is Filed. - Before an action is filed, a person who claims damages for personal injury or wrongful death based on alleged negligence in the provision of health care by a health care provider as defined in G.S. 90-21.11 and the allegedly negligent health care provider may jointly submit their dispute to arbitration under this Article by, acting through their attorneys, filing a stipulation to arbitrate with the clerk of superior court in the county where the negligence allegedly occurred. The filing of such a stipulation provides jurisdiction to the superior court to enforce the provisions of this Article and tolls the statute of limitations.

(b) Once Action Is Filed. - The parties to an action for damages for personal injury or wrongful death based on alleged negligence in the provision of health care by a health care provider as defined in G.S. 90-21.11 may elect at any time during the pendency of the action to file a stipulation with the court in which all parties to the action agree to submit the dispute to arbitration under this Article.

(c) Declaration Not to Arbitrate. - In the event that the parties do not unanimously agree to submit a dispute to arbitration under subsection (b) of this section, the parties shall file a declaration with the court prior to the discovery scheduling conference required by G.S. 1A-1, Rule 26(f1).

The declaration shall state that the attorney representing the party has presented the party with a copy of the provisions of this Article, that the attorneys representing the parties have discussed the provisions of this Article with the parties and with each other, and that the parties do not unanimously agree to submit the dispute to arbitration under this Article. The declaration is without prejudice to the parties' subsequent agreement to submit the dispute to arbitration. (2007-541, s. 1.)

§ 90-21.62. Selection of arbitrator.

(a) Selection by Agreement. - An arbitrator shall be selected by agreement of all the parties no later than 45 days after the date of the filing of the stipulation where the parties agreed to submit the dispute to arbitration under this Article. The parties may agree to select more than one arbitrator to conduct the arbitration. The parties may agree in writing to the selection of a particular arbitrator or particular arbitrators as a precondition for a stipulation to arbitrate.

(b) Selection From List. - If all the parties are unable to agree to an arbitrator by the time specified in subsection (a) of this section, the arbitrator shall be selected from emergency superior court judges who agree to be on a list maintained by the Administrative Office of the Courts. Each party shall alternately strike one name on the list, and the last remaining name on the list shall be the arbitrator. The emergency superior court judge serving as an arbitrator would be compensated at the same rate as an emergency judge serving in superior court. (2007-541, s. 1.)

§ 90-21.63. Witnesses; discovery; depositions; subpoenas.

(a) General Conduct of Arbitration; Experts. - The arbitrator may conduct the arbitration in such manner as the arbitrator considers appropriate so as to aid in the fair and expeditious disposition of the proceeding subject to the requirements of this section and G.S. 90-21.64. Except as provided in subsection (b) of this section, each side shall be entitled to two experts on the issue of liability, two experts on the issue of damages, and one rebuttal expert.

(b) Experts in Case of Multiple Parties. - Where there are multiple parties on one side, the arbitrator shall determine the number of experts that are allowed based on the minimum number of experts necessary to ensure a fair and economic resolution of the action.

(c) Discovery. - Notwithstanding G.S. 90-21.64(a)(1), unless the arbitrator determines that exceptional circumstances require additional discovery, each party shall be entitled to all of the following discovery from any other party:

(1) Twenty-five interrogatories, including subparts.

(2) Ten requests for admission.

(3) Whatever is allowed under applicable court rules for:

a. Requests for production of documents and things and for entry upon land for inspection and other purposes; and

b.   Requests for physical and mental examinations of persons.

(d)   Depositions. - Each party shall be entitled to all of the following depositions:

(1)   Depositions of any party and any expert that a party expects to call as a witness. - Except by order of the arbitrator for good cause shown, the length of the deposition of a party or an expert witness under this subdivision shall be limited to four hours.

(2)   Depositions of other witnesses. - Unless the arbitrator determines that exceptional circumstances require additional depositions, the total number of depositions of persons under this subdivision shall be limited to five depositions per side, each of which shall last no longer than two hours and for which each side shall be entitled to examine for one hour.

(e)   Subpoenas. - An arbitrator may issue a subpoena for the attendance of a witness and for the production of records and other evidence at any hearing and may administer oaths. A subpoena shall be served in the manner for service of subpoenas in a civil action and, upon the motion to the court by a party to the arbitration proceeding or by the arbitrator, enforced in the manner for enforcement of subpoenas in a civil action. (2007-541, s. 1.)

§ 90-21.64. Time limitations for arbitration.

(a)   Time Frames. - The time frames provided in this section shall run from the date of the filing of the stipulation where the parties agreed to submit the dispute to arbitration under the Article. Any arbitration under this Article shall be conducted according to the time frames as follows:

(1)   Within 45 days, the claimant shall provide a copy to the defendants of all relevant medical records. Alternatively, the claimant may provide to the defendants a release, in compliance with the federal Health Insurance Portability and Accountability Act, for all relevant medical records, along with the names and addresses of all health care providers who may have possession, custody, or control of the relevant medical records. The provisions of this subdivision shall not limit discovery conducted pursuant to G.S. 90-21.63(c).

(2) Within 120 days, the claimant shall disclose to each defendant the name and curriculum vitae or other documentation of qualifications of any expert the claimant expects to call as a witness.

(3) Within 140 days, each defendant shall disclose to the claimant the name and curriculum vitae or other documentation of qualifications of any expert the defendant expects to call as a witness.

(4) Within 160 days, each party shall disclose to each other party the name and curriculum vitae or other documentation of qualifications of any rebuttal expert the party expects to call as a witness.

(5) Within 240 days, all discovery shall be completed.

(6) Within 270 days, the arbitration hearing shall commence.

(b) Scheduling Order. - The arbitrator shall issue a case scheduling order in every proceeding specifying the dates by which the requirements of subdivisions (2) through (6) of subsection (a) of this section shall be completed. The scheduling order also shall specify a deadline for the service of dispositive motions and briefs.

(c) Public Policy as to When Hearings Begin. - It is the express public policy of the General Assembly that arbitration hearings under this Article be commenced no later than 10 months after the parties file the stipulation where the parties agreed to submit the dispute to arbitration under this Article. The arbitrator may grant a continuance of the commencement of the arbitration hearing only where a party shows that exceptional circumstances create an undue and unavoidable hardship on the party or where all parties consent to the continuance. (2007-541, s. 1.)

§ 90-21.65. Written decision by arbitration.

(a) Issuing the Decision. - The arbitrator shall issue a decision in writing and signed by the arbitrator within 14 days after the completion of the arbitration hearing and shall promptly deliver a copy of the decision to each party or the party's attorneys.

(b) Limit on Damages. - The arbitrator shall not make an award of damages that exceeds a total of one million dollars ($1,000,000) for any dispute submitted to arbitration under this Article, regardless of the number of claimants or defendants that are parties to the dispute.

(c) Finding if Damages Awarded. - If the arbitrator makes an award of damages to the claimant, the arbitrator shall make a finding as to whether the injury or death was caused by the negligence of the defendant.

(d) Paying the Arbitrator. - The fees and expenses of the arbitrator shall be paid equally by the parties.

(e) Attorneys' Fees and Costs. - Each party shall bear its own attorneys' fees and costs. (2007-541, s. 1.)

§ 90-21.66. Judgment by court.

After a party to the arbitration proceeding receives notice of a decision, the party may file a motion with the court for a judgment in accordance with the decision at which time the court shall issue such a judgment unless the decision is modified, corrected, or vacated as provided in G.S. 90-21.68. (2007-541, s. 1.)

§ 90-21.67. Retention of jurisdiction by court.

The court shall retain jurisdiction over the action during the pendency of the arbitration proceeding. The court may, at the request of the arbitrator, enter orders necessary to enforce the provisions of this Article. (2007-541, s. 1.)

§ 90-21.68. Appeal of arbitrator's decision.

There is no right to a trial de novo on an appeal of the arbitrator's decision under this Article. An appeal of the arbitrator's decision is limited to the bases for appeal provided under G.S. 1-569.23 or G.S. 1-569.24. (2007-541, s. 1.)

§ 90-21.69. Revised Uniform Arbitration Act not applicable.

The provisions of Article 45C of Chapter 1 of the General Statutes do not apply to arbitrations conducted under this Article except to the extent specifically provided in this Article. (2007-541, s. 1.)

§ 90-21.70: Reserved for future codification purposes.

§ 90-21.71: Reserved for future codification purposes.

§ 90-21.72: Reserved for future codification purposes.

§ 90-21.73: Reserved for future codification purposes.

§ 90-21.74: Reserved for future codification purposes.

§ 90-21.75: Reserved for future codification purposes.

§ 90-21.76: Reserved for future codification purposes.

§ 90-21.77: Reserved for future codification purposes.

§ 90-21.78: Reserved for future codification purposes.

§ 90-21.79: Reserved for future codification purposes.

Article 1I.

Woman's Right to Know Act.

§ 90-21.80. Short title.

This act may be cited as the "Woman's Right to Know Act." (2011-405, s. 1.)

§ 90-21.81. Definitions.

The following definitions apply in this Article:

(1)   Abortion. - The use or prescription of any instrument, medicine, drug, or other substance or device intentionally to terminate the pregnancy of a woman known to be pregnant with an intention other than to do any of the following:

a.   Increase the probability of a live birth.

b.   Preserve the life or health of the child.

c.   Remove a dead, unborn child who died as the result of (i) natural causes in utero, (ii) accidental trauma, or (iii) a criminal assault on the pregnant woman or her unborn child which causes the premature termination of the pregnancy.

(2)   Attempt to perform an abortion. - An act, or an omission of a statutorily required act, that, under the circumstances as the actor believes them to be, constitutes a substantial step in a course of conduct planned to culminate in the performance of an abortion in violation of this Article or Article 1K of this Chapter.

(3) Department. - The Department of Health and Human Services.

(4) Display a real-time view of the unborn child. - An ultrasound or any more scientifically advanced means of viewing the unborn child in real time.

(5) Medical emergency. - A condition which, in reasonable medical judgment, so complicates the medical condition of the pregnant woman as to necessitate the immediate abortion of her pregnancy to avert her death or for which a delay will create serious risk of substantial and irreversible physical impairment of a major bodily function, not including any psychological or emotional conditions. For purposes of this definition, no condition shall be deemed a medical emergency if based on a claim or diagnosis that the woman will engage in conduct which would result in her death or in substantial and irreversible physical impairment of a major bodily function.

(6) Physician. - An individual licensed to practice medicine in accordance with this Chapter.

(7) Probable gestational age. - What, in the judgment of the physician, will, with reasonable probability, be the gestational age of the unborn child at the time the abortion is planned to be performed.

(8) Qualified professional. - An individual who is a registered nurse, nurse practitioner, or physician assistant licensed in accordance with Article 1 of this Chapter, or a qualified technician acting within the scope of the qualified technician's authority as provided by North Carolina law and under the supervision of a physician.

(9) Qualified technician. - A registered diagnostic medical sonographer who is certified in obstetrics and gynecology by the American Registry for Diagnostic Medical Sonography (ARDMS) or a nurse midwife or advanced practice nurse practitioner in obstetrics with certification in obstetrical ultrasonography.

(10) Stable Internet Web site. - A Web site that, to the extent reasonably practicable, is safeguarded from having its content altered other than by the Department.

(11) Woman. - A female human, whether or not she is an adult. (2011-405, s. 1; 2013-366, s. 3(b).)

§ 90-21.82. Informed consent to abortion.

No abortion shall be performed upon a woman in this State without her voluntary and informed consent. Except in the case of a medical emergency, consent to an abortion is voluntary and informed only if all of the following conditions are satisfied:

(1) At least 24 hours prior to the abortion, a physician or qualified professional has orally informed the woman, by telephone or in person, of all of the following:

a. The name of the physician who will perform the abortion to ensure the safety of the procedure and prompt medical attention to any complications that may arise. The physician performing a surgical abortion shall be physically present during the performance of the entire abortion procedure. The physician prescribing, dispensing, or otherwise providing any drug or chemical for the purpose of inducing an abortion shall be physically present in the same room as the patient when the first drug or chemical is administered to the patient.

b. The particular medical risks associated with the particular abortion procedure to be employed, including, when medically accurate, the risks of infection, hemorrhage, cervical tear or uterine perforation, danger to subsequent pregnancies, including the ability to carry a child to full term, and any adverse psychological effects associated with the abortion.

c. The probable gestational age of the unborn child at the time the abortion is to be performed.

d. The medical risks associated with carrying the child to term.

e. The display of a real-time view of the unborn child and heart tone monitoring that enable the pregnant woman to view her unborn child or listen to the heartbeat of the unborn child are available to the woman. The physician performing the abortion, qualified technician, or referring physician shall inform the woman that the printed materials and Web site described in G.S. 90-21.83 and G.S. 90-21.84 contain phone numbers and addresses for facilities that offer the services free of charge. If requested by the woman, the physician or qualified professional shall provide to the woman the list as compiled by the Department.

f. If the physician who is to perform the abortion has no liability insurance for malpractice in the performance or attempted performance of an abortion, that information shall be communicated.

g. The location of the hospital that offers obstetrical or gynecological care located within 30 miles of the location where the abortion is performed or induced and at which the physician performing or inducing the abortion has clinical privileges. If the physician who will perform the abortion has no local hospital admitting privileges, that information shall be communicated.

If the physician or qualified professional does not know the information required in sub-subdivisions a., f., or g. of this subdivision, the woman shall be advised that this information will be directly available from the physician who is to perform the abortion. However, the fact that the physician or qualified professional does not know the information required in sub-subdivisions a., f., or g. shall not restart the 24-hour period. The information required by this subdivision shall be provided in English and in each language that is the primary language of at least two percent (2%) of the State's population. The information may be provided orally either by telephone or in person, in which case the required information may be based on facts supplied by the woman to the physician and whatever other relevant information is reasonably available. The information required by this subdivision may not be provided by a tape recording but shall be provided during a consultation in which the physician is able to ask questions of the patient and the patient is able to ask questions of the physician. If, in the medical judgment of the physician, a physical examination, tests, or the availability of other information to the physician subsequently indicates a revision of the information previously supplied to the patient, then that revised information may be communicated to the patient at any time before the performance of the abortion. Nothing in this section may be construed to preclude provision of required information in a language understood by the patient through a translator.

(2) The physician or qualified professional has informed the woman, either by telephone or in person, of each of the following at least 24 hours before the abortion:

a. That medical assistance benefits may be available for prenatal care, childbirth, and neonatal care.

b. That public assistance programs under Chapter 108A of the General Statutes may or may not be available as benefits under federal and State assistance programs.

c. That the father is liable to assist in the support of the child, even if the father has offered to pay for the abortion.

d. That the woman has other alternatives to abortion, including keeping the baby or placing the baby for adoption.

e. That the woman has the right to review the printed materials described in G.S. 90-21.83, that these materials are available on a State-sponsored Web site, and the address of the State-sponsored Web site. The physician or a qualified professional shall orally inform the woman that the materials have been provided by the Department and that they describe the unborn child and list agencies that offer alternatives to abortion. If the woman chooses to view the materials other than on the Web site, the materials shall either be given to her at least 24 hours before the abortion or be mailed to her at least 72 hours before the abortion by certified mail, restricted delivery to addressee.

f. That the woman is free to withhold or withdraw her consent to the abortion at any time before or during the abortion without affecting her right to future care or treatment and without the loss of any State or federally funded benefits to which she might otherwise be entitled.

The information required by this subdivision shall be provided in English and in each language that is the primary language of at least two percent (2%) of the State's population. The information required by this subdivision may be provided by a tape recording if provision is made to record or otherwise register specifically whether the woman does or does not choose to have the printed materials given or mailed to her. Nothing in this subdivision shall be construed to prohibit the physician or qualified professional from e-mailing a Web site link to the materials described in this subdivision or G.S. 90-21.83.

(3) The woman certifies in writing, before the abortion, that the information described in subdivisions (1) and (2) of this section has been furnished her and that she has been informed of her opportunity to review the information referred to in sub-subdivision (2)e. of this section. The original of this certification shall be maintained in the woman's medical records, and a copy shall be given to her.

(4) Before the performance of the abortion, the physician who will perform the abortion or the qualified technician must receive a copy of the written certification required by subdivision (3) of this section. (2011-405, s. 1; 2013-366, s. 4(a).)

§ 90-21.83. Printed information required.

(a) Within 90 days after this Article becomes effective, the Department shall publish in English and in each language that is the primary language of at least two percent (2%) of the State's population and shall cause to be available on the State Web site established under G.S. 90-21.84, the following printed materials in a manner that ensures that the information is comprehensible to a person of ordinary intelligence:

(1) Geographically indexed materials designed to inform a woman of public and private agencies and services available to assist her through pregnancy, upon childbirth, and while the child is dependent, including adoption agencies. The information shall include a comprehensive list of the agencies available, a description of the services they offer, including which agencies offer, at no cost to the woman, imaging that enables the woman to view the unborn child or heart tone monitoring that enables the woman to listen to the heartbeat of the unborn child, and a description of the manner, including telephone numbers, in which they might be contacted. In the alternative, in the discretion of the Department, the printed materials may contain a toll-free, 24-hour-a-day telephone number that may be called to obtain, orally or by tape recorded message tailored to the zip code entered by the caller, a list of these agencies in the locality of the caller and of the services they offer.

(2) Materials designed to inform the woman of the probable anatomical and physiological characteristics of the unborn child at two-week gestational increments from the time a woman can be known to be pregnant until full term, including pictures or drawings representing the development of the unborn child at two-week gestational increments. The pictures shall contain the dimensions of the unborn child, information about brain and heart functions, the presence of external members and internal organs, and be realistic and appropriate for the stage of pregnancy depicted. The materials shall be objective, nonjudgmental, and designed to convey only accurate scientific information about the unborn child at the various gestational ages. The material shall contain objective information describing the methods of abortion procedures employed, the

medical risks associated with each procedure, the possible adverse psychological effects of abortion, as well as the medical risks associated with carrying an unborn child to term.

(b) The materials referred to in subsection (a) of this section shall be printed in a typeface large enough to be clearly legible. The Web site provided for in G.S. 90-21.84 shall be maintained at a minimum resolution of 70 DPI (dots per inch). All pictures appearing on the Web site shall be a minimum of 200x300 pixels. All letters on the Web site shall be a minimum of 12-point font. All information and pictures shall be accessible with an industry-standard browser requiring no additional plug-ins.

(c) The materials required under this section shall be available at no cost from the Department upon request and in appropriate numbers to any physician, person, health facility, hospital, or qualified professional.

(d) The Department shall cause to be available on the State Web site a list of resources the woman may contact for assistance upon receiving information from the physician performing the ultrasound that the unborn child may have a disability or serious abnormality and shall do so in a manner prescribed by subsection (b) of this section. (2011-405, s. 1; 2013-366, s. 4(b).)

§ 90-21.84. Internet Web site.

The Department shall develop and maintain a stable Internet Web site to provide the information described under G.S. 90-21.83. No information regarding who accesses the Web site shall be collected or maintained. The Department shall monitor the Web site on a regular basis to prevent and correct tampering. (2011-405, s. 1.)

§ 90-21.85. Display of real-time view requirement.

(a) Notwithstanding G.S. 14-45.1, except in the case of a medical emergency, in order for the woman to make an informed decision, at least four hours before a woman having any part of an abortion performed or induced, and before the administration of any anesthesia or medication in preparation for the abortion on the woman, the physician who is to perform the abortion, or qualified technician working in conjunction with the physician, shall do each of the following:

(1)   Perform an obstetric real-time view of the unborn child on the pregnant woman.

(2)   Provide a simultaneous explanation of what the display is depicting, which shall include the presence, location, and dimensions of the unborn child within the uterus and the number of unborn children depicted. The individual performing the display shall offer the pregnant woman the opportunity to hear the fetal heart tone. The image and auscultation of fetal heart tone shall be of a quality consistent with the standard medical practice in the community. If the image indicates that fetal demise has occurred, a woman shall be informed of that fact.

(3)   Display the images so that the pregnant woman may view them.

(4)   Provide a medical description of the images, which shall include the dimensions of the embryo or fetus and the presence of external members and internal organs, if present and viewable.

(5)   Obtain a written certification from the woman, before the abortion, that the requirements of this section have been complied with, which shall indicate whether or not she availed herself of the opportunity to view the image.

(6)   Retain a copy of the written certification prescribed by subdivision (a)(5) of this section. The certification shall be placed in the medical file of the woman and shall be kept by the abortion provider for a period of not less than seven years. If the woman is a minor, then the certification shall be placed in the medical file of the minor and kept for at least seven years or for five years after the minor reaches the age of majority, whichever is greater.

If the woman has had an obstetric display of a real-time image of the unborn child within 72 hours before the abortion is to be performed, the certification of the physician or qualified technician who performed the procedure in compliance with this subsection shall be included in the patient's records and the requirements under this subsection shall be deemed to have been met.

(b)   Nothing in this section shall be construed to prevent a pregnant woman from averting her eyes from the displayed images or from refusing to hear the simultaneous explanation and medical description.

(c) In the event the person upon whom the abortion is to be performed is an unemancipated minor, as defined in G.S. 90-21.6(1), the information described in subdivisions (a)(2) and (a)(4) of this section shall be furnished and offered respectively to a person required to give parental consent under G.S. 90-21.7(a) and the unemancipated minor. The person required to give consent in accordance with G.S. 90-21.7(a), as appropriate, shall make the certification required by subdivision (a)(5) of this section. In the event the person upon whom the abortion is to be performed has been adjudicated mentally incompetent by a court of competent jurisdiction, the information shall be furnished and offered respectively to her spouse or a legal guardian if she is married or, if she is not married, to one parent or a legal guardian and the woman. The spouse, legal guardian, or parent, as appropriate, shall make the certification required by subdivision (a)(5) of this section. In the case of an abortion performed pursuant to a court order under G.S. 90-21.8(e) and (f), the information described in subdivisions (a)(2) and (a)(4) of this section shall be provided to the minor, and the certification required by subdivision (a)(5) of this section shall be made by the minor. (2011-405, s. 1.)

§ 90-21.86. Procedure in case of medical emergency.

When a medical emergency compels the performance of an abortion, the physician shall inform the woman, before the abortion if possible, of the medical indications supporting the physician's judgment that an abortion is necessary to avert her death or that a 24-hour delay will create a serious risk of substantial and irreversible impairment of a major bodily function, not including psychological or emotional conditions. As soon as feasible, the physician shall document in writing the medical indications upon which the physician relied and shall cause the original of the writing to be maintained in the woman's medical records and a copy given to her. (2011-405, s. 1.)

§ 90-21.87. Informed consent for a minor.

If the woman upon whom an abortion is to be performed is an unemancipated minor, the voluntary and informed written consent required under G.S. 90-21.82 shall be obtained from the minor and from the adult individual who gives consent pursuant to G.S. 90-21.7(a). (2011-405, s. 1.)

§ 90-21.88. Civil remedies.

(a) Any person upon whom an abortion has been performed and any father of an unborn child that was the subject of an abortion may maintain an action for damages against the person who performed the abortion in knowing or reckless violation of this Article. Any person upon whom an abortion has been attempted may maintain an action for damages against the person who performed the abortion in willful violation of this Article.

(b) Injunctive relief against any person who has willfully violated this Article may be sought by and granted to (i) the woman upon whom an abortion was performed or attempted to be performed in violation of this Article, (ii) any person who is the spouse, parent, sibling, or guardian of, or a current or former licensed health care provider of, the woman upon whom an abortion has been performed or attempted to be performed in violation of this Article, or (iii) the Attorney General. The injunction shall prevent the abortion provider from performing or inducing further abortions in this State in violation of this Article.

(c) If judgment is rendered in favor of the plaintiff in any action authorized under this section, the court shall also tax as part of the costs reasonable attorneys' fees in favor of the plaintiff against the defendant. If judgment is rendered in favor of the defendant and the court finds that the plaintiff's suit was frivolous or brought in bad faith, then the court shall tax as part of the costs reasonable attorneys' fees in favor of the defendant against the plaintiff. (2011-405, s. 1.)

§ 90-21.89. Protection of privacy in court proceedings.

In every proceeding or action brought under this Article, the court shall rule whether the anonymity of any woman upon whom an abortion has been performed or attempted shall be preserved from public disclosure if she does not give her consent to the disclosure. The court, upon motion or sua sponte, shall make the ruling and, upon determining that her anonymity should be preserved, shall issue orders to the parties, witnesses, and counsel and shall direct the sealing of the record and exclusion of individuals from courtrooms or hearing rooms to the extent necessary to safeguard her identity from public disclosure. Each order issued pursuant to this section shall be accompanied by specific written findings explaining (i) why the anonymity of the woman should be preserved from public disclosure, (ii) why the order is essential to that end, (iii) how the order is narrowly tailored to serve that interest, and (iv) why no reasonable less restrictive alternative exists. In the absence of written consent of the woman upon whom an abortion has been performed or attempted, anyone who brings an action under G.S. 90-21.88 (a) or (b) shall do so under a pseudonym. This section may not be construed to conceal the identity of the plaintiff or of witnesses from the defendant. (2011-405, s. 1.)

§ 90-21.90. Assurance of informed consent.

(a) All information required to be provided under G.S. 90-21.82 to a woman considering abortion shall be presented to the woman individually and, except for information that may be provided by telephone, in the physical presence of the woman and in a language the woman understands to ensure that the woman has adequate opportunity to ask questions and to ensure the woman is not the victim of a coerced abortion.

(b) Should a woman be unable to read the materials provided to the woman pursuant to this section, a physician or qualified professional shall read the materials to the woman in a language the woman understands before the abortion. (2011-405, s. 1.)

§ 90-21.91. Assurance that consent is freely given.

If a physician acting pursuant to this Article has reason to believe that a woman is being coerced into having an abortion, the physician or qualified professional shall inform the woman that services are available for the woman and shall provide the woman with private access to a telephone and information about, but not limited to, each of the following services:

(1) Rape crisis centers.

(2) Shelters for victims of domestic violence.

(3) Restraining orders.

(4) Pregnancy care centers. (2011-405, s. 1.)

§ 90-21.92. Severability.

If any one or more provision, section, subsection, sentence, clause, phrase, or word of this Article or the application thereof to any person or circumstance is found to be unconstitutional, the same is hereby declared to be severable, and the balance of this Article shall remain effective, notwithstanding such unconstitutionality. The General Assembly hereby declares that it would have passed this Article, and each provision, section, subsection, sentence, clause, phrase, or word thereof, irrespective of the fact that any one or more provision, section, subsection, sentence, clause, phrase, or word be declared unconstitutional. (2011-405, s. 1.)

§ 90-21.93: Reserved for future codification purposes.

§ 90-21.94: Reserved for future codification purposes.

§ 90-21.95: Reserved for future codification purposes.

§ 90-21.96: Reserved for future codification purposes.

§ 90-21.97: Reserved for future codification purposes.

§ 90-21.98: Reserved for future codification purposes.

§ 90-21.99: Reserved for future codification purposes.

Article 1J.

Voluntary Health Care Services Act.

§ 90-21.100. Short title.

This Article shall be known and may be cited as the Volunteer Health Care Services Act. (2012-155, s. 1.)

§ 90-21.101. Findings.

(a) The General Assembly makes the following findings:

(1) Access to high-quality health care services is a concern of all persons.

(2) Access to high-quality health care services may be limited for some residents of this State, particularly those who reside in remote, rural areas or in the inner city.

(3) Physicians and other health care providers have traditionally worked to ensure broad access to health care services.

(4) Many health care providers from North Carolina and elsewhere are willing to volunteer their services to address the health care needs of North Carolinians who may otherwise not be able to obtain high-quality health care services.

(b) The General Assembly further finds that it is the public policy of this State to encourage and facilitate the voluntary provision of health care services. (2012-155, s. 1.)

§ 90-21.102. Definitions.

The following definitions apply in this Article:

(1)   Department. - The North Carolina Department of Health and Human Services.

(2)   Free clinic. - A nonprofit, 501(c)(3) tax-exempt organization organized for the purpose of providing health care services without charge or for a minimum fee to cover administrative costs.

(3)   Health care provider. - Any person who:

a.   Is licensed to practice as a physician or a physician assistant under Article 1 of this Chapter.

b.   Holds a limited volunteer license under G.S. 90-12.1A.

c.   Holds a retired limited volunteer license under G.S. 90-12.1B.

d.   Holds a physician assistant limited volunteer license under G.S. 90-12.4.

e.   Holds a physician assistant retired limited volunteer license under 90-12.4B.

f.   Is a volunteer health care professional to whom G.S. 90-21.16 applies.

g.   Is licensed to practice dentistry under Article 2 of this Chapter.

h.   Is licensed to practice pharmacy under Article 4A of this Chapter.

i.   Is licensed to practice optometry under Article 6 of this Chapter.

j.   Is licensed to practice as a registered nurse or licensed practical nurse under Article 9A of this Chapter.

k.   Is licensed to practice as a dental hygienist under Article 16 of this Chapter.

l. Holds a license as a registered licensed optician under Article 17 of this Chapter.

m. Is licensed to practice as a physician, physician assistant, dentist, pharmacist, optometrist, registered nurse, licensed practical nurse, dental hygienist, or optician under provisions of law of another state of the United States comparable to the provisions referenced in sub-subdivisions a. through l. of this subdivision.

(4) Sponsoring organization. - Any nonprofit organization that organizes or arranges for the voluntary provision of health care services pursuant to this Article.

(5) Voluntary provision of health care services. - The provision of health care services by a health care provider in association with a sponsoring organization in which both of the following circumstances exist:

a. The health care services are provided without charge to the recipient of the services or to a third party on behalf of the recipient.

b. The health care provider receives no compensation or other consideration in exchange for the health care services provided.

For the purposes of this Article, the provision of health care services in nonprofit community health centers, local health department facilities, free clinic facilities, or at a provider's place of employment when the patient is referred by a nonprofit community health referral service shall not be considered the voluntary provision of health care. (2012-155, s. 1; 2012-194, s. 47(a); 2013-49, s. 2.)

§ 90-21.103. Limitation on duration of voluntary health care services.

A sponsoring organization duly registered in accordance with G.S. 90-21.104 may organize or arrange for the voluntary provision of health care services at a location in this State for a period not to exceed seven calendar days in any calendar year. (2012-155, s. 1.)

§ 90-21.104. Registration, reporting, and record-keeping requirements.

(a) A sponsoring organization shall not organize or arrange for the voluntary provision of health care services in this State without first registering with the Department on a form prescribed by the Department. The registration form shall contain all of the following information:

(1) The name of the sponsoring organization.

(2) The name of the principal individuals who are the officers or organizational officials responsible for the operation of the sponsoring organization.

(3) The street address, city, zip code, and county of the sponsoring organization's principal office and each of the principal individuals described in subdivision (2) of this subsection.

(4) Telephone numbers for the principal office of the sponsoring organization and for each of the principal individuals described in subdivision (2) of this subsection.

(5) Any additional information requested by the Department.

(b) Each sponsoring organization that applies for registration under this Article shall pay a one-time registration fee in the amount of fifty dollars ($50.00), which it shall submit to the Department along with the completed registration form required by subsection (a) of this section. Upon approval by the Department, a sponsoring organization's registration remains valid unless revoked by the Department pursuant to subsection (f) of this section.

(c) Upon any change in the information required under subsection (a) of this section, the sponsoring organization shall notify the Department of the change, in writing, within 30 days after the effective date of the change.

(d) Each registered sponsoring organization has the duty and responsibility to do all of the following:

(1) Except as provided in this subdivision, by no later than 14 days before a sponsoring organization initiates voluntary health care services in this State, the sponsoring organization shall submit to the Department a list containing the following information regarding each health care provider who is to provide voluntary health care services on behalf of the sponsoring organization during

any part of the time period in which the sponsoring organization is authorized to provide voluntary health care services in the State:

a. Name.

b. Date of birth.

c. State of licensure.

d. License number.

e. Area of practice.

f. Practice address.

By no later than 3 days prior to voluntary health care services being rendered, a sponsoring organization may amend the list to add health care providers defined in G.S. 90-21.102(3)a. through G.S. 90-21.102(3)l.

(2) Beginning April 1, 2013, submit quarterly reports to the Department identifying all health care providers who engaged in the provision of voluntary health care services in association with the sponsoring organization in this State during the preceding calendar quarter. The quarterly report must include the date, place, and type of voluntary health care services provided by each health care provider.

(3) Maintain a list of health care providers associated with its provision of voluntary health care services in this State. For each health care provider listed, the sponsoring organization shall maintain a copy of a current license or statement of exemption from licensure or certification. For health care providers currently licensed or certified under this Chapter, the sponsoring organization may maintain a copy of the health care provider's license or certification verification obtained from a State-sponsored Internet Web site.

(4) Maintain records of the quarterly reports and records required under this subsection for a period of five years from the date of voluntary service and make these records available upon request to any State licensing board established under this Chapter.

(e) Compliance with subsections (a) through (d) of this section is prima facie evidence that the sponsoring organization has exercised due care in its selection of health care providers.

(f) The Department may revoke the registration of any sponsoring organization that fails to comply with the requirements of this Article. A sponsoring organization may challenge the Department's decision to revoke its registration by filing a contested case under Article 3 of Chapter 150B of the General Statutes.

(g) The Department may waive any of the requirements of this section during a natural disaster or other emergency circumstance. (2012-155, s. 1; 2012-194, s. 47(b).)

§ 90-21.105. Department and licensure boards to review licensure status of volunteers.

The Department shall forward the information received from a sponsoring organization under G.S. 90-21.104(d)(1) to the appropriate licensure board within seven days after receipt. Upon receipt of any information or notice from a licensure board that a health care provider on the list submitted by the sponsoring organization pursuant to G.S. 90-21.104(d)(1) is not licensed, authorized, or in good standing, or is the subject of an investigation or pending disciplinary action, the Department shall immediately notify the sponsoring organization that the health care provider is not permitted to engage in the voluntary provision of health care services on behalf of the sponsoring organization. (2012-155, s. 1.)

§ 90-21.106. On-site requirements.

A sponsoring organization that organizes or arranges for the provision of voluntary health care services at a location in this State shall ensure that at least one health care provider licensed to practice in this State, with access to the controlled substances reporting system established under G.S. 90-113.73, is located on the premises where the provision of voluntary health care services is occurring. In addition, every sponsoring organization shall post in a clear and conspicuous manner the following notice in the premises where the provision of voluntary health care services is occurring:

"NOTICE

Under North Carolina law, there is no liability for damages for injuries or death alleged to have occurred by reason of an act or omission in the health care provider's voluntary provision of health care services, unless it is established that the injuries or death were caused by gross negligence, wanton conduct, or intentional wrongdoing on the part of the health care provider." (2012-155, s. 1.)

§ 90-21.107. Additional licensure not required for certain volunteers.

(a) A health care provider who engages in the voluntary provision of health care services in association with a sponsoring organization for no more than seven days during any calendar year shall not be required to obtain additional licensure or authorization in connection therewith if the health care provider meets any of the following criteria:

(1) The health care provider is duly licensed or authorized under the laws of this State to practice in the area in which the health care provider is providing voluntary health care services and is in good standing with the applicable licensing board.

(2) The health care provider lawfully practices in another state or district in the area in which the health care provider is providing voluntary health care services and is in good standing with the applicable licensing board.

(b) This exemption from additional licensure or authorization requirements does not apply if any of the following circumstances exist:

(1) The health care provider has been subjected to public disciplinary action or is the subject of a pending disciplinary proceeding in any state in which the health care provider is or ever has been licensed.

(2) The health care provider's license has been suspended or revoked pursuant to disciplinary proceedings in any state in which the health care provider is or ever has been licensed.

(3)   The health care provider renders services outside the scope of practice authorized by the health care provider's license or authorization. (2012-155, s. 1.)

§ 90-21.108. Immunity from civil liability for acts or omissions.

(a)   Subject to subsection (b) of this section, a health care provider who engages in the voluntary provision of health care services at any location in this State in association with a sponsoring organization shall not be liable for damages for injuries or death alleged to have occurred by reason of an act or omission in the health care provider's voluntary provision of health care services, unless it is established that the injuries or death were caused by gross negligence, wanton conduct, or intentional wrongdoing on the part of the health care provider.

(b)   The immunity from civil liability provided by subsection (a) of this section does not apply if any of the following circumstances exist:

(1)   The health care provider receives, directly or indirectly, any type of compensation, benefits, or other consideration of any nature from any person for the health care services provided.

(2)   The health care services provided are not part of the health care provider's training or assignment.

(3)   The health care services provided are not within the scope of the health care provider's license or authority.

(4)   The health care services provided are not authorized by the appropriate authorities to be performed at the location. (2012-155, s. 1.)

§ 90-21.109: Reserved for future codification purposes.

§ 90-21.110: Reserved for future codification purposes.

§ 90-21.111: Reserved for future codification purposes.

§ 90-21.112: Reserved for future codification purposes.

§ 90-21.113: Reserved for future codification purposes.

§ 90-21.114: Reserved for future codification purposes.

§ 90-21.115: Reserved for future codification purposes.

§ 90-21.116: Reserved for future codification purposes.

§ 90-21.117: Reserved for future codification purposes.

§ 90-21.118: Reserved for future codification purposes.

§ 90-21.119: Reserved for future codification purposes.

Article 1K.

Certain Abortions Prohibited.

§ 90-21.120. Definitions.

The following definitions apply in this Article:

(1)   Abortion. - As defined in G.S. 90-21.81(1).

(2)   Attempt to perform an abortion. - As defined in G.S. 90-21.81(2).

(3)   Woman. - As defined in G.S. 90-21.81(11). (2013-366, s. 3(a).)

§ 90-21.121. Sex-selective abortion prohibited.

(a)   Notwithstanding any of the provisions of G.S. 14-45.1, no person shall perform or attempt to perform an abortion upon a woman in this State with knowledge, or an objective reason to know, that a significant factor in the woman seeking the abortion is related to the sex of the unborn child.

(b)   Nothing in this section shall be construed as placing an affirmative duty on a physician to inquire as to whether the sex of the unborn child is a significant factor in the pregnant woman seeking the abortion. (2013-366, s. 3(a).)

§ 90-21.122. Civil remedies.

(a)   Any person who violates any provision of this Article shall be liable for damages, including punitive damages pursuant to Chapter 1D of the General Statutes, and may be enjoined from future acts.

(b)   A claim for damages against any person who has violated a provision of this Article may be sought by (i) the woman upon whom an abortion was performed or attempted in violation of this Article, (ii) any person who is the spouse or guardian of the woman upon whom an abortion was performed or attempted in violation of this Article, or (iii) a parent of the woman upon whom an abortion was performed or attempted in violation of this Article if the woman was a minor at the time the abortion was performed or attempted.

(c) A claim for injunctive relief against any person who has violated a provision of this Article may be sought by (i) the woman upon whom an abortion was performed or attempted in violation of this Article, (ii) any person who is the spouse, guardian, or current or former licensed health care provider of the woman upon whom an abortion was performed or attempted in violation of this Article, or (iii) a parent of the woman upon whom an abortion was performed or attempted in violation of this Article if the woman was a minor at the time the abortion was performed or attempted.

(d) Any person who violates the terms of an injunction issued in accordance with this section shall be subject to civil contempt and shall be fined ten thousand dollars ($10,000) for the first violation, fifty thousand dollars ($50,000) for the second violation, and one hundred thousand dollars ($100,000) for the third violation and each subsequent violation. Each performance or attempted performance of an abortion in violation of the terms of an injunction is a separate violation. The fine shall be the exclusive penalty for civil contempt under this subsection. The fine under this subsection shall be cumulative. No fine shall be assessed against the woman upon whom an abortion is performed or attempted.

(e) The clear proceeds of any civil penalty assessed under this section shall be remitted to the Civil Penalty and Forfeiture Fund in accordance with G.S. 115C-457.2. (2013-366, s. 3(a).)

§ 90-21.123. Protection of privacy in court proceedings.

In every proceeding or action brought under this Article, the court shall rule whether the anonymity of any woman upon whom an abortion has been performed or attempted shall be preserved from public disclosure if the woman does not give her consent to the disclosure. The court, upon motion or sua sponte, shall make the ruling and, upon determining that the woman's anonymity should be preserved, shall issue orders to the parties, witnesses, and counsel and shall direct the sealing of the record and exclusion of individuals from courtrooms or hearing rooms to the extent necessary to safeguard the woman's identity from public disclosure. Each order issued pursuant to this section shall be accompanied by specific written findings explaining (i) why the anonymity of the woman should be preserved from public disclosure, (ii) why the order is essential to that end, (iii) how the order is narrowly tailored to serve that interest, and (iv) why no reasonable, less restrictive alternative exists. In the absence of written consent of the woman upon whom an abortion has been performed or attempted, anyone who brings an action under G.S. 90-21.122 shall do so under a pseudonym. This section may not be construed to conceal the identity of the plaintiff or of witnesses from the defendant. (2013-366, s. 3(a).)

Article 2.

Dentistry.

§ 90-22. Practice of dentistry regulated in public interest; Article liberally construed; Board of Dental Examiners; composition; qualifications and terms of members; vacancies; nominations and elections; compensation; expenditures by Board.

(a)   The practice of dentistry in the State of North Carolina is hereby declared to affect the public health, safety and welfare and to be subject to regulation and control in the public interest. It is further declared to be a matter of public interest and concern that the dental profession merit and receive the confidence of the public and that only qualified persons be permitted to practice dentistry in the State of North Carolina. This Article shall be liberally construed to carry out these objects and purposes.

(b)   The North Carolina State Board of Dental Examiners heretofore created by Chapter 139, Public Laws 1879 and by Chapter 178, Public Laws 1915, is hereby continued as the agency of the State for the regulation of the practice of dentistry in this State. Said Board of Dental Examiners shall consist of six dentists who are licensed to practice dentistry in North Carolina, one dental hygienist who is licensed to practice dental hygiene in North Carolina and one person who shall be a citizen and resident of North Carolina and who shall be licensed to practice neither dentistry nor dental hygiene. The dental hygienist or the consumer member cannot participate or vote in any matters of the Board which involves the issuance, renewal or revocation of the license to practice dentistry in the State of North Carolina. The consumer member cannot participate or vote in any matters of the Board which involve the issuance, renewal or revocation of the license to practice dental hygiene in the State of North Carolina. Members of the Board licensed to practice dentistry in North Carolina shall have been elected in an election held as hereinafter provided in which every person licensed to practice dentistry in North Carolina and residing or practicing in North Carolina shall be entitled to vote. Each member of said Board shall be elected for a term of three years and until his successor shall be elected and shall qualify. Each year there shall be elected two dentists for such terms of three years each. Every three years there shall be elected one dental hygienist for a term of three years. Dental hygienists shall be elected to the Board in an election held in accordance with the procedures hereinafter provided in which those persons licensed to practice dental hygiene in North Carolina and residing or practicing in North Carolina shall be entitled to vote. Every three years a person who is a citizen and resident of North Carolina and licensed to practice neither dentistry nor dental hygiene shall be appointed to the Board for a term of three years by the Governor of North Carolina. Any vacancy occurring on said Board shall be filled by a majority vote of the remaining members of the Board to serve until the next regular election conducted by the Board, at which time the vacancy will be filled by the election process provided for in this Article, except that when the seat on the Board held by a person licensed to practice neither dentistry nor dental hygiene in North Carolina shall become vacant, the vacancy shall be filled by appointment by the Governor for the period of the unexpired term. No dentist shall be nominated for or elected to membership on said Board, unless, at the time of such nomination and election such person is licensed to practice dentistry in North Carolina and actually engaged in the practice of dentistry. No dental hygienist shall be nominated for or elected to membership on said Board unless, at the time of such nomination and election, such person is licensed to practice dental hygiene in North Carolina and is currently employed in dental hygiene in North Carolina. No person shall be nominated, elected, or appointed to serve more than two consecutive terms on said Board.

(c) Nominations and elections of members of the North Carolina State Board of Dental Examiners shall be as follows:

(1) An election shall be held each year to elect successors to those members whose terms are expiring in the year of the election, each successor to take office on the first day of August following the election and to hold office for a term of three years and until his successor has been elected and shall qualify; provided that if in any year the election of the members of such Board for that year shall not have been completed by August 1 of that year, then the

said members elected that year shall take office immediately after the completion of the election and shall hold office until the first of August of the third year thereafter and until their successors are elected and qualified. Persons appointed to the Board by the Governor shall take office on the first day of August following their appointment and shall hold office for a term of three years and until such person's successor has been appointed and shall qualify; provided that if in any year the Governor shall not have appointed a person by August first of that year, then the said member appointed that year shall take office immediately after his appointment and shall hold office until the first of August of the third year thereafter and until such member's successor is appointed and qualified.

(2)   Every dentist with a current North Carolina license residing or practicing in North Carolina shall be eligible to vote in elections of dentists to the Board. Every dental hygienist with a current North Carolina license residing or practicing in North Carolina shall be eligible to vote in elections of dental hygienists to the Board. The holding of such a license to practice dentistry or dental hygiene in North Carolina shall constitute registration to vote in such elections. The list of licensed dentists and dental hygienists shall constitute the registration list for elections to the appropriate seats on the Board.

(3)   All elections shall be conducted by the Board of Dental Examiners which is hereby constituted a Board of Dental Elections. If a member of the Board of Dental Examiners whose position is to be filled at any election is nominated to succeed himself, and does not withdraw his name, he shall be disqualified to serve as a member of the Board of Dental Elections for that election and the remaining members of the Board of Dental Elections shall proceed and function without his participation.

(4)   Nomination of dentists for election shall be made to the Board of Dental Elections by a written petition signed by not less than 10 dentists licensed to practice in North Carolina and residing or practicing in North Carolina. Nomination of dental hygienists for election shall be made to the Board of Dental Elections by a written petition signed by not less than 10 dental hygienists licensed to practice in North Carolina and residing or practicing in North Carolina. Such petitions shall be filed with said Board of Dental Elections subsequent to January 1 of the year in which the election is to be held and not later than midnight of the twentieth day of May of such year, or not later than such earlier date (not before April 1) as may be set by the Board of Dental Elections: provided, that not less than 10 days' notice of such earlier date shall be given to all dentists or dental hygienists qualified to sign a petition of

nomination. The Board of Dental Elections shall, before preparing ballots, notify all persons who have been duly nominated of their nomination.

(5)   Any person who is nominated as provided in subdivision (4) above may withdraw his name by written notice delivered to the Board of Dental Elections or its designated secretary at any time prior to the closing of the polls in any election.

(6)   Following the close of nominations, there shall be prepared, under and in accordance with such rules and regulations as the Board of Dental Elections shall prescribe, ballots containing, in alphabetical order, the names of all nominees; and each ballot shall have such method of identification, and such instructions and requirements printed thereon, as shall be prescribed by the Board of Dental Elections. At such time as may be fixed by the Board of Dental Elections a ballot and a return official envelope addressed to said Board shall be mailed to each person entitled to vote in the election being conducted, together with a notice by said Board designating the latest day and hour for return mailing and containing such other items as such Board may see fit to include. The said envelope shall bear a serial number and shall have printed on the left portion of its face the following:

"Serial No. of Envelope _____

Signature of Voter   _____

Address of Voter   _____

                       _____

(Note: The enclosed ballot is not valid unless the signature of the voter is on this envelope)."

The Board of Dental Elections may cause to be printed or stamped or written on said envelope such additional notice as it may see fit to give. No ballot shall be valid or shall be counted in an election unless, within the time hereinafter provided, it has been delivered to said Board by hand or by mail and shall be sealed. The said Board by rule may make provision for replacement of lost or destroyed envelopes or ballots upon making proper provisions to safeguard against abuse.

(7) The date and hour fixed by the Board of Dental Elections as the latest time for delivery by hand or mailing of said return ballots shall be not earlier than the tenth day following the mailing of the envelopes and ballots to the voters.

(8) The said ballots shall be canvassed by the Board of Dental Elections beginning at noon on a day and at a place set by said Board and announced by it in the notice accompanying the sending out of the ballots and envelopes, said date to be not later than four days after the date fixed by the Board for the closing of the balloting. The canvassing shall be made publicly and any licensed dentists may be present. The counting of ballots shall be conducted as follows: The envelopes shall be displayed to the persons present and an opportunity shall be given to any person present to challenge the qualification of the voter whose signature appears on the envelope or to challenge the validity of the envelope. Any envelope (with enclosed ballot) challenged shall be set aside, and the challenge shall be heard later or at that time by said Board. After the envelopes have been so exhibited, those not challenged shall be opened and the ballots extracted therefrom, insofar as practicable without showing the marking on the ballots, and there shall be a final and complete separation of each envelope and its enclosed ballot. Thereafter each ballot shall be presented for counting, shall be displayed and, if not challenged, shall be counted. No ballot shall be valid if it is marked for more nominees than there are positions to be filled in that election: provided, that no ballot shall be rejected for any technical error unless it is impossible to determine the voter's choices or choice from the ballot. The counting of the ballots shall be continued until completed. During the counting, challenge may be made to any ballot on the grounds only of defects appearing on the face of the ballot. The said Board may decide the challenge immediately when it is made or it may put aside the ballot and determine the challenge upon the conclusion of the counting of the ballots.

(9) a. Where there is more than one nominee eligible for election to a single seat:

1. The nominee receiving a majority of the votes cast shall be declared elected.

2. In the event that no nominee receives a majority, a second election shall be conducted between the two nominees who receive the highest number of votes.

b. Where there are more than two nominees eligible for election to either of two seats at issue in the same election:

1. A majority shall be any excess of the sum ascertained by dividing the total number of votes cast for all nominees by four.

2. In the event that more than two nominees receive a majority of the votes cast, the two receiving the highest number of votes shall be declared elected.

3. In the event that only one of the nominees receives a majority, he shall be declared elected and the Board of Dental Examiners shall thereupon order a second election to be conducted between the two nominees receiving the next to highest number of votes.

4. In the event that no nominee receives a majority, a second election shall be conducted between the four candidates receiving the highest number of votes. At such second election, the two nominees receiving the highest number of votes shall be declared elected.

c. In any election, if there is a tie between candidates, the tie shall be resolved by the vote of the Board of Dental Examiners, provided that if a member of that Board is one of the candidates in the tie, he may not participate in such vote.

(10) In the event there shall be required a second election, there shall be followed the same procedure as outlined in the paragraphs above subject to the same limitations and requirements: provided, that if the second election is between four candidates, then the two receiving the highest number of votes shall be declared elected.

(11) In the case of the death or withdrawal of a candidate prior to the closing of the polls in any election, he shall be eliminated from the contest and any votes cast for him shall be disregarded. If, at any time after the closing of the period for nominations because of lack of plural or proper nominations or death, or withdrawal, or disqualification or any other reason, there shall be (i) only two candidates for two positions, they shall be declared elected by the Board of Dental Elections, or (ii) only one candidate for one position, he shall be declared elected by the Board of Dental Elections, or (iii) no candidate for two positions, the two positions shall be filled by the Board of Dental Examiners, or (iv) no candidate for one position, the position shall be filled by the Board of Dental Examiners, or (v) one candidate for two positions, the one candidate shall be declared elected by the Board of Dental Elections and one qualified dentist shall be elected to the other position by the Board of Dental Examiners. In the event

of the death or withdrawal of a candidate after election but before taking office, the position to which he was elected shall be filled by the Board of Dental Examiners. In the event of the death or resignation of a member of the Board of Dental Examiners, after taking office, his position shall be filled for the unexpired term by the Board of Dental Examiners.

(12)   An official list of licensed dentists shall be kept at an office of the Board of Dental Elections and shall be open to the inspection of any person at all times. Copies may be made by any licensed dentist. As soon as the voting in any election begins a list of the licensed dentists shall be posted in such office of said Board and indication by mark or otherwise shall be made on that list to show whether a ballot-enclosing envelope has been returned.

(13)   All envelopes enclosing ballots and all ballots shall be preserved and held separately by the Board of Dental Elections for a period of six months following the close of an election.

(14)   From any decision of the Board of Dental Elections relative to the conduct of such elections, appeal may be taken to the courts in the manner otherwise provided by Chapter 150B of the General Statutes of North Carolina.

(15)   The Board of Dental Elections is authorized to make rules and regulations relative to the conduct of these elections, provided same are not in conflict with the provisions of this section and provided that notice shall be given to all licensed dentists residing in North Carolina.

(d)   For service on the Board of Dental Elections, the members of such Board shall receive the per diem compensation and expenses allowed by this Article for service as members of the Board of Dental Examiners. The Board of Dental Elections is authorized and empowered to expend from funds collected under the provisions of this Article such sum or sums as it may determine necessary in the performance of its duties as a Board of Dental Elections, said expenditures to be in addition to the authorization contained in G.S. 90-43 and to be disbursed as provided therein.

(e)   The Board of Dental Elections is authorized to appoint such secretary or secretaries and/or assistant secretary or assistant secretaries to perform such functions in connection with such nominations and elections as said Board shall determine, provided that any protestant or contestant shall have the right to a hearing by said Board in connection with any challenge of a voter, or an envelope, or a ballot or the counting of an election. Said Board is authorized to designate an office or offices for the keeping of lists of registered dentists, for the issuance and the receipt of envelopes and ballots. (1935, c. 66, s. 1; 1957, c. 592, s. 1; 1961, c. 213, s. 1; 1971, c. 755, s. 1; 1973, c. 1331, s. 3; 1979, 2nd Sess., c. 1195, ss. 1-5; 1981, c. 751, ss. 1, 2; 1987, c. 827, s. 1.)

§ 90-23. Officers; common seal.

The North Carolina State Board of Dental Examiners shall, at each annual meeting thereof, elect one of its members president and one secretary-treasurer. The common seal which has already been adopted by said Board, pursuant to law, shall be continued as the seal of said Board. (1935, c. 66, s. 2.)

§ 90-24. Quorum; adjourned meetings.

A majority of the members of said Board shall constitute a quorum for the transaction of business and at any meeting of the Board, if a majority of the members are not present at the time and the place appointed for the meeting, those members of the Board present may adjourn from day to day until a quorum is present, and the action of the Board taken at any adjourned meeting thus had shall have the same force and effect as if had upon the day and at the hour of the meeting called and adjourned from day to day. (1935, c. 66, s. 2; 1981, c. 751, s. 3.)

§ 90-25. Records and transcripts.

The said Board shall keep a record of its transactions at all annual or special meetings and shall provide a record book in which shall be entered the names and proficiency of all persons to whom licenses may be granted under the provisions of law. The said book shall show, also, the license number and the date upon which such license was issued and shall show such other matters as in the opinion of the Board may be necessary or proper. Said book shall be deemed a book of record of said Board and a transcript of any entry therein or a certification that there is not entered therein the name, proficiency and license number or date of granting such license, certified under the hand of the secretary-treasurer, attested by the seal of the North Carolina State Board of

Dental Examiners, shall be admitted as evidence in any court of this State when the same shall otherwise be competent. (1935, c. 66, s. 2.)

§ 90-26. Annual and special meetings.

The North Carolina State Board of Dental Examiners shall meet annually on the date and at the time and place as may be determined by the Board, and at such other dates, times, and places as may be determined by action of the Board or by any majority of the members thereof. Notice of the date, time, and place of the annual meeting and of the date, time, and place of any special or called meeting shall be given in writing, by registered or certified mail or personally, to each member of the Board at least 10 days prior to said meeting; provided the requirements of notice may be waived by any member of the Board. At the annual meeting or at any special or called meeting, the said Board shall have the power to conduct examination of applicants and to transact such other business as may come before it, provided that in case of a special meeting, the purpose for which said meeting is called shall be stated in the notice. (1935, c. 66, s. 3; 1961, c. 446, s. 1; 1981, c. 751, s. 4; 1995 (Reg. Sess., 1996), c. 584, s. 5.)

§ 90-27. Judicial powers; additional data for records.

The president of the North Carolina State Board of Dental Examiners, and/or the secretary-treasurer of said Board, shall have the power to administer oaths, issue subpoenas requiring the attendance of persons and the production of papers and records before said Board in any hearing, investigation or proceeding conducted by it. The sheriff or other proper official of any county of the State shall serve the process issued by said president or secretary-treasurer of said Board pursuant to its requirements and in the same manner as process issued by any court of record. The said Board shall pay for the service of all process, such fees as are provided by law for the service of like process in other cases.

Any person who shall neglect or refuse to obey any subpoena requiring him to attend and testify before said Board or to produce books, records or documents shall be guilty of a Class 1 misdemeanor.

The Board shall have the power, upon the production of any papers, records or data, to authorize certified copies thereof to be substituted in the permanent record of the matter in which such books, records or data shall have been introduced in evidence. (1935, c. 66, s. 4; 1993, c. 539, s. 616; 1994, Ex. Sess., c. 24, s. 14(c).)

§ 90-28. Bylaws and regulations; acquisition of property.

(a) The North Carolina State Board of Dental Examiners shall have the power to make necessary bylaws and regulations, not inconsistent with the provisions of this Article, regarding any matter referred to in this Article and for the purpose of facilitating the transaction of business by the Board.

(b) The Board shall have the power to acquire, hold, rent, encumber, alienate, and otherwise deal with real property in the same manner as a private person or corporation, subject only to approval of the Governor and the Council of State. Collateral pledged by the Board for an encumbrance is limited to the assets, income, and revenues of the Board. (1935, c. 66, s. 5; 2005-366, s. 3.)

§ 90-29. Necessity for license; dentistry defined; exemptions.

(a) No person shall engage in the practice of dentistry in this State, or offer or attempt to do so, unless such person is the holder of a valid license or certificate of renewal of license duly issued by the North Carolina State Board of Dental Examiners.

(b) A person shall be deemed to be practicing dentistry in this State who does, undertakes or attempts to do, or claims the ability to do any one or more of the following acts or things which, for the purposes of this Article, constitute the practice of dentistry:

(1) Diagnoses, treats, operates, or prescribes for any disease, disorder, pain, deformity, injury, deficiency, defect, or other physical condition of the human teeth, gums, alveolar process, jaws, maxilla, mandible, or adjacent tissues or structures of the oral cavity;

(2) Removes stains, accretions or deposits from the human teeth;

(3) Extracts a human tooth or teeth;

(4) Performs any phase of any operation relative or incident to the replacement or restoration of all or a part of a human tooth or teeth with any artificial substance, material or device;

(5) Corrects the malposition or malformation of the human teeth;

(6) Administers an anesthetic of any kind in the treatment of dental or oral diseases or physical conditions, or in preparation for or incident to any operation within the oral cavity; provided, however, that this subsection shall not apply to a lawfully qualified nurse anesthetist who administers such anesthetic under the supervision and direction of a licensed dentist or physician;

(6a) Expired pursuant to Session Laws 1991, c. 678, s. 2.

(7) Takes or makes an impression of the human teeth, gums or jaws;

(8) Makes, builds, constructs, furnishes, processes, reproduces, repairs, adjusts, supplies or professionally places in the human mouth any prosthetic denture, bridge, appliance, corrective device, or other structure designed or constructed as a substitute for a natural human tooth or teeth or as an aid in the treatment of the malposition or malformation of a tooth or teeth, except to the extent the same may lawfully be performed in accordance with the provisions of G.S. 90-29.1 and 90-29.2;

(9) Uses a Roentgen or X-ray machine or device for dental treatment or diagnostic purposes, or gives interpretations or readings of dental Roentgenograms or X rays;

(10) Performs or engages in any of the clinical practices included in the curricula of recognized dental schools or colleges;

(11) Owns, manages, supervises, controls or conducts, either himself or by and through another person or other persons, any enterprise wherein any one or more of the acts or practices set forth in subdivisions (1) through (10) above are done, attempted to be done, or represented to be done;

(12) Uses, in connection with his name, any title or designation, such as "dentist," "dental surgeon," "doctor of dental surgery," "D.D.S.," "D.M.D.," or any

other letters, words or descriptive matter which, in any manner, represents him as being a dentist able or qualified to do or perform any one or more of the acts or practices set forth in subdivisions (1) through (10) above;

(13) Represents to the public, by any advertisement or announcement, by or through any media, the ability or qualification to do or perform any of the acts or practices set forth in subdivisions (1) through (10) above.

(c) The following acts, practices, or operations, however, shall not constitute the unlawful practice of dentistry:

(1) Any act by a duly licensed physician or surgeon performed in the practice of his profession;

(2) The practice of dentistry, in the discharge of their official duties, by dentists in any branch of the Armed Forces of the United States or in the full-time employ of any agency of the United States;

(3) The teaching or practice of dentistry, in dental schools or colleges operated and conducted in this State and approved by the North Carolina State Board of Dental Examiners, by any person or persons licensed to practice dentistry anywhere in the United States or in any country, territory or other recognized jurisdiction until December 31, 2002. On or after January 1, 2003, all dentists previously practicing under G.S. 90-29(c)(3) shall be granted an instructor's license upon application to the Board and payment of the required fee.

(4) The practice of dentistry in dental schools or colleges in this State approved by the North Carolina State Board of Dental Examiners by students enrolled in such schools or colleges as candidates for a doctoral degree in dentistry when such practice is performed as a part of their course of instruction and is under direct supervision of a dentist who is either duly licensed in North Carolina or qualified under subdivision (3) above as a teacher; additionally, the practice of dentistry by such students at State or county institutions with resident populations, hospitals, State or county health departments, area health education centers, nonprofit health care facilities serving low-income populations and approved by the State Health Director or his designee and approved by the Board of Dental Examiners, and State or county-owned nursing homes; subject to review and approval or disapproval by the said Board of Dental Examiners when in the opinion of the dean of such dental school or college or his designee, the students' dental education and experience are

adequate therefor, and such practice is a part of the course of instruction of such students, is performed under the direct supervision of a duly licensed dentist acting as a teacher or instructor, and is without remuneration except for expenses and subsistence all as defined and permitted by the rules and regulations of said Board of Dental Examiners. Should the Board disapprove a specific program, the Board shall within 90 days inform the dean of its actions. Nothing herein shall be construed to permit the teaching of, delegation to or performance by any dental hygienist, dental assistant, or other auxiliary relative to any program of extramural rotation, of any function not heretofore permitted by the Dental Practice Act, the Dental Hygiene Act or by the rules and regulations of the Board;

(5) The temporary practice of dentistry by licensed dentists of another state or of any territory or country when the same is performed, as clinicians, at meetings of organized dental societies, associations, colleges or similar dental organizations, or when such dentists appear in emergency cases upon the specific call of a dentist duly licensed to practice in this State;

(6) The practice of dentistry by a person who is a graduate of a dental school or college approved by the North Carolina State Board of Dental Examiners and who is not licensed to practice dentistry in this State, when such person is the holder of a valid intern permit, or provisional license, issued to him by the North Carolina State Board of Dental Examiners pursuant to the terms and provisions of this Article, and when such practice of dentistry complies with the conditions of said intern permit, or provisional license;

(7) Any act or acts performed by a dental hygienist when such act or acts are lawfully performed pursuant to the authority of Article 16 of this Chapter 90 or the rules and regulations of the Board promulgated thereunder;

(8) Activity which would otherwise be considered the practice of dental hygiene performed by students enrolled in a school or college approved by the Board in a board-approved dental hygiene program under the direct supervision of a dental hygienist or a dentist duly licensed in North Carolina or qualified for the teaching of dentistry pursuant to the provisions of subdivision (3) above;

(9) Any act or acts performed by an assistant to a dentist licensed to practice in this State when said act or acts are authorized and permitted by and performed in accordance with rules and regulations promulgated by the Board;

(10)   Dental assisting and related functions as a part of their instructions by students enrolled in a course in dental assisting conducted in this State and approved by the Board, when such functions are performed under the supervision of a dentist acting as a teacher or instructor who is either duly licensed in North Carolina or qualified for the teaching of dentistry pursuant to the provisions of subdivision (3) above;

(11)   The extraoral construction, manufacture, fabrication or repair of prosthetic dentures, bridges, appliances, corrective devices, or other structures designed or constructed as a substitute for a natural human tooth or teeth or as an aid in the treatment of the malposition or malformation of a tooth or teeth, by a person or entity not licensed to practice dentistry in this State, when the same is done or performed solely upon a written work order in strict compliance with the terms, provisions, conditions and requirements of G.S. 90-29.1 and 90-29.2.

(12)   The use of a dental x-ray machine in the taking of dental radiographs by a dental hygienist, certified dental assistant, or a dental assistant who can show evidence of satisfactory performance on an equivalency examination, recognized by the Board of Dental Examiners, based on seven hours of instruction in the production and use of dental x rays and an educational program of not less than seven hours in clinical dental radiology.

(13)   A dental assistant, or dental hygienist who shows evidence of education and training in Nitrous Oxide - Oxygen Inhalant Conscious Sedation within a formal educational program may aid and assist a licensed dentist in the administration of Nitrous Oxide - Oxygen Inhalant Conscious Sedation. Any dental assistant who can show evidence of having completed an educational program recognized by the Board of not less than seven clock hours on Nitrous Oxide - Oxygen Inhalant Conscious Sedation may also aid and assist a licensed dentist in the administration of Nitrous Oxide - Oxygen Inhalant Conscious Sedation. Any dental hygienist or dental assistant who has been employed in a dental office where Nitrous Oxide - Oxygen Inhalant Conscious Sedation was utilized, and who can show evidence of performance and instruction of not less than one year prior to July 1, 1980, qualifies to aid and assist a licensed dentist in the administration of Nitrous Oxide - Oxygen Inhalant Conscious Sedation.

(14)   The operation of a nonprofit health care facility serving low-income populations and approved by the State Health Director or his designee and approved by the North Carolina State Board of Dental Examiners. (1935, c. 66, s. 6; 1953, c. 564, s. 3; 1957, c. 592, s. 2; 1961, c. 446, s. 2; 1965, c. 163, ss. 1,

2; 1971, c. 755, s. 2; 1977, c. 368; 1979, 2nd Sess., c. 1195, ss. 10, 15; 1991, c. 658, s. 1; c. 678, ss. 1, 2; 1997-481, ss. 5, 6; 2002-37, s. 8; 2011-183, s. 57.)

§ 90-29.1. Extraoral services performed for dentists.

Licensed dentists may employ or engage the services of any person, firm or corporation to construct or repair, extraorally, prosthetic dentures, bridges, or other replacements for a part of a tooth, a tooth, or teeth. A person, firm, or corporation so employed or engaged, when constructing or repairing such dentures, bridges, or replacements, exclusively, directly, and solely on the written work order of a licensed member of the dental profession as hereafter provided, and not for the public or any part thereof, shall not be deemed or considered to be practicing dentistry as defined in this Article. (1957, c. 592, s. 3; 1961, c. 446, ss. 3, 4; 1979, 2nd Sess., c. 1195, s. 6.)

§ 90-29.2. Requirements in respect to written work orders; penalty.

(a) Any licensed dentist who employs or engages the services of any person, firm or corporation to construct or repair, extraorally, prosthetic dentures, bridges, orthodontic appliance, or other replacements, for a part of a tooth, a tooth or teeth, shall furnish such person, firm or corporation with a written work order on forms prescribed by the North Carolina State Board of Dental Examiners which shall contain:

(1) The name and address of the person, firm, or corporation to which the work order is directed.

(2) The patient's name or identification number. If a number is used, the patient's name shall be written upon the duplicate copy of the work order retained by the dentist.

(3) The date on which the work order was written.

(4) A description of the work to be done, including diagrams if necessary.

(5) A specification of the type and quality of materials to be used.

(6) The signature of the dentist and the number of his license to practice dentistry.

(b) The person, firm or corporation receiving a work order from a licensed dentist shall retain the original work order and the dentist shall retain a duplicate copy thereof for inspection at any reasonable time by the North Carolina State Board of Dental Examiners or its duly authorized agents, for a period of two years in both cases.

(c) If the person, firm or corporation receiving a written work order from a licensed dentist engages another person, firm or corporation (hereinafter referred to as "subcontractor") to perform some of the services relative to such work order, he or it shall furnish a written subwork order with respect thereto on forms prescribed by the North Carolina State Board of Dental Examiners which shall contain:

(1) The name and address of the subcontractor.

(2) A number identifying the subwork order with the original work order, which number shall be endorsed on the work order received from the licensed dentist.

(3) The date on which the subwork order was written.

(4) A description of the work to be done by the subcontractor, including diagrams if necessary.

(5) A specification of the type and quality of materials to be used.

(6) The signature of the person, firm or corporation issuing the subwork order.

The subcontractor shall retain the subwork order and the issuer thereof shall retain a duplicate copy, attached to the work order received from the licensed dentist, for inspection by the North Carolina State Board of Dental Examiners or its duly authorized agents, for a period of two years in both cases.

(d) Any licensed dentist who:

(1) Employs or engages the services of any person, firm or corporation to construct or repair extraorally, prosthetic dentures, bridges, or other dental appliances without first providing such person, firm, or corporation with a written work order; or

(2) Fails to retain a duplicate copy of the work order for two years; or

(3) Refuses to allow the North Carolina State Board of Dental Examiners to inspect his files of work orders

is guilty of a Class 1 misdemeanor and the North Carolina State Board of Dental Examiners may revoke or suspend his license therefor.

(e) Any such person, firm, or corporation, who:

(1) Furnishes such services to any licensed dentist without first obtaining a written work order therefor from such dentist; or

(2) Acting as a subcontractor as described in (c) above, furnishes such services to any person, firm or corporation, without first obtaining a written subwork order from such person, firm or corporation; or

(3) Fails to retain the original work order or subwork order, as the case may be, for two years; or

(4) Refuses to allow the North Carolina State Board of Dental Examiners or its duly authorized agents, to inspect his or its files of work orders or subwork orders shall be guilty of a Class 1 misdemeanor. (1961, c. 446, s. 5; 1993, c. 539, ss. 617, 618; 1994, Ex. Sess., c. 24, s. 14(c).)

§ 90-29.3. Provisional license.

(a) The North Carolina State Board of Dental Examiners shall, subject to its rules and regulations, issue a provisional license to practice dentistry to any person who is licensed to practice dentistry anywhere in the United States or in any country, territory or other recognized jurisdiction, if the Board shall determine that said licensing jurisdiction imposed upon said person requirements for licensure no less exacting than those imposed by this State. A provisional licensee may engage in the practice of dentistry only in strict accordance with the terms, conditions and limitations of his license and with the rules and regulations of the Board pertaining to provisional license.

(b) A provisional license shall be valid until the date of the announcement of the results of the next succeeding Board examination of candidates for licensure to practice dentistry in this State, unless the same shall be earlier revoked or suspended by the Board.

(c) No person who has failed an examination conducted by the North Carolina State Board of Dental Examiners shall be eligible to receive a provisional license.

(d) Any person desiring to secure a provisional license shall make application therefor in the manner and form prescribed by the rules and regulations of the Board and shall pay the fee prescribed in G.S. 90-39 of this Article.

(e) A provisional licensee shall be subject to those various disciplinary measures and penalties set forth in G.S. 90-41 upon a determination of the Board that said provisional licensee has violated any of the terms or provisions of this Article. (1969, c. 804, s. 1.)

§ 90-29.4. Intern permit.

The North Carolina State Board of Dental Examiners may, in the exercise of the discretion of said Board, issue to a person who is not licensed to practice dentistry in this State and who is a graduate of a dental school, college, or institution approved by said Board, an intern permit authorizing such person to practice dentistry under the supervision or direction of a dentist duly licensed to practice in this State, subject to the following particular conditions:

(1) An intern permit shall be valid for no more than one year from the date the permit was issued. The Board may, in its discretion, renew the permit for not more than five additional one-year periods. However, no person who has attempted and failed a Board-approved written or clinical examination shall be granted an intern permit or intern permits embracing or covering an aggregate time span of more than 72 calendar months. An intern permit holder who has held an unrestricted dental license in a Board-approved state or jurisdiction for the five years immediately preceding the issuance of an intern permit in this State may, in the Board's discretion, have the intern permit renewed for additional one-year periods beyond 72 months if the intern permit holder's

approved employing institution comes before the Board on the permit holder's behalf for each subsequent annual renewal;

(2) The holder of a valid intern permit may practice dentistry only under the supervision or direction of one or more dentists duly licensed to practice in this State;

(3) The holder of a valid intern permit may practice dentistry only (i) as an employee in a hospital, sanatorium, or a like institution which is licensed or approved by the State of North Carolina and approved by the North Carolina State Board of Dental Examiners; (ii) as an employee of a nonprofit health care facility serving low-income populations and approved by the State Health Director or his designee and approved by the North Carolina State Board of Dental Examiners; or (iii) as an employee of the State of North Carolina or an agency or political subdivision thereof, or any other governmental entity within the State of North Carolina, when said employment is approved by the North Carolina State Board of Dental Examiners;

(4) The holder of a valid intern permit shall receive no fee or fees or compensation of any kind or nature for dental services rendered by him other than such salary or compensation as might be paid to him by the entity specified in subdivision (3) above wherein or for which said services are rendered;

(5) The holder of a valid intern permit shall not, during the term of said permit or any renewal thereof, change the place of his internship without first securing the written approval of the North Carolina State Board of Dental Examiners;

(6) The practice of dentistry by the holder of a valid intern permit shall be strictly limited to the confines of and to the registered patients of the hospital, sanatorium or institution to which he is attached or to the persons officially served by the governmental entity by whom he is employed;

(7) Any person seeking an intern permit shall first file with the North Carolina State Board of Dental Examiners such papers and documents as are required by said Board, together with the application fee authorized by G.S. 90-39. A fee authorized by G.S. 90-39 shall be paid for any renewal of said intern permit. Such person shall further supply to the Board such other documents, materials or information as the Board may request;

(8) Any person seeking an intern permit or who is the holder of a valid intern permit shall comply with such limitations as the North Carolina State Board of Dental Examiners may place or cause to be placed, in writing, upon such permit, and shall comply with such rules and regulations as the Board might promulgate relative to the issuance and maintenance of said permit in the practice of dentistry relative to the same;

(9) The holder of an intern permit shall be subject to the provisions of G.S. 90-41. (1971, c. 755, s. 3; 1997-481, s. 7; 2002-37, s. 10; 2006-41, s. 1.)

§ 90-29.5. Instructor's license.

(a) The Board may issue an instructor's license to a person who is not otherwise licensed to practice dentistry in this State if the person meets both of the following conditions:

(1) Is licensed to practice dentistry anywhere in the United States or in any country, territory, or other recognized jurisdiction.

(2) Has met or been approved under the credentialing standards of a dental school or an academic medical center with which the person is to be affiliated; such dental school or academic medical center shall be accredited by the American Dental Association's Commission on Accreditation or the Joint Commission on Accreditation of Health Care Organizations.

(b) The holder of an instructor's license may teach and practice dentistry:

(1) In or on behalf of a dental school or college offering a doctoral degree in dentistry operated and conducted in this State and approved by the North Carolina State Board of Dental Examiners;

(2) In connection with an academic medical center; and

(3) At any teaching hospital adjacent to a dental school or an academic medical center.

(c) Application for an instructor's license shall be made in accordance with the rules of the North Carolina State Board of Dental Examiners. On or after January 1, 2003, all dentists previously practicing under G.S. 90-29(c)(3) shall be granted an instructor's license upon application to the Board and payment of the required fee. The holder of an instructor's license shall be subject to the provisions of this Article. (1979, 2nd Sess., c. 1195, s. 11; 2002-37, s. 7.)

§ 90-30. Examination and licensing of applicants; qualifications; causes for refusal to grant license; void licenses.

(a)   The North Carolina State Board of Dental Examiners shall grant licenses to practice dentistry to such applicants who are graduates of a reputable dental institution, who, in the opinion of a majority of the Board, shall undergo a satisfactory examination of proficiency in the knowledge and practice of dentistry, subject, however, to the further provisions of this section and of the provisions of this Article.

The applicant for a license to practice dentistry shall be of good moral character, at least 18 years of age at the time the application is filed. The application for a dental license shall be made to the Board in writing and shall be accompanied by evidence satisfactory to the Board that the applicant is a person of good moral character, has an academic education, the standard of which shall be determined by the Board; that the applicant is a graduate of and has a diploma from a reputable dental college or the dental department of a reputable university or college recognized, accredited and approved as such by the Board; and that the applicant has passed a clinical licensing examination, the standard of which shall be determined by the Board.

The North Carolina State Board of Dental Examiners is authorized to conduct both written or oral and clinical examinations or to accept the results of other Board-approved regional or national independent third-party clinical examinations that shall include procedures performed on human subjects as part of the assessment of restorative clinical competencies and that are determined by the Board to be of such character as to thoroughly test the qualifications of the applicant, and may refuse to grant a license to any person who, in its discretion, is found deficient in the examination. The Board may refuse to grant a license to any person guilty of cheating, deception or fraud during the examination, or whose examination discloses to the satisfaction of the Board, a deficiency in academic or clinical education. The Board may employ such dentists found qualified therefor by the Board, in examining applicants for licenses as it deems appropriate.

The North Carolina State Board of Dental Examiners may refuse to grant a license to any person guilty of a crime involving moral turpitude, or gross immorality, or to any person addicted to the use of alcoholic liquors or narcotic drugs to such an extent as, in the opinion of the Board, renders the applicant unfit to practice dentistry.

Any license obtained through fraud or by any false representation shall be void ab initio and of no effect.

(b)   The Department of Justice may provide a criminal record check to the North Carolina State Board of Dental Examiners for a person who has applied for a license through the Board. The Board shall provide to the Department of Justice, along with the request, the fingerprints of the applicant, any additional information required by the Department of Justice, and a form signed by the applicant consenting to the check of the criminal record and to the use of the fingerprints and other identifying information required by the State or national repositories. The applicant's fingerprints shall be forwarded to the State Bureau of Investigation for a search of the State's criminal history record file, and the State Bureau of Investigation shall forward a set of the fingerprints to the Federal Bureau of Investigation for a national criminal history check. The Board shall keep all information pursuant to this subsection privileged, in accordance with applicable State law and federal guidelines, and the information shall be confidential and shall not be a public record under Chapter 132 of the General Statutes.

The Department of Justice may charge each applicant a fee for conducting the checks of criminal history records authorized by this subsection. (1935, c. 66, s. 7; 1971, c. 755, s. 4; 1981, c. 751, s. 5; 2002-147, s. 7; 2005-366, s. 1.)

§ 90-30.1. Standards for general anesthesia and enteral and parenteral sedation; fees authorized.

The North Carolina Board of Dental Examiners may establish by regulation reasonable education, training, and equipment standards for safe administration and monitoring of general anesthesia and enteral and parenteral sedation for outpatients in the dental setting. Regulatory standards may include a permit process for general anesthesia and enteral and parenteral sedation by dentists. The requirements of any permit process adopted under the authority of this section shall include provisions that will allow a dentist to qualify for continued use of enteral sedation, if he or she is licensed to practice dentistry in North Carolina and shows the Board that he or she has been utilizing enteral sedation in a competent manner for the five years preceding January 1, 2002, and his or her office facilities pass an on-site examination and inspection by qualified representatives of the Board. For purposes of this section, oral premedication administered for minimal sedation (anxiolysis) shall not be included in the definition of enteral sedation. In order to provide the means of regulating general anesthesia and enteral and parenteral sedation, including examination and inspection of dental offices involved, the Board may charge and collect fees established by its rules for each permit application, each annual permit renewal, and each office inspection in an amount not to exceed the maximum fee amounts set forth in G.S. 90-39. (1987 (Reg. Sess., 1988), c. 1073; 1989, c. 648; 1989 (Reg. Sess., 1990), c. 1066, s. 12(a); 1995 (Reg. Sess., 1996), c. 584, s. 2; 2001-511, s. 1.)

§ 90-31. Annual renewal of licenses.

The laws of North Carolina now in force, having provided for the annual renewal of any license issued by the North Carolina State Board of Dental Examiners, it is hereby declared to be the policy of this State, that all licenses heretofore issued by the North Carolina State Board of Dental Examiners or hereafter issued by said Board are subject to annual renewal and the exercise of any privilege granted by any license heretofore issued or hereafter issued by the North Carolina State Board of Dental Examiners is subject to the issuance on or before the first day of January of each year of a certificate of renewal of license.

On or before the first day of January of each year, each dentist engaged in the practice of dentistry in North Carolina shall make application to the North Carolina State Board of Dental Examiners and receive from said Board, subject to the further provisions of this section and of this Article, a certificate of renewal of said license.

The application shall show the serial number of the applicant's license, his full name, address and the county in which he has practiced during the preceding year, the date of the original issuance of license to said applicant and such other information as the said Board from time to time may prescribe, at least six months prior to January 1 of any year.

If the application for such renewal certificate, accompanied by the fee required by this Article, is not received by the Board before January 31 of each year, an additional fee shall be charged for renewal certificate. The maximum penalty fee for late renewal is set forth in G.S. 90-39. If such application, accompanied by the renewal fee, plus the additional fee, is not received by the Board before March 31 of each year, every person thereafter continuing to practice dentistry without having applied for a certificate of renewal shall be guilty of the unauthorized practice of dentistry and shall be subject to the penalties prescribed by G.S. 90-40. (1935, c. 66, s. 8; 1953, c. 564, s. 5; 1961, c. 446, s. 6; 1971, c. 755, s. 5; 1995 (Reg. Sess., 1996), c. 584, s. 3.)

§ 90-31.1. Continuing education courses required.

All dentists licensed under G.S. 90-30 shall be required to attend Board-approved courses of study in subjects relating to dentistry. The Board shall have authority to consider and approve courses, or providers of courses, to the end that those attending will gain (i) information on existing and new methods and procedures used by dentists, (ii) information leading to increased safety and competence in their dealings with patients and staff, and (iii) information on other matters, as they develop, that are of continuing importance to the practice of dentistry. The Board shall determine the number of hours of study within a particular period and the nature of course work required. The Board may provide exemptions or waivers from continuing education requirements where dentists are receiving alternate learning experiences or where they have limited practices. The Board shall by regulation define circumstances for exemptions or waivers for dentists who are involved in dental education or training pursuits where they gain experiences equivalent to formal continuing education courses, for those who have reached an advanced age and are semiretired or have otherwise voluntarily restricted their practices in volume and scope, and for such other situations as the Board in its discretion may determine meet the purposes of this section. (1993, c. 307, s. 1.)

§ 90-32. Contents of original license.

The original license granted by the North Carolina State Board of Dental Examiners shall bear a serial number, the full name of the applicant, the date of issuance and shall be signed by the president and the majority of the members of the said Board and attested by the seal of said Board and the secretary thereof. The certificate of renewal of license shall bear a serial number which need not be the serial number of the original license issued, the full name of the applicant and the date of issuance. (1935, c. 66, s. 8.)

§ 90-33. Displaying license and current certificate of renewal.

The license and the current certificate of renewal of license to practice dentistry issued, as herein provided, shall at all times be displayed in a conspicuous place in the office of the holder thereof and whenever requested the license and the current certificate of renewal shall be exhibited to or produced before the North Carolina State Board of Dental Examiners or to its authorized agents. (1935, c. 66, s. 8.)

§ 90-34. Refusal to grant renewal of license.

For nonpayment of fee or fees required by this Article, for failure to comply with continuing education requirements adopted by the Board under the authority of G.S. 90-31.1, or for violation of any of the terms or provisions of G.S. 90-41 concerning disciplinary actions, the North Carolina State Board of Dental Examiners may refuse to issue a certificate for renewal of license. As used in this section, the term "license" includes license, provisional license or intern permit. (1935, c. 66, s. 8; 1971, c. 755, s. 6; 1993, c. 307, s. 2.)

§ 90-35. Duplicate licenses.

When a person is a holder of a license to practice dentistry in North Carolina or the holder of a certificate of renewal of license, he may make application to the North Carolina State Board of Dental Examiners for the issuance of a copy or a duplicate thereof accompanied by a fee that shall not exceed the maximum fee for a duplicate license or certificate set forth in G.S. 90-39. Upon the filing of the application and the payment of the fee, the said Board shall issue a copy or duplicate. (1935, c. 66, s. 8; 1961, c. 446, s. 7; 1995 (Reg. Sess., 1996), c. 584, s. 4.)

§ 90-36. Licensing practitioners of other states.

(a) The North Carolina State Board of Dental Examiners may issue a license by credentials to an applicant who has been licensed to practice dentistry in any state or territory of the United States if the applicant produces satisfactory evidence to the Board that the applicant has the required education, training, and qualifications, is in good standing with the licensing jurisdiction, has passed satisfactory examinations of proficiency in the knowledge and practice of dentistry as determined by the Board, and meets all other requirements of this section and rules adopted by the Board. The Board may conduct examinations and interviews to test the qualifications of the applicant and may require additional information that would affect the applicant's ability to render competent dental care. The Board may, in its discretion, refuse to issue a license by credentials to an applicant who the Board determines is unfit to practice dentistry.

(b) The applicant for licensure by credentials shall be of good moral character and shall have graduated from and have a DDS or DMD degree from a program of dentistry in a school or college accredited by the Commission on Dental Accreditation of the American Dental Association and approved by the Board.

(c) The applicant must meet all of the following conditions:

(1) Has been actively practicing dentistry, as defined in G.S. 90-29(b)(1) through (b)(9), for a minimum of five years immediately preceding the date of application.

(2) Has not been the subject of final or pending disciplinary action in the Armed Forces of the United States, in any state or territory in which the applicant is or has ever been licensed to practice dentistry, or in any state or territory in which the applicant has held any other professional license.

(3) Presents evidence that the applicant has no felony convictions and that the applicant has no other criminal convictions that would affect the applicant's ability to render competent dental care.

(4) Has not failed an examination conducted by the North Carolina State Board of Dental Examiners.

(d) The applicant for licensure by credentials shall submit an application to the North Carolina State Board of Dental Examiners, the form of which shall be determined by the Board, pay the fee required by G.S. 90-39, successfully complete examinations in Jurisprudence and Sterilization and Infection Control, and meet the criteria or requirements established by the Board.

(e) The holder of a license issued under this section shall establish a practice location and actively practice dentistry, as defined in G.S. 90-29(b)(1) through (b)(9), in North Carolina within one year from the date the license is issued. The license issued under this section shall be void upon a finding by the Board that the licensee fails to limit the licensee's practice to North Carolina or that the licensee no longer actively practices dentistry in North Carolina. However, when a dentist licensed under this section faces possible Board action to void the dentist's license for failure to limit the dentist's practice to North Carolina, if the dentist demonstrates to the Board that out-of-state practice actions were in connection with formal contract or employment arrangements for the dentist to provide needed clinical dental care to patients who are part of an identified ethnic or racial minority group living in a region of the other state with low access to dental care, the Board, in its discretion, may waive the in-State limitations on the out-of-state practice for a maximum of 12 months. (1935, c. 66, s. 9; 1971, c. 755, s. 7; 1981, c. 751, s. 6; 2002-37, s. 2; 2009-289, s. 1; 2011-183, s. 58.)

§ 90-37. Certificate issued to dentist moving out of State.

Any dentist duly licensed by the North Carolina State Board of Dental Examiners, desiring to move from North Carolina to another state, territory or foreign country, if a holder of a certificate of renewal of license from said Board, upon application to said Board and the payment to it of the fee in this Article provided, shall be issued a certificate showing his full name and address, the date of license originally issued to him, the date and number of his renewal of license, and whether any charges have been filed with the Board against him. The Board may provide forms for such certificate, requiring such additional information as it may determine proper. (1935, c. 66, s. 10.)

§ 90-37.1. Limited volunteer dental license.

(a) The North Carolina State Board of Dental Examiners may issue to an applicant a "Limited Volunteer Dental License" to practice dentistry only in nonprofit health care facilities serving low-income populations in the State. Holders of a limited volunteer dental license may volunteer their professional services, without compensation, only for the purpose of helping to meet the dental health needs of these persons served by these facilities. The Board may issue a limited license to an applicant under this section who:

(1) Has an out-of-state current or expired license, or an expired license in this State, or is authorized to treat veterans of or personnel serving in the Armed Forces of the United States; and

(2) Has actively practiced dentistry, as defined in G.S. 90-29(b)(1) through (b)(9), within the past five years.

(b) The limited license may be issued to an applicant who produces satisfactory evidence to the Board that the applicant has the required education, training, and qualifications; is in good standing with the licensing jurisdiction; has passed satisfactory examinations of proficiency in the knowledge and practice of dentistry as determined by the Board; and meets all other requirements of this section and rules adopted by the Board. The Board may conduct examinations and interviews to test the qualifications of the applicant and may require additional information that would affect the applicant's ability to render competent dental care. The Board may, in its discretion, refuse to issue a "limited volunteer dental license" to an applicant who the Board determines is unfit to practice dentistry.

(c) The applicant shall be of good moral character and shall have graduated from and have a DDS or DMD degree from a program of dentistry in a school or college accredited by the Commission on Dental Accreditation of the American Dental Association and approved by the Board.

(d) The applicant shall meet all of the following conditions:

(1) Show that the applicant has actively practiced dentistry, as defined in G.S. 90-29(b)(1) through (b)(9), for a minimum of five years.

(2) Show that the applicant has not been the subject of final or pending disciplinary action in any state in which the applicant has ever been licensed to

practice dentistry or in any state in which the applicant has held any other professional license.

(3)   Present evidence that the applicant has no felony convictions and that the applicant has no other criminal convictions that would affect the applicant's ability to render competent care.

(4)   Present evidence that the applicant has no pending Veterans Administration or military disciplinary actions or any history of such disciplinary action.

(5)   Show that the applicant has not failed an examination conducted by the North Carolina State Board of Dental Examiners.

(e)   The applicant shall submit an application, the form of which shall be determined by the Board, pay the fee required under G.S. 90-39, and successfully complete examinations in Jurisprudence and Sterilization and Infection Control. The Board may charge and collect fees for license application and annual renewal as required under G.S. 90-39, except that credentialing fees applicable under G.S. 90-39(13) are waived for holders of a limited volunteer dental license.

(f)   Holders of a limited volunteer dental license shall comply with the continuing dental education requirements adopted by the Board including CPR training.

(g)   The holder of a limited license under this section who practices dentistry other than as authorized in this section shall be guilty of a Class 1 misdemeanor with each day's violation constituting a separate offense. Upon proof of practice other than as authorized in this section, the Board may suspend or revoke the limited license after notice to the licensee. For violations of the dental practice act or rules adopted under the act that are applicable to a limited license practice, the Board has the same authority to investigate and impose sanctions on limited license holders as it has for those holding an unlimited license.

(h)   The Board shall maintain a nonexclusive list of nonprofit health care facilities serving the dental health needs of low-income populations in the State. Upon request, the Board shall consider adding other facilities to the list.

(i)   The Board may adopt rules in accordance with Chapter 150B of the General Statutes to implement this section. (2002-37, s. 4; 2011-183, s. 59.)

§ 90-37.2. Temporary permits for volunteer dentists.

(a) The North Carolina State Board of Dental Examiners may issue to a person who is not licensed to practice dentistry in this State and who is a graduate of a Board-approved dental school, college, or institution a temporary volunteer permit authorizing such person to practice dentistry under the supervision or direction of a dentist duly licensed in this State. A temporary volunteer permit shall be issued only to those dentists who are licensed in another Board-approved state or jurisdiction, have never been subject to discipline, and have passed a patient-based clinical examination substantially similar to the clinical examination offered in this State. The issuance of a temporary volunteer permit is subject to the following conditions:

(1) A temporary volunteer permit shall be valid no more than one year from the date of issue; provided, however, that the Board may renew the permit for additional one-year periods.

(2) The holder of a temporary volunteer permit may practice only under the supervision or direction of one or more dentists duly licensed to practice in this State.

(3) The holder of a temporary volunteer permit may practice dentistry only: (i) as a volunteer in a hospital, sanatorium, temporary clinic, or like institution which is licensed or approved by the State of North Carolina and approved by the Board; (ii) as a volunteer for a nonprofit health care facility serving low-income populations and approved by the State Health Director or his designee or approved by the Board; or (iii) as a volunteer for the State of North Carolina or an agency or political subdivision thereof, or any other governmental entity within the State of North Carolina, when such service is approved by the Board.

(4) The holder of a temporary volunteer permit shall receive no fee or monetary compensation of any kind or nature for any dental service performed.

(5) The practice of dentistry by the holder of a temporary volunteer permit shall be strictly limited to the confines of and to the registered patients of the hospital, sanatorium, temporary clinic, or approved nonprofit health care facilities for which he is working or to the patients officially served by the governmental entity to which he is offering his volunteer services.

(6) The holder of a temporary volunteer permit shall be subject to discipline by the Board for those actions constituting the practice of dentistry by G.S. 90-29 occurring while practicing in this State.

(7) Any person seeking a temporary volunteer permit must file with the Board such proof as is required by the Board to determine if the applicant has a valid unrestricted dental license in another state or jurisdiction, has not been subject to discipline by any licensing board, has a proven record of clinical safety and is otherwise qualified to practice dentistry in this State.

(8) There shall be no fee associated with the issuance of a temporary volunteer permit for the practice of dentistry.

(b) The Board is authorized to make rules consistent with this section to regulate the practice of dentistry for those issued a temporary volunteer permit. (2007-346, s. 27.)

Vision Books Order Form

Fax Orders:	1-704-921-9271
Phone Orders:	1-704-921-9271
E-mail Orders:	www.visionbooks.org
Mail Orders:	Vision Books P.O. Box 42406 Charlotte, NC 28215

Shipp To:
Name_____
Address_____
City_____State_____Zip_____
Phone_____Fax_____
Email_____@_____

Bill To: We can bill a third party on your behalf.
Name_____
Address_____
City_____State_____Zip_____
Phone____(_____)_____Fax_____
Email_____@_____

Pamphlet Number ($15.00 Each)	Qty	Total Cost
_____	_____	_____
_____	_____	_____
_____	_____	_____
_____	_____	_____
_____	_____	_____
_____	_____	_____
_____	_____	_____
_____	_____	_____
<u>Full Volume Set 1-92</u>	<u>92 Pamphlets</u>	<u>1,380.00</u>

Free Shipping Shipping & Handling on Full Volume Orders
Add $1.00 Shipping & Handling per pamphlet $_____

Total Cost $_____

DID YOU ENJOY THIS BOOK?

Vision Books, LLC would like to hear from you! If you or someone you know has been fasely imprisoned, we would like to hear your story. If the 'North Carolina Criminal Law and Procedure' has had an effect in your life or if you have suggestions, we would like to hear from you. Send your letters to:

Vision Books, LLC
Attn: Staff Writers
P.O. Box 42406
Charlotte, NC 28215
Email: staff@visionbooks.org

Order Additional Copies:

Fax Orders:	1-704-921-9271
Phone Orders:	1-704-921-9271
E-mail Orders:	www.visionbooks.org
Mail Orders:	Vision Books P.O. Box 42406 Charlotte, NC 28215

www.ingramcontent.com/pod-product-compliance
Lightning Source LLC
Chambersburg PA
CBHW051628170526
45167CB00001B/97